THE NINE LIVES OF MINNIE WINDER OR I DID WHAT I COULD

Mary Hope Williams

Mary Williams

MINERVA PRESS
LONDON
MONTREUX LOS ANGELES SYDNEY

First Published 1997 by
MINERVA PRESS
195, Knightsbridge
London SW7 1RE

Printed in Great Britain by
Antony Rowe Ltd, Chippenham, Wiltshire

THE NINE LIVES OF MINNIE WINDER OR I DID WHAT I COULD

To David, Anne, Paul, Peggy and Robin
With thanks for all their kind assistance

History is the essence of innumerable biographies.

Thomas Carlyle

WINDER FAMILY TREE

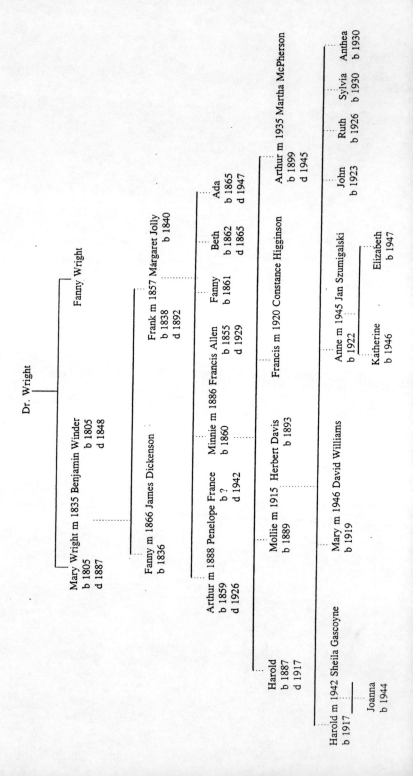

Dr. Wright

Fanny Wright

Mary Wright m 1835 Benjamin Winder
b 1805
d 1887
b 1805
d 1848

Fanny m 1866 James Dickenson
b 1836

Frank m 1857 Margaret Jolly
b 1838
d 1892
b 1840

Arthur m 1888 Penelope France
b 1859
d 1926
b ?
d 1942

Minnie m 1886 Francis Allen
b 1860
b 1855
d 1929

Fanny
b 1861

Beth
b 1862
d 1865

Ada
b 1865
d 1947

Mollie m 1915 Herbert Davis
b 1889
b 1893

Francis m 1920 Constance Higginson

Arthur m 1935 Martha McPherson
b 1899
d 1945

Mary m 1946 David Williams
b 1919

Anne m 1945 Jan Szumigalski
b 1922

John
b 1923

Ruth
b 1926

Sylvia
b 1930

Anthea
b 1930

Katherine
b 1946

Elizabeth
b 1947

Harold
b 1887
d 1917

Harold m 1942 Sheila Gascoyne
b 1917

Joanna
b 1944

ALLEN FAMILY TREE

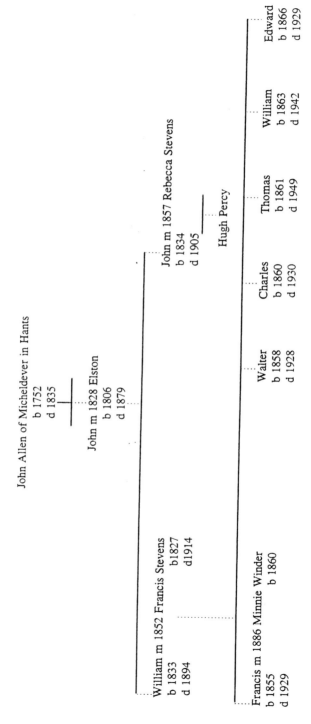

John Allen of Micheldever in Hants
b 1752
d 1835

John m 1828 Elston
b 1806
d 1879

John m 1857 Rebecca Stevens
b 1834
d 1905

Hugh Percy

William m 1852 Francis Stevens
b 1833   b1827
d 1894   d1914

Francis m 1886 Minnie Winder
b 1855   b 1860
d 1929

Walter
b 1858
d 1928

Charles
b 1860
d 1930

Thomas
b 1861
d 1949

William
b 1863
d 1942

Edward
b 1866
d 1929

Minnie Winder on her eighty-eighth birthday - 1948.

Contents

Part One

Part Two

Part Three

Part One

Afraid Of The Past

'Know thyself' it says over the Greek temple at Delphi. For fifty years I kept a diary and now I am afraid to open it again for fear of what it may reveal about myself.

"It is sometimes difficult," I say to my sister Fanny, "to be sure who I really am. I can count at least nine different people I seem to have managed to be in my lifetime."

I can talk to Fanny about some things, you see, although I never would have been able to ask my other sister Ada such a silly question.

"Are you sure you are not sickening for something," says Fanny, "all this introspection isn't good for you. Anyway, you seem the same as you always did."

She has a matter of fact way of looking at life, does Fanny. "Of course you look older, but then don't we all. But you do seem to look even smaller than you used to do."

"None of us three sisters are exactly tall, are we?" I answer defensively. "Not surprising when you think how difficult things were at times. I have always hated being small, you know, it has made everything in life so difficult, as if there has always been an extra effort to be made."

I have been very conscious of the fact that I am so small, ever since I can remember. Small in stature, small in nature, I remember my Aunt saying once, when she was disapproving of something I had done, or more likely something I hadn't done. Of course she was quite wrong, that's the opposite of the truth, if you are very short like me, you have to be all the more assertive to make sure people take notice, so they don't take advantage of you. People will always take advantage of you if they can.

In a way, Fanny is right, this talk about the past is disturbing me. It all started with some old photographs we had been looking at. Now my mind keeps going back to the beginning of things. There is plenty of time at our age to reminisce, you must understand. I am eighty-six, and my sister's only a year or two younger. How much does one really remember of the past, I wonder, and how much is imagination, how much what others have said, have remembered, have repeated. I used to be so certain about everything, but not now.

"What do you mean, things have been difficult," says Fanny. "I don't suppose things have been any more difficult for us than for most other people. Come to think of it you have always been better off than either of us." Ada had come into the room, and now I felt the antagonism of both my sisters.

"You always did make things out to be worse than they were," Ada says.

She's wrong, I ought to know, one has to fight to survive after all. But memories get confused. Am I, I begin to wonder, what I think I am, or am I what other people think I am. Being old makes one ask such silly questions. I am quite upset that Fanny should think I used to be so difficult, perhaps she still thinks I am. I have always done my best through all the uncomfortable happenings of my life. I sometimes joke with Fanny about the nine lives I have led, like the nine lives of a cat, a cat with nine lives.

So I go upstairs to escape my sisters' criticism, and then I start moving things round my room, taking books off the shelves, giving them a cursory glance, and then putting them back. I have always liked to have a lot of books in my room, especially books of poetry. I look at my box, my special diary box, and stroke the satin wood. I put it down beside my chair. I might as well be comfortable. In the box is my old diary. I open the secret drawer and take it out, that old diary of mine. I notice how shiny black its cover still is, although it's very worn in places. I turn the pages, in an idle kind of fashion, finding the faded writing difficult to read.

It's many, many years since I last looked at it. When you are old time passes slowly in retrospect, quickly in terms of every day living. One is always deciding to do things tomorrow rather than today. I am not sure why I have kept my diary all this time. I decided long ago I never wanted to look at it again. But I have always kept it there, just in case.

Perhaps I have been afraid to relive the past. 'Little Minnie Winder' is scrawled on the back of the cover. There it is again, that reference to my small stature. I was always small, even as a child, perhaps that is why they always called me Minnie, although I was christened Mary. Everyone still calls me Minnie.

My sister Fanny was taller than I was by the time I was ten and she was two years younger. She was never what you might call pretty even when she was little, and now the disadvantages of her face have become more pronounced. Her nose is too big, her mouth too wide, and her nondescript hair is even more straggly than it was when she was a child.

Now my other sister Ada, she was quite different, she was so very pretty when she was young, small like me, with dark beautiful hair. That was what you first noticed about her, her long, black shiny curls. My hair was never curly. You wouldn't think she had had such lovely hair when you see her now, she has only those few straggly dark grey strands – she is rapidly going bald.

She was croquet champion of the whole of the South of England one year, was it in 1897, I rather think it was. I used to think croquet a very spiteful game.

I always thought if anyone in our family ever got married it would be Ada, because of her prettiness, and despite her difficult nature. Even Fanny I used to think might get married, because she had a knack of being able to look after people, make them feel comfortable. As it turned out I was the only one that got married.

I wasn't very pretty, but then neither was I very ugly when I was young, but I was certainly small. Being small, my Grandmama used to say, is all the more reason for behaving in a dignified manner. What you lack in stature you may make up in 'presence'; dignity is the secret of a royal presence. She ought to know, she was brought up with princesses, so she said. I thought I understood what Grandmama meant, for if anyone came into a room where Grandmama happened to be, everyone immediately felt a certain respect towards her, listened to what she asked, and did as she expected them to do. I spent a lot of my time when I was young, trying to have a presence.

I look at myself in the mirror: a lined face with drooping skin round my eyes and mouth: a pleasant enough smile, I suppose, if somewhat austere, I don't feel austere: white hair piled on top of my head; I like wearing it like that: Presence? Well I suppose I do have a certain dignity.

I start turning the pages of the diary. The faded writing makes it difficult to read. It's as if the writing has faded to obscure the emotions that I know I once felt so acutely. As I begin to read I start to feel guilty, as if I am prying into someone else's secrets. The diary started on my tenth birthday.

I can remember my tenth birthday, it comes back to me as I read the childish handwriting. The secrets I had written all those years ago. I read with curiosity, it is as if I am reading about someone other than myself. I make myself comfortable in my old armchair and then, as happens when one is old, I fall into a state of half waking, half sleeping when it is difficult to know if one is dreaming or remembering. Is it a dream, or a recollection of what really happened nearly eighty years ago? It is difficult to be sure...

*

But I do vividly seem to recall that day when I was ten. 'To be ten years old is to be of a responsible age,' I remember my aunt saying, in her usual stern and distant manner. 'You are no longer a child, and I expect you to behave accordingly.' 'Witch,' I muttered under my breath, because she always seemed able to spoil everything we did. Aunt. There she stood, that tall gaunt figure, with her long rustling black dress and her unforgiving face, there in the front parlour, on my tenth birthday because Grandmama said we must have a celebration.

We had always called my aunt a witch, ever since the day when we arrived at Grandmama's house, and my brother Arthur and I agreed that that was what she was. 'She's a witch,' he had said, 'I know she's a witch.' We were whispering together despite the fact that we were all alone at last in that big bedroom. 'How do you know,' I whispered back, aware of the round frightened eyes of my two small sisters gazing at us in exhausted bewilderment. 'Because, silly, only witches steal children,' he had said scornfully, 'everyone knows that.'

'Congratulations,' I can almost hear Grandmama saying, 'on reaching your tenth birthday,' and I remember she gave me a little hug, the way she always did when she was pleased. She always smelled of lavender, and her dress rustled in quite a different way to that of my aunt. She had a stern face too, but stern because of what life had had to offer her, I realise, not because of her nature. She was strict, but always kind.

Ten Years Old

Being ten was something to be congratulated upon, I knew that. Not everyone gets as far as ten. Betsy for instance, my little sister, had never got to ten. Betsy, who had gone away to heaven, Mama had told us, to be looked after by the angels. I had always thought of Betsy like that, dressed up in a long white shiny dress. She was only three when she went away.

'Today you are ten years old, and I am giving you this note-book so you can keep a diary. It will improve your writing and your spelling,' my grandmother was saying. I can remember looking at this new possession, with its shiny black cover and neat pages to be filled – by what I wondered. So many pages, so much neat writing to be done. And what would I want to write in it anyway? People only write important things in diaries.

'I shall ask you every day if you have written something interesting,' Grandmama had continued, 'but you can say what you like, and no one will need to read it but yourself. Believe me, you will find it very helpful in years to come to have some kind of record of a happy childhood. My governess persuaded me to keep one when I was young, and I've always been very glad I did. I still read it sometimes.

Grandmama often made me think how unhappy she must have been after she grew up and moved away from London. London, the capital city of England, it sounded such an interesting and exciting place then. She would talk about what she did when she was a girl, having such beautiful clothes, going to parties, visiting so many friends. But she seldom spoke about what happened after she was married.

I did ask her once what grandfather was like, but she just sighed, and changed the subject. I never knew my grandfather. He had been an apothecary in Liverpool, I knew that much, a 'general doctor' Aunt had explained. I always thought of him as the kind of man one should always avoid, a dark ineffectual figure who destroyed people by his very weakness. Perhaps it was something to do with lost memories of what my own father had said, or perhaps my aunt's sniff of disapproval whenever her father was talked of. Drink was sometimes mentioned. I did know he died of tuberculosis long ago in 1848, but that was after Grandmama had come to Huddersfield. He died all alone in a house in Liverpool.

My diary, how difficult it had been to write what I liked when Arthur, that teasing older brother of mine, was sure to snatch it from me, and quiz me about it. My sister Fanny I knew would hate me if I kept it secret from her, and little Ada would want me to read it to her all the time like a bed time story. But my grandmother, as I learnt over the years was a wiser women than one might think. 'Here is a box for your birthday too,' she had said. 'See, it has a secret drawer and you can keep your diary in it. It has a special key, so don't lose it – keep it in a safe place.'

*

Such a pretty box it is, such smooth and silky wood, and lined with dark blue velvet. I stroke the wood again as I did when I first had it.

I am startled to find Ada shaking me. "Had you forgotten we have a visitor for tea?" she said sharply. Her features have become sharper with the years, like her manner. She is sometimes unsteady on her feet. Fanny and I don't mention it, but we think she sometimes has a glass or two of sherry in her room, all by herself.

It takes me a few seconds to remember where I am, and now I have to get ready in a hurry. It's always the same, I protest to myself, when one is in a hurry everything gets mislaid, my hair seems impossible to manage, and I have a struggle doing up my buttons. People are right when they say old age is a second childhood. It is difficult to get one's fingers to obey instructions properly, and my arm aches, and I feel uncomfortable.

The visitor is a neighbour who has come to collect for a children's charity. Today she has brought her two small children with her. They are not very well behaved. Children seem so noisy nowadays. She brings some notices with her, and we have a chat about how difficult everyone is finding it to settle down after the war. One always thinks things will be better at the end of a war, she says, but it seldom turns out like that. Those children really are very noisy.

Fanny and Ada are worried because I decide to go to bed early. What a silly fuss they make. It's just that I get tired sometimes, and all this thinking about the past is making me feel light-headed.

"Shall I call the doctor," Fanny suggests.

"Doctors have far too much to do to bother to come calling at this hour for no reason." I answer crossly. What a fuss they do make. I am glad to get into bed. I have another look at my diary before I fall asleep.

*

My Diary

I knew I could trust Grandmama not to read my diary, she would never ask to look at it, she would only read it if I wanted her to. Aunt was a different matter. If I wasn't careful Aunt would read everything I wrote should she get the chance. 'For your own good,' she would say, but it would be because she wanted to know what I thought about everything, particularly her. It always felt as if she were spying on us all the time.

The way she would suddenly be standing near us, or the things she seemed to know, perhaps guess, about our games. She wouldn't say of course, about the diary, she'd read it while I was asleep, and never say a word. She was always trying to get into other people's minds. But if you said anything to her about anything that mattered she would dismiss whatever it was with a sharp word or two. 'Not a subject for young ladies to talk about,' or 'you are far too young to think about such things,' or 'God will punish you for such wicked thoughts'.

That tenth birthday of mine my brother Arthur sauntered into the room, a way he had of making me feel inferior. I couldn't help but admire him, he was tall and fair, and good looking if you forgot the often discontented expression on his handsome face. 'Happy birthday' he said in his ironic way, as if the last thing he expected was for it to be a happy day. He threw a book at me, to catch. 'Butter fingers,' he said scornfully, as I dropped it. 'You're ten now, in double figures, that's what Aunt says,' he mocked, 'and because you're a girl you'll have to help in the house more often than ever.'

I was jealous of my brother. Why was it, I thought, that girls always have to help in the house, while boys are supposed to go out to play, or sit and read. Why was it, soon after we arrived here, that Aunt had said to me that because everyone was so busy, I would have to look after Arthur's clothes and mend them and see he had socks without holes, and shirts with buttons on. I can't have been more than six. I hardly knew how to sew, let alone darn or sew on buttons, and I found sewing so difficult. Why couldn't Arthur mend his own socks, and sew on his own buttons? But I had soon learned to do it while Aunt stood over me as I tried to weave neat darns, and put on neat patches, and sew on those buttons which I sometimes thought Arthur pulled off on purpose.

I saw that the book Arthur had thrown to me, as I picked the book up off the floor, was called *Alice in Wonderland*. 'It's not mine, I just borrowed it, but I thought you might like to read it. It's a kind of fairy tale, just what girls like reading,' said Arthur. But I could tell he had read it himself and liked it, although I knew he would never admit it. For all his teasing, and pretended superiority, he thought of himself as my instructor, and kept me informed about what he did at school. I have always been grateful to him for that.

I remember the bit in Alice in Wonderland about the tea party where the mad hatter says "no room, no room," and Alice says there is plenty of room and sits down at the table in spite of him. Well done, Alice, I used to think.

I had been born at Chorlton-upon-Medlock near Manchester, so Grandmama had said. That was the first thing I had put in my diary, 'Mary Winder, born in Manchester, on November 25th 1860.' I took such care writing those first few words the way Grandmama had taught me, so slowly and carefully, forming each curve and line so as not to spoil the page. It was like footsteps on fresh snow where you have to walk carefully so as not to spoil the great white sheet under your feet.

'List of presents on my birthday,' I wrote in the diary trying to concentrate on neat writing to please Grandmama. 'Grandmama a box and Diary.' I didn't know if Diary ought to have a capital letter or not, but it seemed important, and it looked much nicer with a capital 'D'. 'Arthur a book', 'Fanny a purse'. I had crossed out a capital 'P' for the purse, and written a small 'p' instead, the first mistake on my clean page.

My sister Fanny was two years younger than me, but just as tall, and her arms and legs seemed to straggle about a bit. I recall the purse she had given me, she had made it from an old stocking. I feel I can still remember her affectionate hug. 'Happy birthday' I hear her saying, 'happy, happy birthday' and she gave me a wet kiss. It's strange the odd things one remembers. She said she wished she was as old as ten. 'I made the purse myself' she told me. 'It's lovely' I said, 'what neat stitches and just what I need to keep my buttons in'. 'You do like it, don't you,' she enquired anxiously. 'It's lovely,' I answered, reassuring her. Fanny always seemed to need reassuring.

'Ada, a cake.' I wrote. Ada my pretty little sister of five, presented me with a small cake that I had seen Elisa help her make in the kitchen the day before. Elisa was our maid. I made it myself Ada said proudly. I gave her a hug too. Many happy returns of the day, she said. It's much nicer than a purse, isn't it, because it's something we can eat now. We shared it between us, and later Aunt scolded me for leaving crumbs on the floor. 'We can't encourage vermin, can we,' she rebuked.

The purse Fanny had given me disappeared next day, and I suspected Ada of having taken it. She often took little things, but sometimes she brought them back later. I was always putting back things she had taken, so Grandmama, and especially Aunt, wouldn't notice.

I remember feeling very happy that day. The best surprise was that Grandmama told me I could go to the High School now I was ten, and so I wouldn't have to go and work in a mill. I had always been afraid that when I got to ten, that's what I would have to do, work in one of those mills down by the canal. Arthur had been at the Collegiate School these past two years. He said he was going to be a doctor when he grew up. If I were a mill girl and he was a doctor, he'd never want to speak to me again when he became a grand gentleman. Perhaps if I worked hard at school I could be a governess, or a teacher, even a writer. Girls couldn't be doctors.

'I AM GOING TO THE HIGHFIELD SCHOOL' I wrote in capital letters, across the middle of the page. I sat there thinking of what the High School would be like, and would the other girls be nice and would I have friends, and would it be very difficult to keep up with school work. Grandmama said I would be well able, she hadn't spent these last few years teaching me to read and write so as to shame her. Arthur was always telling me how hard he had to work. Girls were too stupid to be able to understand things like Latin or mathematics he said, or any other things that were part of his school work. 'I should think at a girls' school you'll learn things like house keeping and sewing and cooking,' he said loftily. 'It won't really matter if you can't read or write properly, and mathematics is no use at all to a girl in any case.'

It wasn't so difficult keeping my diary safe from prying eyes, I found as the weeks went by. I always locked it away in my box. I had a secret place too, to keep the box hidden, because I suspected that Arthur would one day find a way of discovering and opening the secret drawer. No, it was stopping people watching me while I wrote it that was difficult.

'What's that you're writing,' Fanny had asked me one day. Nothing, just a list of things,' I answered as she peered over my shoulder. I would keep it out of her sight in future. 'You better be careful what you put in that book,' Arthur said one morning. I had got up early so no one would be about. He had sneaked up on me, and watched me as I bent over my careful writing. I can almost still feel an embarrassed redness begin to cover my face and neck. I hoped he didn't have time to read anything. I hastily shut it, and after that I put it away in my box, and I didn't get it out again for quite a long time.

*

I wake from my reverie, and Fanny insists on taking my temperature. Ada and Fanny are both looking at me with worried expressions. I wish they wouldn't fuss so. There's nothing really wrong with me. I just feel a bit tired that's all, and if only this wretched cough would go I would be quite all right.

"You can't be too careful at your age," Fanny says. "You should stay in bed for a few days. I will call the doctor."

"I don't want the doctor," I say, crossly. But I can see she is determined and there is nothing I can do to prevent her. She and Ada go downstairs to telephone. I begin thinking of the day we moved to Rochdale.

*

Chorlton

I think I can remember the past, way back sometimes, long before I started writing my diary. That was when we lived at Chorlton in Manchester. Fanny and Arthur have never thought about Chorlton, Manchester, they have always said I have made up stories about it all. I do suspect Arthur remembered something of it, but would never admit it. It's as if I have a secret history of my own, that no one else knows about. Fanny teases me when I say it is the first of my nine lives. Ada wasn't even born. All those disconnected pictures. Perhaps I really do remember them, perhaps not, who can tell. One can only try and recall them as best one can.

I was born on November 25th 1860, so says my diary. One has to be born, whether one likes it or not. People were always being born in Manchester, especially in our street. There was a woman next door who got sent to the workhouse to have her baby because she wasn't married. Everyone was standing round outside the house. Being sent to the workhouse was a terrible thing, like going to hell.

It was hard enough having a baby in the first place, I knew that from the very beginning, because I had watched a baby being born one day. I was crouching in the corner of a room, and there was all that shouting and groaning, and then the baby came. Such a messy, ugly, red little thing. When it cried everyone was happy. I wasn't though.

I can't remember what Chorlton-upon-Medlock where we lived really looked like. It is rather a nice name, don't you think, as if people were usually happy and laughing there. There was my father, as I remember, smelling of tobacco, with tickly whiskers on his face, and a very large sort of presence. He seemed to fill the whole world, almost. His face was kind, with an enveloping smile that made the world seem safe. He used to call me his little Mary, his little madonna, as he let me ride on his shoulders to keep me out of the muck. I have one of those pictures in my mind, of him squelching through evil smelling sticky mud. There was rubbish all over the road. I remember his hands, holding me safe, strong safe hands.

Then there was that horrible spinning shed. There was lots of noise I remember in that giant shed, full of machinery that whirled and churned and clacked, and it went on and on for ever. So much noise it frightened me. I got scolded for trying to run off. All those women, with their shawls, and all those boys and girls with tired white faces, scuttling about and being shouted at by horrid looking men, not that you'd expect anyone to hear what they said. It was very hot and damp. Some of the women were smiling. How could anyone smile in such a horrid noisy place.

Another thing I remember are men lying in the gutters, and a woman groaning. You could see the marks on her where she had been beaten. Drunk, the lot of them, Mama said with a toss of her head, and then added and who could blame them. I wondered why no one offered to help the poor woman. Perhaps she was making more fuss than she needed to, but I didn't think so.

Everyone in Chorlton seemed to have such loud voices. Mama shouted across the street at a neighbour, who shouted back. 'How's the bairn,' 'what think you on Jane's husband running off like that,' and, 'is it true they be laying off hands at t' Mill again?' I suppose I remembered that conversation because those were the three things that mattered, not being ill, having a father to look after you, and getting money from work. My father sometimes shouted at us. He was a brewer's clerk and often he had a few drinks before he left work. I don't like thinking about his shouting at us. I used to put my hands over my ears until he stopped.

My maternal grandfather, that's what Grandmama said I should call Mama's father, when I asked her. We only saw him every now and again when we lived in Manchester, as he lived across town, and was always working we were told. We did spend Christmas day together once at his house. It seemed very small, there were so many people in it. He and my maternal grandmother worked in the cotton mill together, and so did most of my aunts and uncles. Some of them were cousins but I don't know which except for the babies.

Some things in Chorlton were as clear as could be. There was Arthur and me and Fanny and Betsy and Betsy was ill, coughing so hard, with a fever. Little Betsy, she was more mine than anyone else's, after all I looked after her a lot of the time. She belongs to me, I used to think.

I remember standing in a field with lots of grave stones standing up in rows. There was a box Mama said Betsy had been shut up in, and it was at the bottom of a hole. I wondered how she could get out of the box to go to heaven. After she died no one else ever talked about her, even Arthur didn't want to listen when I asked him how you got to heaven.

I used to have dreams about Betsy. Sometimes they had to shake me to wake me up and even then I would go on screaming. There was a dream that I had been shut up in a box in black darkness, not being able to get out. Sometimes I remembered holding Betsy's hand when she was ill, and it was my fault I couldn't stop her going away. Sometimes it seemed we were in a dark hole together, and we called and called and no one heard us.

Sometimes I was frightened when Papa came home. I remember angry raised voices in the next room. One morning Papa didn't go to work, because he said he had lost his job. 'I've been turned off,' he said. Mama looked so worried. Papa and Mama talked all day long, they were not angry any more, just feeling hopeless. They talked about what should be done, and how we could get enough to eat, and the workhouse. Arthur and me and Fanny crowded into a corner and tried not to be noticed. All that talking as if none of us were there in the corner, scared of we knew not what.

After that all I can recall is that Elizabeth, Mama's sister came to stay for a while and Mama went back to work in the Mill. She was always tired and cross when she came home from that Mill. But she didn't work for long, she got laid off as well. 'Summat will have to be done,' she said, 'if things don't get any better. It's only bairns now what seem to get any work.' She must have seen that I looked scared. 'There's nought to be afeared of,' she said, 'none of you bairns is old enough to work in the Mill as yet.'

Cotton famine is hard on us all, Papa said. I asked what a cotton famine was. I think he must have said something about America, that half the world was starving because men had been fighting each other a long way across the sea. For a long time I couldn't understand why anyone should be fighting because they wanted to eat cotton in some far away place called America.

It was years later that I understood that we escaped working at the Mill because a new law had been passed, and there were so many applications for the few jobs available it wasn't worth the owners to cross the factory authorities. No one could have thought any of us as being ten years old yet.

I asked Mama later how she could work in such a horrid place. She said she worked there before she was married. 'I started when I was eight,' she said proudly, 'and worked my way up to be a spinner. It can be quite good fun, and having money of your own, that's quite something. You can be your own master then.' 'Weren't you glad to leave it,' I asked, thinking of the noise of all those great clanking machines and how frightened I was of the very idea of being inside one of those great sheds. 'You get used to it,' Mama said, 'it's easier when you're young.'

*

I wake with a start. For a few minutes I am not sure where I am.

"I've brought you a cup of tea," says my sister Ada. I don't care much for my sister Ada now, perhaps I never did. I look at her waspish old face, and I can't imagine how she could once have been such a pretty, engaging child. I suspect she has been drinking.

"Wake up," she says, her face too close to mine, I'm sure her breath smells of alcohol. We three old sisters, Fanny and Ada and I, living together in our little house by the seaside, are getting on each other's nerves. After all Ada is the youngest, and she's eighty-one. We have to manage things in the house between us, most of the time it is Fanny and myself who keep things reasonable. Ada does help sometimes.

"The doctor will be coming later this morning" she says. "You should stay in bed." I am glad when she goes downstairs again. The more one thinks of the past the further back memories can go. I lie here in bed, waiting for the doctor. I do feel rather hot. And I am grateful for the cup of tea. I seem to feel so sleepy all the time.

*

Moving Away

Papa had got a new job as a clerk in a spinning shed in Rochdale. 'And lucky to get it,' he said, 'we must move over to Rochdale tomorrow.' We spent all day putting our things together.

Of course we had to leave Betsy behind when we moved away from Manchester. There she would be all alone in that grave in the churchyard. No one to visit or to talk to her as I did when me and Mama went to put flowers on her grave. I used to wonder if Betsy knew I couldn't help leaving her when we had to go to Rochdale. I did tell her we had to go, the last time I went to her graveside before we left for good, but I didn't know if she could hear me.

I planted a primrose on her grave because I remember thinking she would have something pretty to look at every year when the flowers came out. I asked Arthur to come and help me, but he just shrugged and said Betsy was gone, and that was all there was to it. Putting flowers on her grave was a silly sort of girl's idea. Perhaps he just didn't want to talk about her, he wanted to forget she was ever born.

Living in Chorlton was what I think of as the first of my nine lives. It is my own secret life. Fanny and Ada say they remember nothing of it at all. I went back there years later, and the streets were all changed, so there was no way I could find where we used to live. I couldn't even find Betsy's grave. I think I left part of myself behind in that churchyard. It was something I understood even then in a strange kind of way, something I knew I had lost and could never get back. It felt as if a piece of me would always be missing for ever after.

*

When I wake up this time, the doctor is standing by the bed. He insists on sounding my chest, and I feel embarrassed.

"You have a mild attack of bronchitis," he says, "and you should stay in bed for a few days" Fanny looks triumphant. "It wouldn't do," continues the doctor, "at your age, to let complications set in." At my age. What has age got to do with it, I'd like to know. When he has gone Fanny brings me a cup of tea, walking carefully so as not to spill it. It is another penalty of old age, that it is difficult to be sure of one's balance while concentrating on what one's hands are doing. She trips, but manages to keep her feet.

"Careful" I say, "there is no need for you to keep waiting on me like this. I'll get up in a few minutes."

"You'll do nothing of the kind," she says. "And the doctor says you must drink plenty of fluids, so you must drink as much as you can. Now I shall go and get your medicine."

When she comes back she gives me the medicine, and water somehow gets spilled all down the front of my night gown. The bed has to be rearranged, and I feel quite tired and start thinking about Rochdale again before I fall asleep.

*

It was quite exciting moving to Rochdale, away from Manchester. There was a big cart with all our things that we had helped pile up on it. The horse started away to somewhere else, miles and miles away, and we might have been going anywhere, I thought, to a strange land with castles, or near the sea Papa had told us about, or where there were great big houses, with princes and princesses in them. 'It's quite a small place,' Mama explained, 'but the district isn't too bad. We'll rent the cellar until we can find something better.'

Rochdale

Rochdale is a very hilly kind of place. Everywhere you go it is either up a hill or down a hill. Rows and rows of houses, each one like the other, up or down the street. If you looked out in the early morning there would be someone on each doorstep, scrubbing away at the dirt on the step, and washing it back into the street. But we didn't live in a street like that. We lived in a cellar of a back-to-back block of houses right at the bottom of the hill.

Mama was right when she said there wouldn't be much room when we moved. Papa had a new job, but it was much less money. Everywhere people seemed to be moving into rooms or out of them. It was dark in our cellar and we had to have candles if we wanted to see very much. It was damp too, water ran down the walls, and left little pools at the bottom, which had to be mopped up all the time. Mama and Papa slept on the floor on one side, and we slept all together on the other side, keeping each other warm. We had mostly bread and porridge to eat, and lentil stew. When I try, I can still smell the stew cooking on the fire for our Sunday treat. I don't think I have ever smelled or tasted anything so good since.

Mama said it was better for us to be outside when we could, because inside it was so cramped, and damp, and the air so stale. Arthur and I used to climb with our little sister Fanny up the steep streets to where the moors began. In summer there were flowers and bees, and birds singing, and we never wanted to go back to the cellar. Mama would give us a piece of bread, and we could stay out all day. There was always the beck if we were thirsty. Up there the water always tasted clean and fresh, not like the water we got from the pump in the yard. Besides, we could collect wood for the winter.

Sometimes Papa and Mama would come with us on a Sunday. Papa would tell us all about the caterpillars that turned into butterflies and moths, and the tadpoles that turned into frogs and toads and newts. Once we saw a badger. But come the winter it was so cold up there in the wind, we couldn't stay for long.

Rochdale was where our Ada was born. We came back from the moors one day to find the new baby that was expected was a sister. She slept on a pillow in a drawer from the old chest we had brought with us from Manchester. She cried a lot.

Mama felt uncomfortable in our cellar, you could tell she hated it there. 'Whenever are things going to look up,' she would say, 'it's bad for the bairns in this damp, dark place, and I wonder if the baby can live. It will be Betsy all over again,' she would say accusingly. 'Our Ada has had a cough these last few weeks and I begin to wonder if she has the fever too.' Ada always seemed to be snuffling, and complaining with that wailing cry of hers. When ever any of us got a cold Papa would laugh and sing:

Julius Caesar made a law,
Augustus Caesar signed it
That anyone who made a sneeze
Should run away and find it.

Then we would all laugh. Papa often made us laugh, he was always making jokes. But we all hated the winter, there was always one or other of us poorly, sometimes all of us at once. Sometimes Mama would look so tired we thought she was going to be ill too.

Papa would say in a kind of desperate voice that he was doing his best, and not to go on at him, and we just had to be patient until the cotton famine got better. I still shivered whenever I heard the whistle of the buffer early in the morning calling everyone to the Mill. I was getting older now, and they might take me on. I would have gone if I had been allowed because we were all so hungry. Arguments with Mama and Papa always ended up in their shouting at each other. They always seemed so cross and tired since we came to Rochdale.

Arthur was put on as errand boy, which brought in a little money each week, but would barely pay for his own keep, Mama would complain. Arthur had a distant hard look in his eyes, as if he wasn't really there at all. He worked, brought home the money, tossed it on the table, and then went to sleep.

'Pa's drunk again,' Mama used to say more and more often when we lived in Rochdale. I knew there was something wrong, because there would be arguments, and shouting all night. At first I used to be so happy when Papa used to sing me to sleep at nights, hymns sometimes, about evening, and nursery rhymes about Jack and Jill, or Little Jack Horner. But now we used to listen with dread to his rambling voice singing as he came down the street, and we knew it would be a bad night again.

Some of the arguments made us really afraid, as Mama would cry, and say he would lose his job again, and why couldn't they just be happy, and why did he have to go and drink all the time, just like his father, and look where that had got us all.

We didn't like the people in the street at Rochdale either. 'Talking Dutch hoity-toity, too big for your boots' boys would call us as we walked down our street. It never seemed to matter in Manchester that we talked the way Papa said we should. He couldn't abide it if we didn't call him Papa. 'Better' not 'be'er,' he would repeat rather wearily, 'we're gentry' he used to say, 'even if we have fallen on bad times, and I want my girls to be brought up as ladies'. Trying to be gentry here only seemed to make everyone laugh at us. Perhaps it was because our clothes were cleaner than most, they were always being washed to get rid of the fleas and lice and bed bugs. Our clothes were getting very ragged.

Besides Papa said we shouldn't mix with the rougher sort, but keep ourselves to ourselves. Sometimes they threw stones. 'Boney will get you,' they called, 'Boney will get you.' I thought Boney must be like one of those rough men Papa warned us about, but very thin and bony, with a red nose with a drop on the end of it, and long bony fingers that might scratch your eyes out. Everyone had been frightened once that Boney might come across the sea and catch us all.

It was when I was about five, on a damp dark day when I got burnt and the whole world caught on fire. My bad luck day, I always call it. It was after that that everything got worse and worse. It was very cold, and Ada was poorly again. I was holding a candle that fell over and it must have caught the corner of my pinny. I remember I screamed, I remember the pain in my arm and my shoulder, trying to tear off my clothes as the flames leapt up. It almost seemed as if someone else was hurting, not me, because it hurt too much, yet I knew it was me all the time. People started running about.

Everything seemed dark after that, except I could always feel the pain in my shoulder. Then I only remember a few things, like a neighbour saying 'If it hadn't a been for her shawl, I doubt the poor bairn would still be with us'. I remember Mama weeping, and holding my hand: Arthur staring at me with curious disbelief: Fanny holding onto my hand: Papa's voice, and people everywhere, and Ada crying.

I did wonder sometimes as I lay there in a corner of the cellar, if I was going to join Betsy with the angels. I supposed I might go to hell, and that that wouldn't feel very different from now. Hell fire must be just like the pain in my arm and chest. But I hadn't been really wicked, had I – I couldn't think of anything so awful that I would have to go to hell.

There were the times of course when I had wet myself, and the day I lost my temper with Fanny and she ran off in floods of tears. The day I had hidden one of the marbles which Arthur was so fond of, to stop him being so horrid. Perhaps I would still have a chance to go to heaven. Going to live with the angels didn't seem such a bad idea, I would be happy, and my shoulder wouldn't hurt, and I wouldn't be tired any more, but best of all I would stop hurting. I remember Papa sitting by me as I cried in the night, and Mama would put fresh linen over the burns, but that often made it hurt more.

One day I looked at myself and knew the burn was never going to heal properly, I'd be scarred for life, I'd always have that red puckered scar in a hole in my shoulder. I didn't mind so much how it had hurt, you can forget that in the end, but you can't forget a scar that will be there for ever. I could never ever wear those low cut dresses like the gentry. I couldn't pretend to be a 'princess' any more, find someone handsome to marry and look after me, if I had such an ugly shoulder. I would never ever let anyone see it, I'd always keep it covered.

I could move my arm all right, after a time, but not very high, and it still aches sometimes if I use it too much. It's difficult to sew for long, and writing makes my arm get very tired. I always think of my burnt shoulder when I think of Rochdale, I hated Rochdale.

My shoulder did seem to take a very long time to heal. Papa couldn't bear to look when the dressings were being changed. He would come and comfort me when I cried in the night, and tell me stories, and hold my hand, but he didn't call me his little Madonna any more. I felt as if I had got spoiled, dirty, no good any more, like a cup with a dirty crack in it. It was never the same with Papa anymore. He was very gentle, but it just didn't seem the same, he never looked at me the way he used to do, just turned away.

*

"I hardly dreamt at all last night" I tell Fanny next morning. "It is a beautiful sunny day."

"Perhaps that is why you seem so much better today" Fanny says. "All that dreaming about the past is very bad for you." I insist on getting up.

"Perhaps it will do no harm for you to get up for a while", Fanny says, "as long as you wrap up warm."

It's pleasant sitting in the sun. The sitting-room faces South, unlike my bedroom which is North. I am content to drink my tea, and eat some scones Ada has made. Ada is a better cook than Fanny.

"I made them specially for you," she says. Fanny is knitting, she does a lot of knitting.

"I am making you a new bed jacket," she says. I admire the pattern, Fanny is really very good at knitting still, even with the rheumatism she has in her fingers.

"They have put up a new shelter on the front, quite near," says Ada. I am glad. We have found lately when we go for a walk that getting as far as a shelter in windy weather has been quite a difficulty.

"Perhaps you will be well enough to go for a short walk in a day or two," says Ada.

"We have asked John and Philip and Peter to come for tea tomorrow," says Fanny. I don't like the idea that they have been making arrangements behind my back.

"I told Peter not to come," Ada says. Fanny looks annoyed.

"I don't know if I feel up to visitors," I say.

"They won't be coming until half past four."

"But they always come at four," I complain.

"I thought you would be pleased," says Fanny, even more affronted.

"My dears, I'm sure you made the arrangement for the best," is all I can think of replying. Perhaps by tomorrow I shall feel like talking to visitors. So I smile, and they smile back and we are friends again.

I am tired climbing up the stairs. I can't sleep so I get out of bed again to get my diary. Now that I have once opened it, it is like Pandora's box, once memories have begun to escape they can't be stopped. I fall asleep thinking of Rochdale, where we started that new kind of life which always seemed to be threatened by an imminent move to the workhouse.

*

A few months later, Mama and Papa had a terrible row one night. Papa had come home very tired, and sat on the chair saying nothing all evening. I heard him and Mama talking after we went to bed. Arthur was awake too, and we looked at each other, with a great fear, because we might have to go to the workhouse.

'I've lost my job,' Papa said to Mama, in a quiet and listless sort of way, 'and there's no prospect of another. Reckon it will be the workhouse now. I've done my best, been round all the likely mills this last few days, but there's no work to be had anywhere.' 'I guessed as much', we heard Mama say, 'these last few days when you've come home, I've known you've been tramping the streets. I warned you, I warned you that drink would be the end of us. I've only to look at you to know there's trouble coming.'

Mama cried, Papa cursed, Mama said she would get work, Papa shouted that didn't she know there was no work to be had. 'There's two weeks rent to pay, and how am I to feed us all,' Mama said. There was more shouting, and crying, and then it was quiet. Arthur and I held hands in the dark. We must have gone to sleep at last.

Next morning Mama said Arthur was not to go for his job, that we must think what to do, because we couldn't stay as we were. 'Your father has left us, gone off he says to America, to make his fortune, and he'll come back and find us and look after us when he can. There's no work to be had here. He thinks they will be glad of anyone who has a good hand – can write well – in the new country. He says he may find family contacts there.'

But Papa never said goodbye, he never came and said goodbye. Why didn't he say goodbye?

Papa had gone away, to where there wasn't any cotton, but he'd come back soon to look after us. I wondered where America was, perhaps it was near Manchester, only like an island in the sea. I tried to think what it would be like without Papa for a while. At least be and Mama wouldn't be shouting at each other every night. I hoped it wasn't too far away, and he would be coming back to take us away from the workhouse.

Mama was holding a letter which she kept tapping against her other hand. It was if she were making up her mind about something. I was thinking that now nothing could stop us from going to the workhouse, because there wouldn't be enough money. Arthur would never make enough to keep us all, and there were no jobs to be had in the mills for Mama. Perhaps Mama could get some other work somehow, and I could look after our baby and Fanny. I looked at Arthur. We both knew Mama wouldn't find any work. I was only six, well, nearly seven and I knew they wouldn't have me.

The workhouse would be the worst possible place to go, everyone talked in hushed voices when they mentioned it and no one would go there if they could possibly help it. It sounded worse than prison, and nearly everyone who went there died.

'Your Papa left me this,' Mama said at last, and brought the long dreadful silence to an end. 'It's a letter to your grandmama,' she said. 'Are we going back to Chorlton,' I asked. I thought if we were going to stay with Mama's brothers and sisters it would be very difficult to fit us all in. 'No, I did think of it', Mama said, 'but they are having hard times too.'

'It is to your other grandmother, Papa's Mama.' 'I didn't know we had another grandmama', Arthur said. 'She lives in Huddersfield.' 'Is that near America,' I remember asking. 'It's about as far away as Manchester,' she said. 'She lives in a nice house and Papa said before he left that I must take you there straight away.'

Why, I wondered, did Mama sound so sad about it, when it sounded like a fairy story, like being saved by a rich queen from a kind of ogre. It sounded exciting, like an adventure, so very different from a journey to the workhouse where I'd been afraid of going just a few minutes ago. Nothing could be worse than that, so why had Mama been so sad to tell us about it? When Papa came home he would be pleased to be coming to a nice house.

It was to be the end of living with Mama and Papa in our own room, I realised, even if it had been only a cellar. Everything would change. I'm beginning to feel like a butterfly or a frog, turning from one thing to another, I thought. I wondered if butterflies and things had any memory at all of what they used to be. There must be something in me that will get left over from before I thought. There was the scar on my shoulder of course, that would stay with me for the rest of my life.

*

A Sea Change

It is odd how quotations keep coming into mind when one is old, I think as I close the diary.

> Nothing of him that doth fade,
> But doth suffer a sea-change
> Into something rich and strange.

The Tempest was always one of my favourite Shakespeare plays. I suppose we all felt like drowned sailors when we went to live in Huddersfield, we certainly suffered a sea change. I decide to put the diary away for a while.

Next day I am dressed, and ready to receive our two visitors. I try and concentrate on the present, and stop my mind wandering off into the past, at least for the afternoon. One needs friends at our age, it makes all the difference. My friend Captain John Maurice, retired from the navy, still quite handsome, with his easy manner and his kindly face and a naval swagger despite the fact he has to walk with a stick. "Rheumatism, fearful nuisance," he announced at our first introduction. An open, seafarer's kind of face he has, scarred by the elements. All sailors seem to look like that, as if the storms at sea had always been matched by the storms of their own personal lives. He is someone to trust, I think.

Philip Harbenden, a retired solicitor, Fanny's friend, is quite different. He looks as if he had the secrets of the world locked up beneath his smooth and kindly manner. I'm not sure if I would trust him, too smooth. We were going to have Peter Morris here as well, but Ada never seems to keep her friends for long. We rather liked Peter, he's a retired insurance man, but he and Ada had an argument about the date on a card in the Museum last time we were out together. Ada always thinks she knows best about everything.

We went to the Museum together some weeks ago, before I got bronchitis. We go on these little outings sometimes, either to the

Pavilion for tea, or to a theatre matinee, it breaks the monotony. That time we had decided we would to try something different.

It gives one a strange feeling to be part of history. Exhibits of household goods, like mangles and irons and leaded grates that were part of our own childhood, set out as if they belonged to some foreign tribe or are part of an ancient civilisation. I suppose they are, but then of course so are we, part of an ancient civilisation. Perhaps that's what the young people think of us, fossils to be labelled and described like museum pieces. John with his old sea captain's blazer must seem like that to them, and Philip too with his bent shoulders and slow walk, and his black rolled umbrella.

We usually take great care with our little tea parties. There is the silver teapot and things to clean, the best cups to get out, the scones to make. Fanny has bought a cake today, instead of making one. What with the rationing, and the very warm weather, last time the cake didn't turn out so well. Such a waste of the butter and sugar we had saved. None of us like bought cakes very much.

I knew things wouldn't be right this time, I see the crumbs on the carpet, the uncleaned silver, the stain on the tray cloth, the dust on the book shelf. I never can trust my sisters to do things properly.

"No help in the house," repeats John over tea, when I tell him how difficult things are. "We can't have that, can we? I'll see about putting in an advertisement in the store for you."

We are lucky that we do have a small local shop quite near within walking distance. They even stock pretty paper table napkins.

It is a pleasant enough afternoon, I suppose, although I wish there had been three men instead of two. It always makes for difficulties, with two men and three women. Ada is not in a very good temper, and Fanny gets resentful. However our visitors seem to have enjoyed their tea. Besides, men like to feel they are contributing something. Men should always feel they are being useful to their women folk, it makes for contentment all round. And now perhaps at last we shall have someone to help in the house again.

After our visitors have gone, we discuss it at length.

"You can't expect me to contribute much money," my sister Ada says, "All my savings are tied up in the nursing home I have arranged to go to when I feel I can no longer stay here."

"But it is Fanny and I who have bought the house between us. You don't seem all that short of money when it comes to paying out for our coffee or tea at the pavilion, or any of our other little treats," I protest.

"I pay my share of the housekeeping, don't I?" she says indignantly. "We all do our bit, one way or another, don't we? Besides if we do get someone, they are sure to be more trouble than they are worth."

"We can't go on like this," I say, "because the house really does need a good clean. When our friends were here to tea, I felt quite ashamed, those crumbs on the carpet, and the dust on those top shelves."

"You've only got to tell me what needs doing," says Fanny. I ignore this. It's not her fault that we are all liable to injure ourselves, if we take on too much. And that's another thing, we have had so many breakages lately.

"We can't go on like this," I say again firmly. "I am tired, I don't want to argue any more. I am going to bed. For once I'll leave the washing up to both of you." So I go to bed.

*

'I live at Belmont Terrace, Brunswick Place, Huddersfield, Yorkshire.' I had written in my diary. That was the beginning of my next life, so different from being with Mama and Papa. After Papa had gone we had spent the day wrapping our few belongings in our shawls. Mama had gone out and sold the chest with the drawers and all the other things like our cooking pot and jars, and come home with a loaf of bread. 'We've just enough for our train fares', she announced, 'and now we'll not need to pay the rent.'

We walked to the railway station. The station was full of noise, and steam, and sparks, and a fiery glow, whistles blowing, trains clanking. Trains are like dragons, I thought, belching fire and smoke. We sat together on a seat, the dragon gave a whistle, and clanked out past the houses, and the gas works, and the mill, past more and more houses and then we were out in the green fields with trees and cows and sheep. We even went over a river, with ducks swimming in the water. If it is like this where we are going to live, I thought, I wish we had left Rochdale a long time ago. I was quite sorry when we got near to Huddersfield and all the buildings started again. It seemed to be a very busy place.

Everywhere men were building things. Half finished mill buildings, half finished houses, piles of sand, coal dust patches covered with muddy pools, fences being pulled down, put up, stray bricks, piles of rubbish being burnt on small bonfires, everything seemed to be in a state of permanent change. Men walked along beside the railway, often with a wife and children trailing behind, cows and sheep were being driven alongside, everything seemed noise and bustle the nearer we got.

You can hear the trains puffing away all the time in Huddersfield. All the commotion of people and luggage, and carts and pony traps, whistles and steam and people and guards shouting 'all clear'. Trains are such exciting things. I remember thinking we would never have got to Huddersfield without a train.

*

I am quite recovered and we have resumed our walks along the front, our little treats and outings. We had only one, unlikely, application in response to our advertisement for help in the house. Rose has been with us two weeks.

"Them germs," she says, "are everywhere, crawling up the walls and down them drains." Each day she demands an endless supply of disinfectant to keep the germs at bay. The whole house smells of it.

"Them germs are everywhere," she repeats, "everywhere, even if you can't see the beggars." She talks as if they are the enemy, as if they were German spies. "They'll get us, one of these days, mark my word. They are there, everywhere, climbing up them walls, everywhere."

She starts putting disinfectant on her duster to dust down the walls. The wall paper is already beginning to show signs of wear and tear where it has been scrubbed and cleaned with all that disinfectant. Everything smells of disinfectant.

Rose is to be dismissed. Fanny and Ada have gone to the corner shop leaving me to tell her so.

"You are much better at doing such things," they say, as they make the excuse that we have run out of tea to go round to the store. Perhaps I can get Rose to clean the bathroom before she goes. She doesn't like cleaning the bathroom.

"Them germs are worst in the bathroom, I daren't clean in there." It is of course the one place in the house at the moment that could do with some disinfectant.

I give her instructions, and hover uneasily while she complies. She reappears very quickly.

"I've finished the bathroom, Ma'am," Rose says. I inspect the bathroom. I suppose it is a little cleaner than it was. The disinfectant is overpowering. For a moment I wonder if I shall need to wear my gas mask next time I enter. Perhaps it is as well I haven't thrown my wartime mask away yet. I give her her wages for this week, and an extra ten shillings.

"Thank you for all you have done for us," I say, "but we won't be requiring your services any more." Rose looks so crestfallen I almost relent. But a waft of disinfectant persuades me otherwise. She looks as if she might be going to cry.

"I am sure you will find other work easily enough," I say, "and I have given you an excellent reference." Rose gives a sniff and departs, much to my relief. I go back to my diary.

*

Huddersfield

There we stood, on that dark September evening when we knocked on the door of Grandmama's house. We were carrying all our belongings in our shawls. It seemed a very big house. It was red brick, and it seemed very clean and neat, standing on its clean pavement. There was a big door with a brass knocker, and Mama knocked hard on it until someone came. A maid opened it, she was wrapped in a large white apron and her hair was up in a bun with ends sticking out everywhere. She smelt of onions.

'Who is it?' asked a lady's voice. 'She says she's Margaret Winder, Ma'am. Your daughter-in-law,' the maid added as Mama explained. 'And Ma'am, she's brought four children with her.' There was a long pause. 'My grandchildren did you say,' the lady's voice asked as if it were impossible to believe it. 'That's what she says, Ma'am.' Another pause. 'Show them in, don't keep them waiting on the doorstep, show them in at once,' the voice said.

We were ushered into a big room where an old lady was sitting in a chair in front of a flickering fire. It was difficult to see anything else much in that room except the old lady and the fire. There was a small table with an oil lamp on it next to her, and that flickering fire in a big grate beneath a mantelpiece. She looked very stern, dressed in black, with a lace cap on her head. 'Come in, Come in', she said, 'and Elisa, shut that door for goodness sake and keep the cold out.'

I can still see us standing there, myself included, just as if I had a photograph of us all, just inside that big room. The four of us in front of the door that had just closed behind us. At one end of the row was Arthur, a little way away by himself. I knew that look on his face, he was trying to pretend that visits to Huddersfield were an every day occurrence, and nothing at all to be bothered about. I thought Mama must be proud of him, standing there like a young gentlemen, despite his ragged clothes. Fanny was clinging to my hand on one side, while

Ada hid her face in my skirt and gave me a sharp pinch to make sure I hadn't forgotten she was there.

At first I could only see Grandmama sitting by the fire and the lamp, with the light flickering round. She seemed to take up most of the room. She sat there in her black dress and black lace cap like a kind of sad queen. Her eyes looked straight at me, and they were smiling even though her face looked stern.

There was another lady I could just make out after a while, very dark in the shadows, and all I could see were her eyes like two straight lines, with the light shining on her nose. She was tall and thin and we knew straight away that she disapproved of us all. Her black dress rustled in a threatening kind of way, as if she wished we would go away.

'That will do, thank you, Elisa,' said the old lady by the fire, and the maid disappeared through a door at the back of the room. Mama was walking over to the big chair in a determined kind of way, holding out the letter. 'I think you should read this,' Mama said.

It all seemed very unreal at the time, like something from a story, with the firelight, the glowing oil lamp on the little table, Mama standing there, talking softly to the old lady, and the tall cross lady moving nearer and listening to a conversation we couldn't hear properly. 'No,' said the cross lady, at last, 'I never heard of such a ridiculous idea in all my life. Dickinson would never allow it.' I wondered who Dickinson was.

'Well, aren't you going to introduce me to my grandchildren?' the old lady said, the whispering conversation coming to an end at last. Mama pushed Arthur forward towards the chair. 'Ma'am, this is our Arthur' she said. 'He's eight.'

Arthur shook hands politely the way Papa used to shake hands with him. 'I'm glad to see', said my grandmother, 'that he's not totally devoid of manners. This is your Aunt Dickinson,' she said, turning to the cross lady. Arthur held out his hand to her but she ignored him, and turned away. Grandmama gave a disapproving grunt. 'And this is our next, Minnie,' said Mama, as she encouraged me forward. I gave her a curtsey, the way people do to the gentry. 'Minnie, hmm, you are small aren't you', she said, making me feel even smaller than usual, 'let me see, how old are you did you say?' 'Six' I said, 'last birthday.' She looked me up and down but said no more.

'And this is our Fanny, she's five,' continued Mama. Fanny was taller than I was. She gave a bob too, and then gave a miserable sniff. Ada just cried, a long wailing cry, that made the thin lady put her hands over her ears. 'Hush,' said Mama. 'Ada is only two,' she explained by way of apology. 'Well, there's one thing for certain', said my Grandmother, 'you will all have to stay here for tonight, whatever is decided. You won't be able to travel any further at this late hour.'

She rang a little bell and the maid came back through the door. 'Elisa, can you find enough blankets for them, and I expect they will all be hungry.' Elisa put her arms round us and gathered us up between her arms to usher us all through that door at the back of the room.

'Why did you never answer Frank's letter after we got married,' we heard Mama say as we went. 'What letter', said Grandmama, 'I've never heard from Frank since he walked out ten years ago.' There was a sudden silence.

Elisa took us down some steps into the basement kitchen and gave us bread and dripping and a cup of tea by the kitchen range. We were very hungry. Then she lighted a candle to take us upstairs to a big room, empty except for a large and musty four-poster bed, where our echoing footsteps made us feel we were intruders. We shivered. 'This is the kind of room', Arthur announced, 'where ghosts might come.' 'What nonsense, a big boy like you talking of ghosts. Hush now, think of your little sisters.' I agreed with Arthur, it was the kind of room that made you shiver, it had a lot of dark corners. Boney could get you here, I thought. If I dared I'd have a good look under the bed before I got into it.

We were brought blankets and pillows, Elisa helped us undress as far as our petticoats, she brought water in a pretty jug and poured it into a big basin to wash our faces and hands. Us three girls were put at the top of the bed, while Arthur, refusing to undress at all, was settled at the other end. Fanny and Ada were so tired they were soon asleep. 'I don't like that tall lady,' said Arthur, in a loud whisper, after Elisa had gone. 'She's a witch, I'm sure she's a witch.' Arthur and I crept out presently to listen at the top of the stairs to see if we could hear what was being said in the room below.

Mama's voice was explaining that Papa had gone to America, that she had no money and no hope of work. It would be the workhouse for all of us unless someone could help. 'Well, they can't all stay here', I recognised the harsh voice of Aunt saying with great finality, 'I forbid it. Think of your health Mama. At your age. Sixty three is no time in life to start caring for a family of four small children. Think how old you will be by the time they are grown.'

Then there was a man's voice. 'Who ever can that be,' whispered Arthur. We tried to creep down to see, but it was no good, they would have seen us if we had crept any nearer. 'What do you think Dickinson?' said the cross lady's voice. There was a long pause. 'He must be someone important,' I whispered back. We were shivering, I suppose partly from cold and partly from fear we would be sent to the workhouse next day.

'There must be some way to keep them from the workhouse,' the old lady's voice was saying. 'There's Elisa to help, she's a good girl, I'm sure she'll be quite pleased to have them here. And I can see to their schooling.' Aunt's harsh voice spoke again – 'and what about the rest of it, where will they sleep, think of all the cooking, the washing, have you thought they might be ill? Be practical mother, even Frank couldn't expect us to do the impossible. Besides I doubt we can afford it, we'll all of us find ourselves in the workhouse if we are not careful.'

'I wouldn't wish the workhouse on anybody,' said the Dickinson man's voice. It was a soft voice, and it sounded as if it came from far away, as if he were taking a long time to think. 'Frank says in his letter he will be back as soon as he has money, he may not be away for long,' Mama said. But she didn't sound very certain. Aunt's harsh voice again, 'if you believe that you'll believe anything. Just like my father was, is Frank, once the drink gets hold there's nothing can be done. And gambling too, no doubt, if father was anything to go by.' 'You should be grateful your father didn't leave us destitute, like these poor children,' grandmother answered angrily. 'It wasn't his fault he died of the lung disease.'

'Frank is a good man, he's just had bad luck, that's all. He'll be back soon from America, you'll see,' Mama protested. 'That'll be the day', said Aunt, 'you can say goodbye to that idea for a start.'

Arthur and I looked at each other. It hadn't occurred to us that Papa wouldn't be back again in a matter of a few weeks. The idea that he would never come back at all was too stupid for anyone to believe. 'And how do you know they are your grandchildren, we've only got her word for it.' It was as if Aunt couldn't bring herself to call Mama by her own name of Margaret, as if that would somehow have made her a real person. 'It's all her fault', she said accusingly, 'enticing Frank away from us, his own kith and kin.'

'They are my only grandchildren, all there is of the next generation,' the old lady's voice said firmly. Mama's voice again: 'Frank told me to give you these. They are a copy of our marriage certificate, and the birth certificates of all the children, he said they would show we are a respectable family.' I imagined Mama handing over the papers she had brought with her. 'Hm', said Aunt, 'I see by your marriage certificate that you can't even write your own name but have to have it recorded as a mark.'

'I think we should consider carefully if we can afford to let them stay,' said the quiet man's voice. 'We can't, so that's settled,' the Aunt stated. 'We surely won't let them starve,' said Grandmama, sounding obstinate. 'Just think what life in a workhouse would be like, we can manage if we try.' Then the cross voice again – 'they can't all stay, there just isn't room.'

We knew she was making excuses to send us away, why even the big bedroom we had just sneaked away from was bigger than the room we had all lived in at Rochdale. Arthur and I looked at each other in horror, that was something else we'd never thought of. The very idea of us not being all together seemed quite impossible to imagine. It was bad enough, that Papa might be away a long time, but we had always been together. 'I think we should let them stay for the present,' said the man's voice. 'All of them?' said Aunt, in an unbelieving voice. There was a long pause. 'If you say so, James', she said, at last, 'but I'll not allow it unless I am in full charge.'

We listened, but we couldn't hear any more, because a door had been shut. We were very tired and cold, Arthur and I. We crept back to the bedroom and I jumped in quickly, in case Boney was under the bed. We were too tired not to go to sleep. And we knew we could stay here for a while at least, and not go to the workhouse.

*

Settling In

It is a few weeks later and we still have no one to replace Rose. We have invited our friends to tea again. I am determined that this time things will be done properly. I don't want John Maurice to think we don't know how to do things in a ladylike way. I am in the kitchen peeling tomatoes.

"Tomato sandwiches are much nicer if you take off the skins first," I tell Fanny.

"The ordinary cups will do," I say to Ada.

"I thought you were the one who was so particular," rejoined Ada. "It is always best to do things properly, I'll get the best ones down from the shelf." None of us is really capable of climbing up step ladders any more.

"I don't want any of us to get up on that ladder and reach for the cups," I say. My sister Ada has always been like that, as soon as she could talk, making me feel uncomfortable, feeling perhaps I should make more of an effort, do something other than I think is sensible, when we both of us know perfectly well that there is nothing else that can be done. It would be madness to try and get the cups down. But now all over teatime I shall be looking at our ordinary cups, and thinking perhaps I should have made some kind of effort to get the best ones out instead.

"Can I help?" says Fanny. She has a knack of always offering to help just when everything has been done. I'm holding a plate of sandwiches in my hand. Why doesn't she, I wonder, just take the plate and put it with the others on the trolley in the sitting room, it's obvious what I intend to do with them. I tell her to take the plate, and I watch with apprehension as I think she is about to drop some of those carefully made sandwiches. Even spreading butter is more difficult than it used to be. The plate is tilted at a dangerous angle. Fanny's hands are not very strong these days. I have to stop putting out the cream cakes as I can't be sure the sandwiches will arrive safely. As I thankfully note she has reached the trolley I resume my own preparations.

"It is a pity only two are coming," says Ada, "one of us will have to play gooseberry." I could shake her, just as I used to want to shake her all those years ago. I remind her that at our age having two gentlemen to tea does not mean we are likely to want to behave like courting couples. But I do begin to worry that again an odd number at tea will not produce as congenial an atmosphere as I would have liked.

"It's a pity Mr Patey, the vicar, couldn't come," I say. Mr Patey is Ada's new friend.

"Oh, I'm not really bothered," says Ada. I suspect she has put the vicar off, just as she did Peter.

"I don't agree with all this church going, anyway," she says. I survey the tea trolley standing in the sitting room with pleasure. The silver teapot and hot water jug, the plates of sandwiches and cakes, the bright paper table napkins, the lumps of sugar in the silver sugar basin look very inviting. Fanny and Ada sit looking out of the window to make sure they see the visitors arriving, while I clear up the kitchen, and see that the kettle is on. I take the silver teapot and the hot water jug back into the kitchen ready to make the tea when the time comes.

I hear Fanny's voice in the other room.

"She thinks she's a little Queen, you know, she always did think too much of herself."

"She always did give herself such airs," rejoins Ada. I never could get my sisters to see, even when they were young, that manners are important, and it is always best to do things in a ladylike manner, if one can. Perhaps that's why they never got married, as I did. It's always best to ignore remarks like that. I look out at the street.

It is a bright sunny day, and people are parading up and down the road as it is near the sea front and a popular place for tired old folk like us to take their exercise. There is a man in a wheel chair being pushed by rather a desperate looking younger woman, his daughter, I suppose: there is an old woman carrying some shopping, as she drags her rheumatic legs slowly across the road: there is the old man with the stick, tapping his lonely way back to number fifteen. No sign yet of our visitors. A bicycle goes by.

Three sisters living together like the three of us does make for monotony. We all know each other so well, or think we do.

Conversation gets exhausted. Mannerisms and irritating foibles get exaggerated out of all proportion. I can't stand the way Fanny will drop crumbs on the floor, or Ada will leave all the doors open and let in the draughts. I even suspect she does it so she can hear what we might say about her while she isn't there. She creeps about the house so.

And then I worry. It is such a worry when one of my sisters is out on her own. A few minutes late back and I begin to fear the worst, perhaps she has been run over, or had her purse snatched, or even at times that Fanny has lost her way home all together. Sometimes Ada goes out for hours on end, and never says where. She gets a taxi, what an extravagance. She says she has business to transact. Why should I worry, I tell myself, it's stupid. But I do, and find my hands have been shaking with anxiety until who ever it is is home again.

The bell rings and our gentlemen callers are here. There is a chorus of 'come in, can I take your stick for you, would you like to sit here, how are you? Did you have a pleasant walk here along the front?' 'Is the wind cold,' someone asks, 'is the tide in, are there many people on the beach?' Then it's 'do have a sandwich, I think you take sugar, we find this kind of cake very good, do try some.' All my life I have had this strange habit, of feeling that I am looking on at what is happening whenever we have visitors, instead of being a part of it all. I feel as if I am looking on at some kind of theatrical entertainment.

It turns out to be a pleasant enough occasion. It is nice to have the company of men. They tell us there is a rumour that more houses are to be built a few streets away; there has been an inspection of the Pavilion to make sure standards are good as someone has mentioned there might be cockroaches. I like the sound of the sea captain's cheerful voice. Fanny can't stand cockroaches, she once worked in a hospital.

"Mrs Allen," the Captain says after a while, "we do all sound very formal, don't we. May we call you by your Christian names, we feel we are beginning to know you well enough to drop some of the formalities." Soon we are Minnie, and Fanny and Ada, to their seafaring John and their legal Philip.

I have noticed a tendency among older men to talk at length about their health, I don't know how we got onto the subject.

"I don't want another go of gout," says Philip. "You've no idea how painful it can be. All last week I was laid up."

"Have another sandwich, Philip, they will only get wasted if we do not eat them all this afternoon."

"It's my back," says John, "some days I find it difficult to walk, even with a stick."

"Would you like another cup of tea," I ask.

"A little less milk, this time, if you wouldn't mind."

"Have you tried Firey Jack" says Fanny, "Many people seem to get relief with that."

"Backs are funny things..." he continues.

"Fanny pass the sugar to John, please," I interrupt.

I like to feel I am in command of my little party. I flatter myself I can control the trend of conversation.

"What do you think Mr Atlee will do next?" I enquire of Philip. I like talking about politics to John and Philip. Fanny and Ada don't know much about politics.

"I don't like the idea of everyone being dependent on the state," says John. We have quite an interesting conversation.

A pleasant, a very pleasant afternoon. We played cards, we conversed. We three sisters managed to feel less antagonistic towards each other for a whole afternoon.

Now they are gone, and we are in the kitchen once more, clearing up.

"You don't change, do you, Minnie?" says Fanny, "you always did like to have everything your own way." Did I always like having my own way? That's the second time Fanny has said that in one day. I never thought so. Ada helps herself to the last cake, and hopes we won't see her eating it with her back turned to us in the corner. Fanny drops one of the cups.

None of us has changed much, I suppose, I say. But I don't feel myself that I am in the least the same.

*

When it was morning Elisa brought a jug of hot water for us to pour into a basin, so we could wash ourselves. Such a pretty jug and basin it was, with little flowers on it, and butterflies too. I helped Ada to dress. Fanny only needed her pinafore to be fastened.

'Lord a mercies, we'll have to see to some new clothes for you all,' Elisa said, when she saw our rags, not to mention the lice which despite all Mama's efforts were very apparent. We had breakfast in the warm clean kitchen which smelled of cooking. We sat on brown chairs round a table scrubbed white, and drank tea with lots of sugar and ate bread and dripping. Elisa asked us how we were. 'Very well, thank you, Ma'am' we answered, too scared to say much, and wondering what would happen next.

In the next few hours we three girls were all scrubbed together in a bath in the kitchen until we shone. 'Lord 'a mercy' Elisa said again when she saw my shoulder. We all came out of the bath several shades lighter and were given new clothes to put on. I don't know where they came from, but they seemed to fit all right. They felt very clean and comfortable. If we've got new clothes, we won't be sent away, I thought. Arthur got clean later.

Then we were summoned back to the big room, where Grandmama was still sitting in her chair by the fire. I wondered if she had been there all night. Aunt was there too, but not that mysterious man called Dickinson. 'Where's Mama,' we asked. 'She's gone back to Manchester to see her sister,' Aunt said coldly. 'When is she coming back,' we demanded. 'We shall have to see,' Grandmama said. 'You will be staying here with us for the time being.' I wondered how long the time being would be.

'We will have to see you are all occupied if you are to stay,' said Grandmama. 'You are to have lessons with me every morning, and Elisa will take you for walks in the afternoons.'

'Your Mama said you should have this,' Grandmama said to me later that day. That was when I knew Mama wasn't coming back although I always went on hoping she would. It was a picture of me, a picture of me in Manchester, of Mama holding me when I was only a baby. I knew what store Mama set by that photograph, how proud she had been to have it taken. She'd never have given it to me if she was coming back, never. I've still got that picture, and I keep it in my secret drawer to remind me of her.

As time went by I wished I could remember more about Papa. I try and see his face sometimes but I can't any more. Even when I look at Mama's picture, I can't really see what she was like. There's just a great empty space in my mind. I think I tried to forget them at first, it was easier not to think about it. And later when I wanted to remember I couldn't. We none of us could really believe we would never see either of them again.

But I was thinking about the time we arrived in Huddersfield. It was a very big house we had come to. Soon we went exploring, peering into various rooms. At the very top of the house was the attic, where Elisa slept. She was very cross at first when we went up there. Thinking about it now I realise it was the only privacy she ever got, the only place she could retreat to when she needed to be on her own. But kind as she was, we soon found that when we were in tears, or didn't know what to do, we could knock on her door and she would always console us with a hug and a kiss and sometimes she would provide us with a piece of home-made toffee. We'd sometimes have a romp with her round the kitchen when Aunt was out, and she would chase us and we could all laugh together.

The kitchen basement with its scrubbed table, brown chairs, and the warm iron cooking range was the place we liked best. That was where we had most of our meals. We had stew and rice pudding and prunes, and we always had an orange before we went to bed. 'At least no one can accuse me of not seeing you are all properly fed,' Aunt said.

Every morning before breakfast Aunt would come and say grace. We had to shut our eyes and pray for Grandmama and Dickinson, and Aunt and Elisa, and please God make us good. I always added a prayer for Mama and Papa, whispering it to myself if there was enough time left. Aunt had lots of sayings from the Bible.

Then Aunt would say grace.

> To God who gives our daily bread
> A thankful song we sing
> We pray that he who sends us food
> May fill our hearts with praise.

As if we were to thank Aunt for her kindness in looking after us. Then we would say the Lord's Prayer. We already knew that because Papa had taught us.

There was the parlour where Grandmama sat by the fire, and the next-door dining room where Grandmama and Aunt and Dickinson had their meals. We had lunch in the dining room on Sundays, where we had to be good and sit still and not say anything except please and thank you. 'Use your knife properly, Ada; Arthur don't be so greedy,

you're not a wild animal, eat slowly and chew your food properly;
Fanny where is your napkin; Minnie you should be ashamed leaving
scraps on your plate, that fat is very good for you.' Aunt's voice
never seemed to stop. We hated those Sunday lunches.

The water closet was something we had never come across before.
We were always using the closet when we first arrived. When you
pulled the chain it made a clonking sound, and the water made all
kinds of gurgling noises. And then there was the tin bath which hung
in the kitchen and which Elisa got ready every Saturday night so we
could be scrubbed clean for Sunday. When it was cold we used to run
as fast as we could up the stairs to bed, so as not to get too cold.

I feel myself shivering at the memory of that cold bedroom, 'the
girls' room' Aunt called it. The big bed went soon after we came,
and we each had our own small one. It always seemed very dark in
the night. Ada got frightened in the night, and sometimes wet the
bed. I often crept into bed with her or Fanny when they cried for
loneliness. Once Ada was poorly with a bad chest and Aunt came to
sit by her bed all night and give her medicines. Ada was better in the
morning.

.Arthur had his bed in a small box room. 'He's getting a big lad
now,' said Aunt not long after we arrived, and he was banished up the
stairs. It meant we couldn't talk at night, and I missed being able to
tell him things and find out what he thought.

Our schoolroom was opposite our bedroom, where every day
except Sundays Grandmama would give us our lessons. We read from
the Bible, or copied our letters, or copied drawings of wild animals
from other countries.

There were two rooms we never dared go into. They were quite
big and very dark, and seemed to be full of all kinds of mysterious
clothes and things. Grandmama's smelled of lavender. Aunt's
smelled of carbolic soap.

'When will we see Mama again,' we asked sometimes. You have
to pretend something might happen, even if deep down you know it
never will. 'Not for a while,' the answer would always be. 'Are we
going back to Manchester?' we would suggest. 'Only if your Mama
comes to fetch you,' was the answer. 'Is Papa back from America?'
we wanted to know. We were met by a shake of the head.

I supposed it was my fault for getting burnt that had made Papa go
away. I knew he never looked at me the same after I got burnt. And

then Mama had gone away because Papa had left us. It was all my fault from the very beginning. Whenever Aunt was extra cross I thought God must be punishing me because that is what I must deserve. After all it had been very careless of me to let the candle catch my pinny alight. Aunt often told me what a careless child I was.

Looking For The Past

Every day I thought there might be a letter just to say where Papa was and when he would come back so we could all live together again. I knew Mama couldn't write letters, Papa had always done all the writing we needed. I remember he once said Mama's mark on their marriage certificate was prettier than any hand he had ever seen written. I thought perhaps she might find someone to write for her, and it would tell us when she would come and fetch us. Weeks, months, years went by before I accepted we would never see either of them ever again.

Uncle Dickinson lived with us in Huddersfield, although we hardly ever saw him. He and Aunt and Grandmama only had meals with us on Sundays, and he went out every morning early to his chemist's shop in Kirkgate, and came home late every evening. But he came to church with us on Sundays. It felt as if he thought we were invisible, but he was never unkind, he just ignored us all. He was very tall, and always seemed to be dressed in a dark suit. He hardly ever said anything to us in that distant voice of his.

Aunt was very strict. I pretended sometimes that because she was a witch she must have stolen the letters that never came. It was because she wanted to keep us so she could do what she liked with us. She seemed to be cross most of the time, but I did get to know she was quite proud of us really.

Sundays for instance. I remember the first day we went to church with Aunt. Grandmama never went out at all, and never came to church with us. She always excused herself saying that she was too old to sit so long in such a draughty building. I don't think she liked our church. We were marched down the road in our Sunday best, new clothes that Aunt had made for us herself. She had got me to help her, so I could learn, she said, how to make clothes for us all in the future.

We girls were all dressed alike, with our skirts and petticoats and buttoned boots. We had hats and gloves too. Doing up our boots seemed to take hours. Arthur was lucky, boys' clothes are so much easier to manage. How I wished I was a boy. We would be constantly corrected as we walked along two and two. 'Minnie, don't skip, remember you are a young lady now, you must learn to be dignified; Fanny, where is your handkerchief, stop that snivelling; Arthur, don't walk so fast, remember your sisters have to keep up with you; Fanny, hold Ada's hand, don't let her stray off the path; Minnie, look how you've splashed your dress, what am I to do with you; put your hat on straight, Fanny, you've knocked it to one side.'

I think she was beginning to think of us as her own children, the children she never had. After all her initial objections, she wanted to keep us now, and make us into what she thought we ought to be, she wanted everyone to see how well brought up we were.

There were all those important looking people in church, with their dark clothes, and watch chains and big hats, and all their children looking brushed and clean and well behaved. I could see some of them nudge each other. There were whispered remarks such as 'The Winder orphans, deserted, poor little things'; 'It's not right for an old lady of her age to have to bring up her grandchildren'; 'Wonderful woman, Mrs Dickinson, to take all that trouble with them'; 'What a shame they were deserted by their father'; 'I've heard tell their mother was no better than she should be'; 'They won't have much of a future, I don't suppose'. These and similar remarks we often heard when we first went to church.

There was a reading once about the sins of the father being visited on the children and I could feel all those eyes burning into the back of my head. But we quite liked singing hymns.

There was a picture in that church called *The Light of the World*. It was a picture of Jesus knocking at a door. His eyes seemed to follow me everywhere, no matter where we sat. It made me feel as if He could see all my secrets, all the things I should feel ashamed of. There was one place in the church where He couldn't see me, and if we were a bit later than usual we could sit there behind a pillar. But then His eyes would follow me again as we walked out at the end of the service, and I would think how wicked it was of me to have walked so slowly on the way so that He couldn't look at me all the time I was in church.

Sometimes we went to visit Aunt Eleanor, Dickinson's sister. She was called Halstead because she was married, and her husband had died a long time ago. She didn't have any children. There were always china cups on the table and one day Fanny dropped one and it broke. We had bread and special jam, and parkin to eat. One day we had something called tomatoes, with sugar on them. I didn't like them very much, and Ada spat hers out and refused to eat it. Aunt was very cross. 'Gregory powder for you when we get home' she said. Gregory powder was supposed to stop people feeling sick, but we were always sick anyway.

Sometimes we were given presents. There was a Noah's Ark with all the animals to go in two by two, to play with on Sundays. There were the little dolls we were given, one each, all dressed in their frilly clothes. Mine was called Margaret like Mama. Fanny called hers Annie, though I never discovered why. Ada's was called Crystal because that was what was on the label round its neck. Arthur had a game of dominoes.

One day I found Ada had taken one of the little china cats Aunt Eleanor kept on her mantelpiece. I spent sleepless nights in an agony of apprehension, expecting Aunt to come and ask me to explain the missing ornament. Then when nothing happened in the next few days, I spent weeks wondering how to put it back again without anyone finding out. Fortunately we went to tea again quite soon and I sneaked in and put it back while everyone was saying goodbye. No one ever guessed.

Each morning Grandmama gave us lessons in what Aunt called our schoolroom. We read from the Bible, did sums on slates: we had spelling bees and chanted our tables: we recited lists of English places and counties, and the capital cities of the world. I liked the certainty of learning things that never change and answers were always either right or wrong. Nowadays everything is always changing, sometimes for the better I suppose.

*

We, my sisters and I, have decided to hire a chalet down on the beach for the summer months. We are not to worry about stray hand grenades any more, nor other arms washed up on the sand, they have all been cleared we are told. The barbed wire has gone at last. The beach is quite a pleasant place to visit once again.

They are really very comfortable, the chalets, and we have chosen one that is out of the wind. There are chairs and tables provided, and we can boil a kettle and have our little tea parties in the sun. It makes a change from always being in the house, perhaps we shan't get on each other's nerves so much. There is plenty to watch, with people swimming and sunning themselves, ships passing by on the horizon, and small fishing dinghies coming and going inshore. We can invite our friends here for tea, it will be much less trouble, and we can always buy buns from the corner shop.

It is very fortunate indeed that we have the chalet just now. One of my grandchildren has come on a visit, my granddaughter Mary and her husband to be precise, they are here for a weekend break. Poor dears, they work so hard, and they live so far away, they can't visit very often. He teaches at Leeds University, strange they should have moved up North near where I grew up.

I told Mary to be careful marrying an academic, an idealist, they are all alike, more interested in ideas than people, I always think. Like my brother Arthur. The two young people seem happy enough despite that, I am glad to say. They deserve some happiness, the youngsters, after all they have been through. Mary was in London during the bombing, and the hospital where she worked was hit: David was out in the tropics, and then fighting in Italy: What they must both have gone through, everyone has had such a difficult time these last few years.

They do look tired poor things. I could see that the moment I opened the door. I don't suppose they get enough to eat with all this rationing. He's a likeable enough fellow, despite his idealism, very clever, very amusing, but you know what clever people are like.

She goes for a swim in the sea, while he keeps us amused with tales of his travels. She always has been a keen swimmer. I can see she enjoys herself, though the water must be quite cold. I remember – how could I forget – when she stayed with me sometime before the war started, always off to the Blackpool swimming baths. She used to worry me sometimes, diving off that high board. It was suggested that she join the English swimming team, but I didn't think that would be a good idea, the people she would mix with would not really be her sort. Besides there was her education to think about. In any case, the war came soon after that, so she lost nothing by refusing.

She brought photographs to show us of her travels while she was working as an army nurse, pictures of Egypt and Syria, Petra, Persia, Palestine, there seemed so many places that she has been to. Such lovely places some of them, and they must make history much more vivid for her. For instance, Bible stories must seem more relevant after actually seeing such places as the Sea of Galilee and the Dead Sea. What must Palestine be like now though, with all the turmoil between Jews and Arabs, and all those bombs going off. Perhaps some of the photographs are of historic buildings that have now been destroyed forever.

In the pictures I see that she is sometimes wearing trousers, at which I cannot feel but somewhat shocked. Women should not dress like men, no good will ever come of it. If women insist on becoming just like men they will lose all the respect they deserve. Of course, Mary explained that while climbing in and out of army lorries, trousers were a much more modest kind of dress than skirts. I had to agree. But it makes me sad.

Their visit has been all too short, but the sun has been shining, and I could see that the two of them looked less tired by the time they left. Nothing like relaxing in the sun to restore one's health, I told them. They promise to come again soon. I am sorry to see them go. None of my other grandchildren seem able to pay us a visit, but I do sometimes get long letters from my eldest grandson Harold. Now he is a boy I feel sorry for, he was a war baby you see.

We spend a lot of time at the beach this summer, it is so warm and sunny. Sitting quietly listening to the waves is a soothing experience. I find one can reminisce as one likes without interruptions. One can watch other regular visitors, especially children, one gets to know their names. There is a little boy called James, so very well behaved, we take quite an interest in him. He sometimes comes to have a piece of our cake.

Our friends often come to tea. Maurice has such bright blue eyes, I noticed today, when we were all having tea together. He sings in a deep voice to himself sometimes, when he thinks no one is listening. I sometimes wonder what life at sea must have been like for him, a rough life no doubt, and yet he couldn't be more of a gentleman. His eyes have a twinkle all of their own, just like the sea.

School

'School', I wrote in my diary. We all went to school in 1870 because the government said we must. I didn't much like the Board school. Aunt said Grandmama was tired, and what a blessing it was, that we could be out all day at school. Even Ada seemed to know how to read and write better than almost everyone else at that school. It was always so noisy, and we were always being marched about in lines, and standing up and sitting down on our benches, with a great scraping of shoes, but some children didn't have any shoes. There weren't many people to be friends with, either, not anyone I wanted to talk to out of school. None of us felt we really fitted in at that school.

I was twelve by the time I could go to the high school, Greenhead High School, with one hundred and fifty girls. Miss Chieveley the head mistress came in, and tapped her desk, and there was instant silence. 'Miss Chieveley's got "presence"' I remember thinking, she only had to tap her desk and there was instant silence. She gave us a long talk about making this new school a success, and she was relying on all of us to work hard. 'Girls have a right', she said, 'to the same education as boys, for it is likely many of you will have to earn your own living. The subjects you will take are the same as those of the boys at the collegiate. What the boys learn you will also have the opportunity to learn. You must make the most of the chance this offers you.'

The school was very near our house, and I only had to walk along the terrace and through the lane, though I did have to cross the top of Castlegate. That was where the Irish all lived. The Irish had all come because of the Irish potato famine, Aunt said, to find work on the canals and railways. They talked in their soft sing song voices, and often seemed to be drunk. You could see them down the hill weaving about the road, or even lying in the gutter, getting in the way of carts and horses. I wondered why there weren't more accidents. Aunt never tired of warning us never to go into Castlegate. Grandmama, I discovered, had taught me well, and I was quite up to standard in things like writing and English. It was very different to the Board School. We were given timetables with all the subjects noted in neat little boxes; Scripture, English, French, German, Italian, History, Geography, Mathematics, Natural Sciences (with sub-headings of Botany and Zoology and Geology) Music, Drawing, Needlework, and Domestic Economy. 'It's still not fair', I thought, 'because I know the boys don't learn things like needlework and domestic economy. If girls try to catch up with boys, they can only do it by always doing extra work.'

There was a school choir: I would have liked to have been in it, but when we had our first practice the music teacher said I couldn't sing in tune. The choir sang Handel's *Messiah*, Stainer's *Crucifixion*, Mendelssohn, Stanford – 'it is good practice, you never know, one day a few of you may want to join the Huddersfield Choral Society, I do have hopes for one or two of you', he said. Aunt was very good at singing. It was the kind of music sung in her choir.

It sounded very beautiful sometimes, but as I couldn't sing and couldn't play the piano either, I never learnt enough about music to have a 'real appreciation' as Aunt would say. 'It's a good thing', Miss Chieveley said once, 'that you are not at a young ladies' academy, they would soon give you up with your lack of accomplishments. No music, no drawing, though I admit your plain sewing is quite good, and you have a very good French accent. You can concentrate on mathematics, science and English, you are much above the average in your understanding of all those subjects.' I could see she meant that I could never make a good marriage.

I had wondered why Arthur had always seemed so different after he went to school. At high school you learn to think and talk about things that no one at home understands and school and home become two quite different places. Perhaps everybody has to learn to be two people, one for work and one for home, like Uncle Dickinson.

I had friends at school now, Dorothy, Jane, Kate and Elizabeth, we always seemed to do things together. Jane and Kate were my best friends. I even asked them home to tea sometimes, especially when I thought Aunt might be out. They all liked Grandmama.

I seem to have noted such a lot of things during that first year at school. For one thing everything became more expensive, and treats became less frequent. 'Don't waste that crust of bread, why have you left some of your porridge, finish everything on your plate,' Aunt would say. 'But it's just fat and gristle,' we would protest. 'There are many people would welcome such scraps', said Aunt, 'think of all those who are so much worse off than we are.'

So many people were moving into Huddersfield the population had trebled in the last few years. Compared to the cotton industry the wool trade was flourishing. 'It's because the mills use shoddy, and can make cheaper goods,' Dickinson explained. I pictured all those people hidden inside the great mills each day, sorting out old clothes into different coloured heaps so they could be turned into new cloth. And good quality cloth too, he said. Because of shoddy you could still see fires glowing from the engineering works, the coal pits were working, and even the silk mills were still trading. And all because of shoddy.

Now that the end of the Franco–Prussian war had brought peace to Europe, trade should be improving, Uncle said. The head governess Miss Robinson had had a class about French and German wars, with maps and diagrams, and estimates of how many people had been killed. Why, I wondered, are men always having wars. I can't think that anyone gains anything by it, everyone seems poorer, and all those people killed.

We had lots of militia men in the town, good-looking men in their bright uniforms and with their swaggering ways. The older girls at school often ogled them, giggling and smiling and laughing. If I had told Aunt about it she would probably have stopped my going to school ever again in the company of such girls. I could almost hear her saying that such frivolous behaviour was not fit for any young lady to indulge in. Sometimes the soldiers paraded through the streets with the band playing. They really did look very handsome.

Elisa sometimes brought fish and chips home for supper. There was a new kind of shop where you fetched cooked fish to eat at home. Aunt of course didn't approve, but we all enjoyed them on evenings when Aunt was out.

Other things I noted was the opening of the Apollo Gymnasium for 'dancing, fencing and exercises'. Arthur and his friends often went there, but Grandmama said she thought that perhaps I shouldn't.

There were the swimming baths too, but I couldn't go there, although I would have liked to learn to swim. My shoulder got in the way of so many things.

Everyone talked about the married woman's property act. Grandmama had said many a time that it was a scandal that a man could gamble away all his wife's money, or do anything else he liked with it, spend it on drink, or women, or fritter it away in useless enterprises. 'Why shouldn't women keep control of their own affairs', she said indignantly, 'they know far better how to use their own money than any man.' At school they talked about John Stuart Mill, and an end to the 'subjugation of women.'

'I hate her,' I wrote in my diary. Hated who, I wonder. I looked several times through the pages, and at last could just make out some tiny initials in one corner, it was if I wanted to keep my hatred secret. 'JJ' I could just make out. I remember now, Janie Jones. She was a tall girl who thought herself quite something. I used to wonder what her secret was. She wasn't particularly pretty, or clever, her clothes weren't special, and I don't think her father was very rich. But she somehow managed to persuade most of the girls that they should do exactly as she said. 'Little Minnie Mouse, Minnie can't sing; Minnie can't play the piano so she'll never get married; Minnie is a teacher's pet,' the taunts were endless.

But I had my own friends. Jane Morley was older than me, tall and fair, she was pretty and she had a rich father. 'Don't take any notice,' she would say, coming up and taking my arm, and the other girls would fall suddenly quiet. 'Just ignore them,' she would say. By the end of the year there were no more taunts.

Kate Pearson was quite different. She was dark and angular and kind, and we had a lot of fun together. She was always inventing new games, she was such a good mimic, pretending to be Janie Jones, or one of the teachers, or even Aunt, and we three, Jane and Kate and I could laugh together and ignore the rest.

There was a great to-do in school one day about going to church. I had always thought that people were supposed to go to church. One of the governesses at school, Miss Warrender, got into trouble for taking some of the girls to church. I remember lots of whispers in the corridors, 'what is she supposed to have done; will Miss Warrender have to leave; what will the school governors say.' I was glad she didn't leave. Grandmama explained that ours was a nondenominational school, and parents would strongly object if girls were ever taken to a church which they didn't belong to.

Wishful Thinking

What pleased us most were the stories Grandmama read to us every evening before we went to bed. My struggles with darning and hemming were made bearable by the adventures of David Copperfield and Nicholas Nickleby and all the other Dickens stories. Little Nell made me cry. Then there were all those great adventures by Sir Walter Scott, I think our favourite was *Ivanhoe*, with rescues and knights and wild countryside.

Arthur and I used to label the people in church as Mr Macawber, or Martin Chuzzlewit, or perhaps Mr Pecksniff. There was one man we always called Uriah Heep because he was always rubbing his hands together. We even began to look forward to church each Sunday so we could see them sitting there.

'Oh look', Arthur would say, 'there's Mrs Jellybub.' Aunt had once said how charitable that particular lady was, and then added how neglected her children seemed to be. They were always very noisy in church. We never could remember her real name. I would nudge him when I recognised a likeness of Mr Jingle or Mr Squeers. We were quite disappointed sometimes when our favourite characters didn't come to church on Sunday.

At home we often played trains, when we would all be going back to Manchester to Mama to live in a lovely new house Papa had bought with the fortune he had made in America. Arthur was always the engine driver, and we were the passengers. Sometimes Ada had to be Aunt, who got left behind at the station. Sometimes I was Grandmama, who was allowed to come with us.

Sometimes Grandmama would tell us about her princesses. We, my sister Fanny and I, were born in New York, she would tell us, 'because your great grandfather Dr Wright, was physician to the court of Louis Philippe. Napoleon III, his son, wasn't King of France then of course, not when I was young. He was afraid to go back to France because the revolutionaries might execute him. There was all the uncertainty and fear of the French Revolution, you must understand. We were taught with the princesses you know,' she would say proudly.

'Your great grandfather was an American, and when Louis Philippe came to Philadelphia, your great grandfather treated the Duc D'Orleans' brothers for a lung complaint. He was sent for again to come and treat them when Louis Philippe was in London, and that is when I met the princesses. We were educated with the princesses,' she would say proudly, 'and we went with them to parties and soirées and balls, and met many of the important politicians of the time.'

Grandmama always gave the impression that this was the best time of her life. 'It was a great time,' she would say. 'When I was young we lived at Twickenham in London, and many's the time we drove along the riverside to visit one grand house or another.' I was never sure if we were being told a fairy story that sounded real, or being told a tale that was real but sounded like a fairy story.

'What were the great houses like?' we would ask. 'I remember one called Marble House where we often went, a very big, very grand house,' she would say, 'with steps leading up to a ballroom, and a great staircase. There would be servants in livery and bright lights everywhere. There were great chandeliers hanging from the ceilings, beautiful polished floors and carpets from the East, great mirrors round the walls, and such rich decoration, you'd never believe, all gold and red and blue silk. The orchestra would play, and we would dance late into the night. Nearly every night,' she would add as if as an afterthought.

'What would the princesses be wearing?' we would ask. Such glittering silks and satins and jewels she would describe. There was one dress Grandmama often talked about, of blue silk and velvet, with sparkling jewels and lace ornaments, and I knew it must be one that she had often worn herself. She did so like describing that dress in all of its details. She would tell us about the beautiful necklaces and rings she had. She would tell us how difficult it was to perform the elaborate curtseys required in front of the King of France and other nobility. Of course he wasn't Emperor then, she would explain.

'Where are they now?' we would ask, 'and why don't you go and visit the King of France? I expect he would be very pleased to see you.' 'He's no longer King, they are all dead or forgotten now,' she would sigh.

Sometimes I imagined Grandmama in her dress, at one of those balls in the great staterooms she had told us about. It was hard to think of Grandmama as a young girl dancing through the night. Mostly I thought of what I should look like in such a lovely dress, with all its sparkling jewels.

'Blue doesn't suit you,' Ada said sometimes to me. 'You would only trip over yourself with those great skirts to manage,' she would say to Fanny. 'Now I would look just right at one of those balls.' She was right, really, she was the one who would have looked the best. I could imagine her dancing all night in those glittering rooms.

I wished I could be a real princess. After all, Grandmama was nearly a princess, wasn't she? Perhaps I could meet a king one day. Perhaps Arthur could grow up and be a physician to a prince, and then I could really meet some princesses.

*

It has been a long hard winter, and we three old ladies, my sisters and I, are only just emerging like troglodytes from their cave. So much snow and ice, such cold winds. We were lucky our friends had insisted on finding us as much wood and coal as they could before the winter set in. With all the power cuts and the low gas pressure, it was almost impossible to keep warm. We hardly dared venture out, we were lucky the corner shop could deliver all the essential things we needed. We wore so many clothes we must have looked as fat and round as the snowmen the children had built everywhere. Children never seem to mind the cold. We learnt the trick of never sitting still for long, and we must have drunk an ocean of hot tea. Hot tea and biscuits almost every hour seemed to keep us going, as we crouched over our gas fire with its tiny blue flame, or made the most of the coal fire which we lit only on Sundays.

The cold weather seemed to go on for ever, from January to March, and even then there was still snow on the ground. Our boredom was relieved by watching the children at play, with their games of snowballs, and the sledges they pulled along the street. Across the road they got disenchanted with the snowmen they had built, and instead we would see a statue of Hitler, or Mussolini, or the

Japanese Emperor appear as if by magic overnight. Very inventive, those children. Perhaps they will all turn out to be art students. People passed with an arm in a sling or a plaster on their leg, casualties of the slippery pavements. A long hard winter.

Trying To Escape

It isn't far down the hill by Westgate and Kirkgate in Huddersfield to the canal basin, where the Ramsden canal and the Narrow canal meet at the Apsley Basin. Grandmama was always explaining about Huddersfield, and its buildings and the cloth trade. Everything had to be unloaded from the barges to the narrow boats and from the narrow boats to the barges, all the coal, cotton, wool and cloth, everything.

I remember when we first went to Huddersfield there was a great drought and the canals couldn't be used for lack of water. Water is very uncertain, you either have too little of it and have a drought, or too much, when there would be floods. A long time before we came, there was a great flood and lots of people were drowned. We ought to have enough water, I used to think, what with the River Colne and the River Holm, and all the dikes like Thunder Bridge dike we once went to see, and Carr dike and I don't know how many more. Perhaps the water is too dirty to use any more.

When the canals were working it was such a scene of bustle and commotion down by the Britannia Mill. Boats were constantly arriving while cranes lifted out great bales of wool, or ships would be discharging coal, or cloth would be loaded to deliver to Manchester or Leeds, and then perhaps onward across the sea. There were cargoes to be taken to the woollen mills like the Starkey and Brook Mills which lined the canal banks. Each mill had to be kept working all day and night.

So many people, so much pushing and pulling, water splashing, carts and horses, shouts of 'whoa' and 'git up', as horses were harnessed to the barges. Handcarts rattled by, while ragged children stared from the decks of the boats. Elisa said we must never come here on our own, there were drunks about, we might fall in, or be stolen away to work on a barge. If it was going to Manchester I wouldn't mind being stolen away at all, it might be a way of seeing Mama again.

Arthur said he would one day get on a barge and disappear, and nobody, not even Aunt, would ever find him again. He could go to Manchester and find Mama. I told him I would come with him, but he said 'don't be ridiculous, girls can't run away. Who would keep you away from all those rough boys and drunken men, I'd like to know.'

Sometimes he said he would sign on as a leg man. 'You'll never come back if you do,' I told him. Even strong men get injured, pushing a boat like that through the tunnel with their legs, or else they fall in and get drowned. 'You can't do that, anyway,' I told him, 'you have to look after us, Papa told Mama so before he went away'. 'If you came with me', he objected, 'who would look after Fanny and Ada, and whoever heard of a girl sailing the seven seas or going to America or living on an island like Robinson Crusoe. Besides, you're much too small', he added contemptuously, you'd never reach high enough to haul the ropes'. 'We could go on a steam ship,' I ventured. I'd never seen a steam ship but the bargees used to talk about them sometimes.

Errand boys brought most of the things we needed to the kitchen door, and Arthur would sometimes chat to them. 'I'm glad I'm not still delivering things,' he would say. But Elisa and Aunt would both be angry when he said that. 'Everyone has to know their place,' said Elisa. You must not forget that, now you are a gentleman.

*

The weather is warm enough for Fanny and Ada and I to meet our friends for coffee at the Pavilion today. Lots of people have coffee at the Pavilion on a bright morning; it is a pleasant enough place, although it could do with repainting, like most things at the end of a war. The coffee is quite good, and the cakes, too, considering ration restrictions. The waitresses are helpful, especially when they get to know you.

"How are you today, Dolly?" Philip says to his favourite waitress, "we missed you last time we were here."

"It's my husband," she says, "come home at last. But he can't get a job, see, so I've come back here temporary like."

"You've had your hair done differently," says the captain to the waitress called Amy. Amy is a bit of a flirt, and simpers as she pats her curls.

"Suits you," says the captain.

We always give them a good tip. I don't suppose they earn all that much, and poor dears, they often look so harassed and tired.

You can watch people on the beach from our table at the Pavilion. Even the children seem a bit timid, as they paddle in the waves, and get excited over the shells they find. It is as if they still can't really believe that the war is over, although the surrender was two years ago now. In places there are still barbed wire and lumps of broken concrete about and notices about not picking up strange objects on the sand, in case they turn out to be explosive.

Ada didn't want to come, she hasn't been so well these last few weeks. Her face looks pinched, and she is beginning to look really old, the way she creeps along. It is difficult to tell whether it is her secret need for whisky that is to blame, for on bad days I know she drinks far more than usual. It's her only comfort, she says. "It's all very well for you and Fanny, you seem to find plenty to talk about, but you ignore me all the time." I suppose she has a point. But it is difficult to talk to Ada. "I've worked hard all my life", she says, "and where has it got me? None of my ex-pupils ever wrote to me as they did to you, Minnie. Since Marjorie died I've had no one to talk to, no one." I point out that none of my friends are still living, and that I never hear now from my various ex-pupils with whom I used to correspond. The war changed all that.

The gentlemen arrive and join us at our table. They talk about the economic situation, and rationing, and the shortage of everything. At least we're better off than Germany, they say. We have put another advertisement in the local shop for a cleaner.

"We should have kept on the last one," says Ada, "at least she did some cleaning."

"I still keep seeing her germs climbing up the walls everywhere," Fanny says,

"Everything looked worse when she left than it did before she came," I insist.

We stroll along the front together, and watch a passing fishing boat.

Double Views

Occasionally we walked into town when Elisa wanted to do some shopping. We would go and stare into the window of Uncle Dickinson's shop. All those coloured bottles and jars. Uncle must be very rich, we thought, there were always so many customers in his shop.

I sneaked in sometimes, and stood at the back of the shop, listening to them asking for all kinds of different things – headache pills; laudanum for keeping the babies quiet; stomach pills; Gregory powders and fever pills. Blackcurrant lozenges sounded quite nice. The bottles were labelled with lovely names like Arnica, Syrup of Toly, Tincture of Ipecac and Tincture of Valerian. There was a little room where there were dies and rods and rollers for making pills and things, it was like a witches' kitchen. I know because I sneaked in there once, but was quickly removed with dire threats against further exploration.

Uncle Dickinson was quite different in his shop when he was talking to his customers, he would be laughing and teasing the children, joking and telling all kinds of tales. He must be a very important man, we thought, because so many people were always asking for his help and advice. Uncle was like two people, quiet and almost invisible at home – that is, whenever we saw him which was usually only on Sundays – and the jolly, authoritative person he was in his own shop. I sometimes wondered what it would be like if the 'shop' Dickinson came home and the 'home' Dickinson started working in the shop.

Sometimes I would see a face in the crowds down by the canal or in the streets, who looked familiar in an odd kind of way. I thought that if it were Mama or Papa they wouldn't recognise me because I had grown a bit, and I didn't think I could remember their faces well enough to recognise them. Just imagine, I would think to myself, perhaps that man over there really is Papa and neither of us recognises each other. Or that woman going into a shop, she has a kind face and walks in a strangely familiar way, perhaps that is Mama and we pass each other like strangers. But it is no good imagining. There were all kinds of advertisements on the shop fronts.

Attend all ye who enter here
It's time you changed your ways
And asked your loving husband
For the finest things in stays.

I looked to see what kind of stays they were. I thought that perhaps if Aunt had different stays she might not seem so stiff and unbending. I always thought her stays must be much too tight, and she'd much better buy some new ones. But then I thought she might not rustle so much and we wouldn't be able to hear her coming so easily, and she might catch us out more often.

Sometimes we went to the cloth market. So many bolts of worsted cloth, of mohair and alpaca, lustres (which I always thought were so pretty) and jacquered goods. You could hear the men calling out their Kersey wares, and you could admire the wonderful colours of the latest fashions in men's waistcoats. 'Huddersfield is built on the wool trade,' Elisa would say. All those new buildings, all those mills with their mysterious processes of scribbling, fulling and carding, combing oiling, blending and dying, going on in all those great buildings with all the noise and shouting. You could, I thought, like Puck in *A Midsummer Night's Dream*, put a girdle round the earth, only of cloth.

There were other things, like chemical dye works, iron foundries, and machine factories. What I hated was the way they made the water in the rivers and dikes so black and treacly, and how horrible they smelt. All that mess, couldn't they bury it somewhere, instead of letting it kill off so many plants and trees? I remembered the green fields we passed on the train, but in Huddersfield all the grass was sickly yellow and brown, and all the trees nearby were becoming dead and brown too. Grandmama read us a poem by Wordsworth about dancing daffodils. There weren't any places like that in Huddersfield.

There weren't many girls to play with, there were mostly babies and boys in our road. There was Harry Chapman from next door, whose father was a music seller. You could sometimes hear music coming from their house, because they had a piano. Harry was at school with Arthur. They had games together, like marbles and checkstones or cots and twys. Only two could play together at games like that, Arthur said, and in any case who wanted girls.

Harry had a little sister called Lillian, who was always calling us. 'Your shoes cleat' she would shout as we walked past. 'Our shoes don't squeak' I would protest. 'Talking Dutch don't make you no better than us' she would shout back. I wished I could have her as a friend, but she didn't like me much. She had a baby sister, and I hated being asked to mind her. She was always crying and being sick. 'Even a child is known by his doings,' Aunt said mysteriously.

There was Albert Garbutt only a year younger than me, whose father was a coachman, and he had a baby sister. The coachman was a jolly man, and he once asked me if I would like a ride in his empty coach. Aunt was very angry when she found out the next Sunday. 'Be sure, your sins will find you out, remember you are a lady now,' she said, 'and ladies don't take rides with strange men in coaches.' 'But he's not a stranger,' I protested, 'and I thought ladies were supposed to ride in coaches'. 'Don't answer back Minnie,' she snapped. 'Go to your room at once. If you can't behave like a lady, you shouldn't be sitting at this table at all.' Arthur was pretending he had nothing to do with it, Fanny was ready to burst into tears in sympathy, and Ada was looking triumphant. I was glad to go.

I would much rather have been in the kitchen with Elisa, which is where I went. It was warm there because the kitchen range was always lit for the cooking. Elisa always seemed to have some hidden treat, like cake or toffee, to comfort us. I even liked the smell of onions on her hands. I knew I was supposed to go upstairs to my room, but it was so cold up there. Elisa finished the cleaning she was doing, then put her arm around me. 'Never mind, love,' she consoled me, as tears came into my eyes, despite myself. 'Do you know how we could find Mama,' I asked her. She just shook her head. 'It will be time for your walk soon,' was all she said. We always went for a walk on Sunday afternoons.

Arthur and I decided one day to run away and find Mama. But when we asked where Mama might be (very carefully, of course, in case she suspected anything) Aunt said she didn't know, because Mama had moved away from Manchester some time ago. Fanny and Ada had very soon forgotten all about Mama and Papa, especially Ada. I think Fanny remembered we once did have a Mama and Papa, but Ada couldn't even remember that. All the other families on our terrace had Mamas and Papas. 'It isn't fair,' I said to Grandmama. 'Life is never fair,' she answered, 'and the sooner you understand that the better, we all have to make best of what we've got.'

The tower on Castle Hill above Huddersfield was where we sometimes went for a walk in the summer. It was quite high up, and said to be an Iron Age fort. Up there in winter it sometimes snowed, while where we lived in the town it was only cold, with that fierce cold wind that sometimes blew round the streets for days on end. It looked like a white magic world up there, so clean and far away. But in the summer we sometimes took a picnic up the hill and climbed to the top of the tower. And then if you looked you could see the town below, and it looked like a far away secret place, with its church spires and smoking chimneys, and the water in the rivers looked clean and sparkling. Most things seem to look better when they are far away.

Aunt would sometimes come with us to Castle Hill in the summer, when Elisa had her Sunday off. She would tell us all about the plants and animals and insects. There were birds called ring ousels and nightjars, willow warblers, redstarts, and blackcaps, besides the bees and butterflies and grasshoppers, and sometimes even a death's head hawkmoth to wonder at. Sometimes we collected herbs like comfrey to take home for Dickinson to use in the shop.

Arthur and I often discussed the reason why Mama went away and left us. 'It was the witch,' Arthur used to say, 'Aunt put a spell on Mama so she couldn't come back.' I heard Elisa say once that it was unfortunate but Mama had had no choice, we could all have gone together to the workhouse, or she could leave us with Grandmama. But why did she never come and visit, or get someone to write us a letter? That would be better than nothing. 'Anyway, she must like it wherever she is,' I said, 'or she would certainly have come to see us by now.' 'Perhaps she's just waiting for Papa to come back from America,' he said, 'so we can all be together again.'

Aunt always wanted us to go for long walks, mostly with Elisa. 'Good for your health,' she said, 'we don't want you getting tuberculosis like your grandfather.' 'But you said grandfather was a doctor, so why didn't he know how to cure himself?' 'Tuberculosis is not something you can cure,' she said, 'but you can try and prevent it.

Dickinson says fresh air is what is needed. It is easier to prevent illness than to cure it.'

Aunt was a bit surprising. Sometimes she talked about medicines with Dickinson as if she knew more about it than he did. Sometimes he asked for her advice. They talked about hygiene and antiseptics. 'Dickinson is far ahead of his time,' Aunt would say.

We found Aunt did surprising things, like sing in the church choir, when she didn't sound a bit like a witch. There were always concerts being given in aid of the lame, or the blind, or destitute children. Sometimes she helped in Dickinson's shop, and everyone would ask for her advice. She sounded very kind when she talked to customers. But she was very strict with us, always telling us what was right and wrong.

I tried to catch her out one day. 'Is it always wrong to tell lies,' I asked her, 'because Elisa asked me how she looked in her new hat and I think she looks horrible. Is it better to be kind or truthful?' 'Being truthful is more important,' she declared. 'Next time she might choose a better hat.' Grandmama wasn't like that. 'The only kind of truth that really matters,' she explained when I asked her, 'is observation. Knowing whether you like a hat or not is a matter of taste. But the sun is either shining or it is not; your eyes are blue, Arthur's are brown; dogs have four legs, you have two.' I wasn't quite convinced. Elisa's eyes were hazel, and sometimes they looked blue and sometimes brown, depending on what clothes she wore. I asked Arthur what he thought, but he said not to bother my little head about such complicated ideas.

Grandmama said it was very important to behave like a lady, because unless everyone behaved like ladies and gentlemen we would have a lot of revolutions, with people killing each other all the time. 'Ladies and gentlemen respect each other,' she insisted, 'and unless people everywhere learn to respect one another there will always be fighting and revolutions and wars. That is why, she said, everyone should have a good education.'

*

It has been a warm and drowsy summer, with plenty of time to day dream and think of the past. It has taken me a long time to try and recall my third life; what I did and how I felt about our days in

Huddersfield. Some things seem so vivid in one's mind, others seem to be buried too deep to be recalled at all.

I am glad that today is one of our tea-party days. One can get too immersed in the past and almost forget the present. We are having tea with our friends at the beach hut. It makes for a change of company. John Maurice has arrived. We have noticed for some time that he is finding walking increasingly painful these days. It was quite perturbing to see how he struggled along the path and sank thankfully into the deckchair we always have ready for him. We get on well together, he and I. He is always cheerful, in his blustering kind of way. Philip, Fanny's friend, has already come, and he and Fanny are having their little joke together about something or other as Fanny makes the tea. I know Philip finds it increasingly difficult to see and hear, I think perhaps he just laughs, without knowing what has been said. I suspect Fanny is talking about me, I hope they don't break anything.

We are all getting older, finding it more difficult to see and hear what goes on around us. I wrote to my granddaughter yesterday, though I have grave doubts about whether she can read what I have written. I felt I had to write, and scold her a little, as she sent me a photo of her and her mother wearing trousers. I know she explained to me that climbing on and off lorries while serving in the forces made wearing them almost essential, but her mother, she has no need to wear them. That a daughter of mine should so degrade herself, I cannot understand it. I feel quite upset that a daughter of mine should wish to wear such unwomanly things.

I have grown rather fond of John, and I think he of me, but I know Ada and Fanny don't really approve. Perhaps they are jealous. I always did get on with men better than either of them ever did. For one thing he is always interesting to talk to, and makes a point of discussing various recent items from the newspapers, or something he has heard on the wireless.

"Don't agree with all this social provision nonsense the government is making such a fuss about," John says, "mark my words, it will lead to no good in the long run, let people stand on their own feet, that's what I say."

"It's just a way of making people save for their own medical treatment and their own old age, that is a way of standing on their own feet isn't it?" I say defensively. John has never lived as I once did, with cotton factory workers. "After all, we pay insurance on our property, why not for care for ourselves?"

"That's what you are supposed to think," he says, "you don't suppose it will stop there, do you? Before you know it the Unions will run the country, and then where will we all be?"

Who should stroll by but Andrew Patey, Ada's once upon a time friend. We asked him to join us. I could see Ada wasn't best pleased, and that made him feel uncomfortable. I don't know what it is about Ada, she always makes people feel uncomfortable. He didn't stay long. The four of us, John and Peter and Fanny and I played whist until it began to go a bit chilly. Ada sulked. John, I remember, raised my hand to his lips in a most gallant style as he and Peter said goodbye and went off together. The lame leading the blind and deaf, I thought.

"You should be ashamed of yourself, at your age," says Ada, "making up to a man in that shameless fashion, making a spectacle of yourself like that. You are not an eighteen year old girl you know, but a respectable widow of over eighty, and you have no business to behave so."

"How could you?" says Fanny. "You've spoiled everything. I can't imagine what Philip will think of us all now."

"What a fuss you do make about nothing," I say, 'it was only a friendly gesture after all. It is you two who have spoiled things, if anyone has, we shall all feel self-conscious about it now."

If old fogies like us can't show a little affection now and again without seeming to be indelicate, then the world is sillier than I thought.

*

Life And Death

One day we were sent home from school. Miss Chieveley explained that one of the girls who lived at Paddock had a sister who was ill with smallpox. The Medical Officer of Health had come to school to make the best arrangements he could to protect us from catching it. It is a very contagious and serious disease, he explained, and we must do our best to minimise the risk of infection. We all knew it was a serious illness to catch, and it always left your skin looking horrid and wrinkled. 'A doctor will come round to all your homes to vaccinate anyone who might have had any contact with the family. Meanwhile all those who have been anywhere near Sarah Jones will be quarantined for three weeks. I expect,' Miss Chieveley said, 'that we will have taken precautions in time, and that there is nothing to worry about. But we must do as the medical officer says.'

We were given notes to take home. I didn't really mind the idea of having an extra holiday, I could have more time to write my diary. I was quite looking forward to that. 'Those most at risk are in form four,' the man had said. Well, I was in form four, but Sarah was not one of my particular friends. I thought they were all making a fuss about nothing; smallpox was an illness that was much less common than it used to be. Besides, Miss Chieveley had said there was nothing to worry about.

When we got home and Aunt had read the note I was sent straight up to our old school room. Aunt became very busy. She hung a sheet wrung out in disinfectant across the door of the room. A bed was moved in and I was told to stay in that room and not to leave it without permission on any account, not even to go to the lavatory. Aunt brought in the necessary equipment like jugs and basins and a chamber pot. 'If anyone comes near this door, tell them to go away', Aunt said, 'we'll take no risks.' I suppose, I thought, this is what it must feel like being in prison. I had no idea there could be so many things I wanted to do, or things I wanted to fetch from the rest of the house: I had a pencil I couldn't sharpen; I wanted some pieces of paper; I wanted a book Aunt couldn't find; I could only discover one stocking instead of two; I needed to sew a button back on but had no thread. I began to get very irritated by all the restrictions, and especially having to ask Aunt to get so many things for me. She never scolded me.

Everyone was vaccinated, including Elisa, who objected strongly about doctors who gave you diseases instead of curing them. 'Mark my words,' I heard her say, as her voice floated protestingly up the stairs, 'them contagious doctors will have all of us in our graves given half a chance.' Fanny and Ada were sent to stay with Aunt Halstead, and Arthur too, though I could hear him protesting loudly at the very idea. Things were being packed and a cab sent for. 'It is just for the time being,' Aunt said, 'until we see how things work out.'

What a fuss Aunt does make, I thought sometimes. She must like having me shut up here where she can see everything I do, with no one else to talk to me. I sometimes told her things I would never have done before. There is something about being shut up alone with another person that makes people say things to each other in a most unguarded way. I felt cross and irritable, Aunt must have found me very trying company. I even told her that we thought she was a witch. She just smiled in a knowing way, which made me feel even crosser. I wrote my diary sitting all alone in that room. Aunt was the only one ever allowed in my room. 'If you do catch smallpox,' she said, 'which may God forbid, I have told the doctor I will took after you.' Elisa brought me my meals and left them outside the door. I could hear whispering voices downstairs sometimes, though most of the time it was so quiet, so very quiet, that I began to be frightened by the quietness. Suppose, I thought, everyone has gone away and left me here, all on my own. But then Aunt would come in, bringing me yet another book to read. I even asked her if there were any socks to darn, I was getting so bored. 'Better not,' she said, 'until we are sure you haven't caught the infection. We would only have to burn them.'

I wrote a lot in my diary alone in that room. After all there was no Arthur to look over my shoulder, and I could always hear Aunt coming and hide it under the bedclothes. I wrote at the beginning of one page, 'WHAT I WOULD LIKE TO BE' I wrote a list in order of preference – 'Doctor, teacher, writer, nurse.' And then 'NOT A SEAMSTRESS'. 'If Arthur can be a doctor, then so can I', I wrote. About a week later I wasn't very well. I had a headache. In the next few days I felt iller and iller. Aunt came and read to me. Her voice began to sound as if it were a long way away. Great black clouds seemed to come rolling over me. Aunt always seemed to be there. My lips became dry and cracked, my eyes hurt. Aunt would give me drinks and put salve on my lips. I didn't want to eat anything. I was never sure if I was awake or dreaming. I couldn't stand up, and even sitting up made the room go round me in a most disturbing kind of way, as if I were falling and falling for ever. Everything smelled horrible, and the smell wouldn't go away.

While I was ill Aunt used to sing to me sometimes. I had nightmares when I seemed to do terrible things and people chased me, and the vicar told me I was going to hell. I think I screamed sometimes, or perhaps I only dreamt I did. There were lumps in the bed, and the pillows were like lumps of rock, and mostly my head hurt.

All the time Aunt kept the blinds down, and it seemed to be perpetual evening. She told me later that it was to prevent the sun hurting my eyes, and stop my getting bad scars on my face. I wondered if I was going to die. I don't mind if I die, I thought, I feel so dreadful, I feel so tired I could go to sleep for ever. Something I read somewhere I think, 'The window slowly grows a glimmering square, and leaves the world to darkness and to me' kept going through my head.

Aunt read me quotations from the Bible. The ones I remember best are 'Thy word is a lamp to my feet and a light unto my path; blessed is he that considereth the poor, the Lord will deliver him in time of trouble'; 'Out of the depths I cry unto thee, oh Lord'; 'The Lord is my strength and a very help in trouble'. She did make it sound as if God might help me, and not have me thrown into hell for all the wicked things I had done. I can still recall the touch of those firm hands of Aunt, how could such a strict person soothe me so, I wonder. She always seemed to be there when I needed her, I can't think she ever slept. She seemed to be there with me all the time.

One night I had a proper sleep, no dreams, no headache, and I woke up to find I didn't want to die after all. Aunt smiled at me. 'God be praised,' she said, 'that's better Minnie. I have brought you some broth to drink.' That and the gruel she provided over the next few days tasted wonderful. But then the itching got really bad; it was almost as bad as feeling ill. Aunt tied my hands to the bed. 'For your own good,' she said, 'scratching those spots will only make them worse.' There was a little more light allowed into the room, but not much.

Aunt read to me, again and again. There was Dickens and Jane Austen, and Trollope, Thackeray and Sir Walter Scott and many more, Tennyson she read too. I made her read *The Lady of Shalott* so many times she must have been heartily sick of it.

> Willows whiten aspens quiver
> Little breezes dusk and shiver
> Throw' the wave that runs for ever
> By the island in the river.

That was one of my favourite pieces. Her voice seemed to have changed, it used to sound so harsh, but now as she read her voice sounded soothing and quite cheerful. The itching began to get less and less.

One day my hands were untied and the curtains drawn back. The light seemed almost blinding. I lay in bed, thinking I would soon be getting up. I noticed as I lay there a scar on the back of my hand where one of the spots had been, and suddenly felt a terrible panic overwhelm me. I remembered things those whispering far off voices had been saying when I was ill. I had had smallpox, and smallpox always leaves people with scars and a horrid coarse skin which you have to try and hide for the rest of your life. I would be ugly, really ugly, for always and always. I was never really pretty, I thought, not like Ada, but now I would be ugly for the rest of my life.

It's not fair, how could God let me get smallpox. I'd never been really wicked, had I? First I got burnt, that was bad enough with a hole in my shoulder, an ugly part of my body which I would never want anyone to see, and now I would have an ugly face as well. I cried, how I cried. 'Don't,' said Aunt, as she came into the room, 'you'll only make your face look worse.'

Presently Aunt brought me a mirror. 'I don't ever want to look in a mirror again,' I said, hiding under the bedclothes. 'I've only brought it,' she said, 'so that you can see how lucky you have been, there is hardly a mark on your face. Come, have a look.' I stayed under the bedclothes until she went away but I could see she had left the mirror by the bed.

It took me a long time to look in that mirror. I thought of the mirror in *The Lady of Shalott*, 'The mirror cracked from side to side'. I thought of throwing the mirror on the floor, but then there would always be more mirrors to avoid for the rest of my life. I had seen so many people with their scarred faces to have any illusions, I thought I would rather remember my face as it used to be.

Next day I took a quick look secretly when Aunt wasn't there. 'You see,' she said triumphantly as she came into the room, 'what marks there are have nearly all disappeared.' I had looked, and now I looked again and then I looked again, this way and that and Aunt was right, I had to believe her. There were none of those horrid pox marks I had seen on so many faces in the streets. 'You were a good girl,' Aunt said, 'you didn't scratch, and Dickinson is going to write a paper for the medical journals about the need to keep strong light away to prevent scarring on all infectious lesions of the skin.'

I got better rather slowly. I was very thin and wobbly at first. Grandmama said I was small enough before, but now there was nothing left of me at all. Elisa took me for short walks, and Grandmama and I played backgammon. All my clothes were burnt, and all my books, and everything in my sick room scrubbed with disinfectant. 'You can't be too careful,' said Aunt. I tried to thank her one day for all she had done in looking after me.

'It is a Christian duty to care for the sick,' she said, 'I would have done the same for anyone who needed nursing. Don't think I treated you any differently than I would anyone else who needed such nursing care.' There didn't seem anything else to say after that. Then Arthur and Fanny and Ada came home from Aunt Halstead.

*

Now it is August and we are being subjected to the foul smell of rotting seaweed, piled high on the shore.

"I blame the atomic bombs," says Fanny, "Stands to reason, interfering in nature like that will have all kinds of unforeseen consequences."

"So I suppose you think the bombs are responsible for the cold last winter, and the floods afterwards and now all this very hot weather," says Ada.

"Get away with you," I say crossly, "women always blame things on what they don't understand."

"So you understand all about atoms, do you?" says Ada sarcastically. "Well, there is one good thing about it, at least it kills the taste and smell of this awful whale meat we are supposed to be eating. I really can't stand the taste of it."

"It's said to be very nutritious," I say. "It is either this or no meat at all. The meat ration is hardly sufficient for one meal now, and we have to eat something." Ada seems to eat less and less these days, she is always complaining about the food.

"No one could be expected to eat the disgusting kind of food we get these days," she protests.

"I ask you," Fanny says, "carrot tart, whale meat, sausage meat, that's all there seems to be. Perhaps we would have been better off if we had lost the war."

It's not like Fanny to complain. Philip doesn't come to see us any more. He has got so deaf and blind that he has gone to live with his daughter at Brighton. I think Fanny misses him. It doesn't do for us three old fogies to rely only on each other's company.

We clear away the lunch and throw the whale meat away. Well, one has to try these things. I suppose tomorrow it will have to be sausage meat again, if we can get any.

I have been to the hairdresser's today. The smell of the seaweed seems to get everywhere, especially in one's hair. I pat my hair as I come in, to feel it is in place, and realise how sore my head really is. The girl who does my hair for me comes from Poland, she was rescued from unspeakable conditions in a Nazi camp. What a truly dreadful time the Poles had during the war.

"I don't like your new hair style", says Ada, "makes you look ridiculous." I don't say anything, but I had rather a nasty experience today. She is only a young girl, the hairdresser, not used to hairdressing, anyone can see. They are always short of trained staff. Poor child, she didn't mean to scald my head. I can feel the patch on top where the hot water burnt, where it feels so sore. She was so apologetic. I suppose I could have complained, but what good would that have done? I doubt she'll ever make the same mistake again, using the water without testing it first. She would only have got the sack, and the damage has been done. She took so much trouble, poor child, rearranging my hair so the red patch doesn't show. I gave her an extra tip. I daresay my head will heal all right, but it does feel rather uncomfortable just now. I have made up my mind not to say a word to anyone, not to Fanny, nor Ada, they would only fuss so. 'Least said, soonest mended,' as Aunt would have said. What made me think suddenly of Aunt, I wonder.

John calls in. "One of my good days," he says, in his blustering way. You can see how painful his progress is, so what must it be like on a bad day, I can't imagine. He has taken lately to just calling in. "Saves all the fuss of your having to get tea," he says. "Besides I never know until the last minute whether I will feel able to walk this far." We play whist with Ada and Fanny, Ada doesn't really want to play, although she and Fanny seem to get all the best cards. John seems very tired.

"I don't approve of all these foreign workers coming in, mark my words we are only building up trouble for ourselves and for them too for that matter," John says. Sometimes I think people can read one's thoughts. "It's not so much the Europeans" he continues, "it's those who don't share a common cultural background with us that will make things difficult. And then of course they'll take it out on us."

"I think the powers that be put out as many gloomy bulletins on other countries as they can, just to make us feel better off than the rest of the world. All those starving Germans in the ruins of their towns, political unrest everywhere, Jews and Arabs at each other's throats, people searching everywhere for missing relatives in Europe, you would think the world war is just beginning, not that it had ended three years ago."

"What a gloomy mood you're in today," I say to John.

"It is the end of an era," he says, "things will never be the same again. We may not have been perfect in the way we ruled our Empire, but for most of the people most of the time they were far better off than they will ever be again. You ladies should go to the cinema next week," he says, "there is a very good film called *Brief Encounter*, so I am told. Not about the war so much as about people. Thinking about ordinary people with ordinary feelings is the only thing that keeps one sane these days."

As I help John to his feet our hands linger together. I can see the disapproving eyes of my sisters. But John and I know without saying it in words that this is likely to be the last time he comes. He has always been too proud to ask us to his place. "It would shatter your illusions," he always says. He is very apologetic about it, but very adamant. We suspect he has some woman there, his wife perhaps, but more likely not. He always seems well looked after. 'I would ask you round to my place,' he says, 'but I don't somehow seem to keep up with things.'

"Goodbye," we say, "take care," and watch John struggle alone the road. I know we shall miss his company very much. But at our age what can you expect. We are lucky to have had his company as long as we have.

That girl in the hairdresser's, just an ordinary girl, but brought up many many miles away in some far country. She made me think of myself as a young girl, starting out on a new career.

*

The Scars Of Life

After the smallpox it was a while before we could go back to school. Aunt kept finding us things to do. Aunt said that the devil made work for idle hands. That was how we were told about Grandfather Winder. The silver needed cleaning, she said, as Elisa had had too much to do lately to attend to it. 'What are the pictures on these spoons,' I asked as we sat down in front of a pile of silver teapots and jugs and cutlery, and the engraving on the spoon handles caught my eye. I had never seen them before. 'It is the Winder crest, a bull with a cherry in its mouth. It is depicted on the Lorton great seal. Your father,' she said with a bitterness in her voice I had never noted before, 'took it with him to America, and I doubt we'll ever see it again.'

It was Grandmama who explained everything. 'Your grandfather Winder came from a well known family in Cumberland,' she said. 'The Winders owned Lorton Hall, a big long grey stone house at Lorton village in the Secret Valley.' Grandmama had told us about her own family many times, but she had never wanted to talk about Grandfather Winder before.

'There are many lakes in the Lake District, you will know all about that Minnie, with your interest in Lake poets like Wordsworth.' Nowadays Grandmama seemed to forget so much, but then suddenly she might remember some things quite clearly. 'Lorton is near Loweswater, a very pretty place, your grandfather and I went there once after we were first married. The Winders have lived at Lorton Hall for hundreds of years, even before the days of William the Conqueror.' And what date was that, I almost expected her to say as she would have done when she used to give us lessons. 1066, I would have promptly replied.

'The Winders were always ready to support the Kings of England against the Scottish raiders who came over the border, stealing cattle from the English. A wild lot they were then, so I was told. Lorton is in a very remote valley, not for nothing was it called the secret valley, for there was but one way in and out across those hills. But the Winders were well born, why even their name is taken from Winander, a small place beside Lake Windermere. The Winders are descended from Kings,' she said, proudly. 'You remember John of Gaunt, who died in 1399, the fourth son of Edward III. He was never king himself, but it seems all English Kings since then are his descendants. And so are we,' she said proudly.

'What is Lorton Hall like,' we asked. 'I remember it as a long grey stone building, a peaceful enough looking place, with quiet grounds around it. There is a great beech tree near the house, in which King Charles I is said once to have hidden to escape the Parliament forces. It feels quite different when you go inside to a dark and gloomy hall with antlers and spears and armour hanging round the walls. That part of the house gives one a most uncomfortable feeling and makes one wonder what violent deeds have been committed there, But the rest of the house is pleasant enough.'

'Wild men, border fights, a secret valley, it is all too good to be true,' Arthur said. 'It is a story like the border ballads or some romantic tale by Sir Walter Scott. I don't believe a word of it,' he said in his superior voice. Grandmama ignored his rudeness. 'There is a ghost there too, they say, a young girl dressed in grey walks the corridors,' she continued, 'I never saw her myself, but there are those who say they have. I always meant to take you there one day, but it is a difficult journey for an old woman to undertake. There are no trains that go to Lorton, Cockermouth is the nearest station and that is a good few miles away.' 'Always filling the children's heads with your romantic nonsense,' said Aunt, as she opened the door. 'It's time for your rest mother, and Elisa is ready to take them all for a walk. I see I shall have to finish the cleaning for myself.'

'Do you believe that it could really be true,' I said, as we climbed the hill together, 'I mean to go there someday to find out. I wonder why we never lived there.' 'You are as bad as Grandmama,' Arthur said, 'you always did have romantic notions about being an aristocrat. Best to forget it. Even if any of it were true it's nothing to do with us now. You don't suppose we would be living here if there was even the remotest chance of our ever having a home in Cumberland.'

We went back to school. They weren't as lucky as me at school. There were empty desks when I walked into the classroom. 'Where is everyone?' I asked. No one said anything. 'Where's Jane,' I wanted to know, 'Jane Morley. Did she have smallpox too?' Still silence. I asked again, 'when is she coming back?' 'My dear Minnie,' Miss Robinson said, 'I'm afraid she won't be coming back.' 'Where's she gone?' I asked, though I already knew the answer. 'She had it very badly,' said Miss Robinson.

Not Jane, my dear Jane. I thought of her lying there as I had done, how wretched she must have felt, perhaps she was glad to die. I thought about her all day at school, but no one scolded me for not paying attention to my lessons. I cried all that night when I was alone at last in my bed, and for many nights to follow. I would go to school thinking I felt all right, and then something someone said, or even something I just saw would set me off again. Everyone was very kind. I hardly cared what day it was, or where I was. Nothing seemed worthwhile any more. Sometimes I thought of Betsy. 'Moping about won't help,' Aunt said severely sometimes. 'I am the resurrection and the Life,' says the Lord 'Whom the Lord loveth he chastiseth.' These and other similar quotations were always being aimed at me. Time just went slowly by. Sometimes I talked to Kate, Kate was the only one that really understood.

Everyone was sad. Many of the girls had pockmarked faces, I remember one girl called Alice, a pretty lively girl who only last term had been ogling the militiamen as they strutted about the town. She sat quietly in class now, her face no longer pretty, sewing most of the time. 'I'm not clever enough to be a teacher,' she said, 'and the only thing I am any good at is sewing. Since now I will never have a chance to marry, I must earn my living this way.' There were many more like her, subdued and sad and changed. There were those who had lost sisters or brothers, even parents. School was never quite the same again.

One day Miss Chieveley called me into her room. 'I thought it time we had a little chat, she said. 'I wouldn't want you to throw away all your chances. You are lucky that you have the ability to make something of yourself. You are getting older now, and soon you will have to think what you will do with your life. Of course you may get married. Even if you do, it is always useful to be able to earn your living if the necessity arises.' She asked me what I would like to do. 'It is always easier to work towards some kind of a goal,' she said. 'I want to be a doctor like my brother,' I answered. I realised at that moment that that is what I had had in mind for a long time now. 'I'm sure if I worked hard I could pass the same subjects that he has been studying.' She explained that although I could probably pass the exams if I worked hard enough, it would be very difficult for me to actually practise medicine. 'Maybe in fifty years time or so, there will be plenty of women doctors, but not now. There are some pioneering women, only a very few mind you, like Elizabeth Garrett Anderson who are trying to work in that field. But they already have an assured position in society and even for them it is a very uphill struggle. I wouldn't advise it. There are other qualifications you can get, like nursing, or teaching, or government service. Think about it, and come and tell me what you decide.'

It was about then I think that Ada stopped taking things. I watched her carefully, just to make sure, but she knew what I was doing and she became increasingly resentful. So I stopped watching her, and stopped worrying about it.

*

My daughter-in-law, Connie, has arrived on the doorstep. All the way from Canada. She did say she might be coming one day soon, but it's just like her to turn up without a word of warning. I don't suppose she realises how difficult it is to provide hospitality at a moment's notice. I am fond of Connie in a way. Not that I didn't feel antagonistic when she first married my son, that is my second son Francis. She is American you see, and we were all well aware that she and her sisters had come over to England in the twenties to find themselves English husbands.

Looking back on it I think she was genuinely fond of him when she married him. Anyway he was a most attractive young man, a good catch as they might have said. He could have married anyone he chose – perhaps someone from a wealthy family – a trained doctor, successful, intelligent, with many intellectual friends, a most eligible young man. Connie had no money in her family. Perhaps that was the trouble, poor Connie, she was never up to his intellectual level, good-hearted enough, perhaps too much in love. Francis soon found her company boring. He was intensely irritated too by the way she brought up their only son. He soon opted out of home life altogether, and while she was left at home he enjoyed the company of his married and unmarried friends.

He found the perfect solution at the outbreak of the second World War in 1940, when it was suggested that some families should be evacuated to Canada. The arrangements were swiftly made for her and Francis junior to sail off to Montreal. It wasn't long before the divorce followed, and my son married again, a well known actress. I never liked her, I don't even like to mention her by name. She was so condescending the first time we met that I never wished to see her again. Too full of herself, she thinks herself so superior. Connie has a much nicer personality.

Well, here she is and I ask her in. She always did look American, and here she is neatly dressed in that nondescript style of all Americans, still good looking in that bland American way. An unhappy life she must have had, but she brought it on herself I suppose. But she did her best, I grant you that, she did her best.

I ask about my grandson, Francis. Poor boy, how she made his life a misery. She was always on at him to make sure he wore his warm clothes, to be careful not to fall, not to put himself in any kind of danger. She spoiled him and over-protected him, and made it impossible for him to make friends with anyone of his own age. They always teased him, not surprisingly, and then he came running back to his mother which only made it worse. His father ignored him, as he ignored Connie. Still I'm told he's making quite a good job of being a reporter for the Montreal Star. Poor boy, he came to see me when he was demobbed, I think that is the term they used for the disbandment of troops in 1945. At least he had joined up. I don't suppose I am likely to see him again.

It wasn't my son's fault, I suppose. He was in a strange state when he got married. Wounded in the trenches in 1918, he still has a metal plate to cover the hole the bullet made in his head. I think that bullet changed his personality. It made no difference to his brains thank goodness, he has always been a good and successful doctor in the fashionable area of Highgate, with many intellectual friends and many public figures as his patients. But he has always seemed a stranger to me since his war experiences.

Connie is her usual cheerful self. She is a fighter, I'll give her that, she doesn't complain about her life, just gets on with living it.

She has a certain tenacity one cannot help but admire. We are fond of each other in a strangely intimate way, as if we recognised the other in ourselves.

My sisters and I find some lunch, we use up our week's supply of eggs, and Fanny and Ada have been to the shop with good effect. We have some cheese and potatoes, and the inevitable carrots. Connie offers to do the washing up, "I like washing up," she protests as she leans away from the sink so as not to endanger her clothes. We suggest she does the drying instead.

She leaves quite soon. "I want to visit as many people as I can", she says, "while I am here. I doubt if I'll have the opportunity to come again." We bid each other an affectionate farewell. "We'll write as usual once I'm back in Montreal," she says. We've kept up a correspondence for years, I wonder if she values it as much as I do. I like to hear about Canada, and the French customs, and the people there. Poor Connie. It's sad it is the last time I will ever see her. I watch her lingeringly as she walks away down the road. Poor Connie.

Escape

I promised Miss Chieveley I would work hard, especially at my favourite subjects of zoology, botany and chemistry, and get the best examination results that I could. I would choose what I wanted to do when I knew what subjects I had passed. And I did work hard, very hard. What else could I do: there didn't seem much pleasure in other things, not now when Jane had gone. Besides I wanted to prove to my brother that girls were capable of doing as well as any boy. Above all I had begun to realise I wanted a passport to other things, not to have to spend the rest of my life in Huddersfield. Qualifications brought freedom, I told myself, a reasonable salary, a choice.

It is a curious thing about Aunt. She had been so kind to me while I was ill I thought things would be different now, but not a bit of it. Sometimes it seemed as if I had dreamt about it, dreamt that she had been so kind, you would never know it by her manner since, the same antagonism, the same sarcasm, the same feeling that we children were a cross she had to bear. I sometimes thought of pretending to be very ill again, just to see if her other self was still there underneath that brusque unyielding presence.

There is not much I remember over the next few years, except hard work, discussions with Arthur about work, and with Kate about the situation of women. We read John Stuart Mill on 'The Subjection of Women' and decided we would fight for women's rights whenever the opportunity arose. I remember reading *The Wrongs of Women* by Elizabeth Toma with great enthusiasm, though I can't recall now much of what she said. Why should men think they had a God-given right to better standards of living, to the best jobs, and think that they owned their wives and had a right to treat them as their servants, or worse.

What I do remember vividly, oh so vividly, is what occurred when I took the examinations and got the results. I passed the senior

Cambridge papers in a variety of subjects, including the sciences. I got a distinction in zoology, the first woman, so Miss Chieveley said, ever to do so. There were a few of us together in her study as she told us the results. 'A credit to the school' she said. She told me to wait when the others left.

'I have,' she told me, 'negotiated for you a scholarship to Bedford College in London to take a teaching course. The details will, I know, be a mere formality after these excellent grades of yours. I know the Principal well, and I know Miss Sharpe is looking forward to welcoming you there.'

It was like a talisman to a new life, a new world. I could be my own Master, I could study the subjects that I really liked. I don't think I have ever felt so elated as I did that morning in school, one of the best few minutes of my entire life I have often told Fanny. I didn't even envy Arthur going to Edinburgh to study medicine. I would be in London, the capital city of England, and I felt I could conquer the whole world. I couldn't wait to tell Grandmama and Aunt, and even Dickinson I thought would be pleased. They had all of them said to work hard, and now I had fulfilled all that they could possibly have expected of me.

I couldn't wait for the school bell to ring, and go home to tell everyone. I ran home, 'very unladylike' Aunt would say if she knew. I was breathless, explaining, telling everyone the good news. Aunt said 'congratulations' on my hard work. 'Of course,' she said, after a pause, 'there is no question of your being able to take up the scholarship, there simply isn't the training money available.' At first I thought she was joking, even though Aunt had never been known to make jokes. I turned to Grandmama. She just looked blank. 'But,' I said, 'it's a scholarship, no one has to pay out any money.' 'And what about your keep,' said Aunt. 'We are hard pushed enough as it is to pay for your brother's training.'

'Why' I demanded, 'should Arthur have all the money spent on his education.' We three girls needed to earn our living just as much as he did. 'He will eventually have a wife and family to support, while you will only have to keep yourselves. He will need the money more than you three girls,' said Grandmama. 'Besides you wouldn't go away would you, and desert us. You are needed here, to help Aunt, and care for your sisters.' I appealed to Dickinson when he came home, but he only said the same.

I was angry, with a cold hard anger I had never felt before. Aunt, if she had known about it, would have called it the sin of wrath. 'They all want to trap me here,' I thought, 'they don't care about me, what I might want or need, all they care about is making sure I am available to provide help in the house when it is needed. Well, I will find my own way to escape.' Whatever gratitude or affection I might owe them would count for nothing now. The sooner I made my own plans the better. I would tell no one what I was doing, not until I had worked something out. But I was going to leave, sooner or later, that I knew.

When it come to making the arrangements, they proved easier than I could ever have imagined. Miss Chieveley said I could stay on at school for a term at least, teaching the younger girls, until I knew what I would do next. I would be able to save a little money. 'I would offer you a permanent post here,' she explained, 'except that it has come to my notice that this school may one day soon be closing down. You would be well advised to look elsewhere.'

I noted advertisements for teaching jobs in London, writing to several to see if they had vacancies for an English or science teacher. I appealed to Miss Chieveley to find out what kind of schools they were, if they were respectable, if they had a good academic record,

There was one she particularly recommended. I wrote again, asking if I could have a teaching post and also bring my younger sisters with me. They were most helpful. I knew I could manage to pay our fares and get all the things we needed out of my pay, not a princely sum for a year's work but enough. I could pay for my sisters at the new school with my new salary.

There was no way we could be prevented from leaving now if that is what we wanted. I did ask my sisters what they thought under dire threats as to what I might do should they give our secret away. 'I shall be going to London anyway,' I told them, 'and you can come with me if you wish.' 'I want to stay with you,' Fanny answered, 'London would be a better place to live than here,' Ada said. Arthur was in Edinburgh. I wrote, but by the time he received the letter we would be gone. So our plans were laid.

I never told Aunt what we were doing. I had spent much of the time while we were at Huddersfield, planning how we could escape, and now the time had really come. If I told Aunt our plans I felt that in some uncanny way she might upset them. My wages were one hundred and fifty pounds for my year's work. I did pay something towards my keep, twenty pounds over the year. I offered Aunt twenty-five, but she said to keep five for myself. I couldn't refuse without arousing suspicions about the rest of the money.

The week before we left we had a wonderful time shopping in the town, getting our new outfits and working out how to purchase all that we might need. I can't think how Aunt missed the excitement that we felt, or somehow didn't notice when we smuggled everything up to our room. We had never had so much money to spend on ourselves before, and I think it went rather to our heads. I remember our hats, we thought ourselves so bright and gay, I remember thinking even Fanny looked quite pretty, and Ada of course would catch everyone's eye. How happy we were for those brief weeks, thinking of our escape.

'Does Madam care for this style,' 'we have other hats for you to try,' 'I assure you the quality of this skirt is exceptional, you can't beat Huddersfield wool cloth for ensuring lasting wear'; 'This jacquard jacket is beautiful is it not?' 'This is the latest London fashion in footwear'; 'These stays are the best design for health that are on the market'; 'Would Madam care to try on this new style blouse?' What a trial we must have been to all those hard worked shop assistants, but they joined in our fun. They even seemed to delight at our trying so many new things.

What fun we did have in those shops. We were somewhat fearful that word would get to Aunt about what we were doing. She would have been horrified at our frivolity, even had she known we could pay for everything ourselves. Fanny threw her new hat in the air with excitement as we left one shop, so unlike Fanny. Perhaps, like butterflies emerging from their chrysalis, each of us would be metamorphosed into something new when we began to enjoy our new freedom in London.

'We are leaving for London on Monday morning,' I informed Aunt one day. She thought I was joking. 'We will not be a burden to you any more. You will have more money to spend on Arthur in Edinburgh when we are gone,' I explained to Grandmama. I showed her our train tickets, and the letters from the school. We packed. Despite ill looks from Aunt, and tears from Grandmama, and Dickinson's comment that he thought we were being too hasty, we insisted we would go.

My third life, my educational upbringing was about to end. The cab I had ordered was piled high with all our possessions as it took us to the station and we were off on our great adventure. What it is to be young and hopeful, thinking the world is at one's feet. My anger had turned to excitement, to a new adventure. My third life was over. The next of my nine lives was about to begin.

Part Two

All Is Vanity

It is a rather cold bleak day, but Fanny and I have managed to struggle to the library and home again. Wonderful idea, a library, what would we do without them. There is not very much left to talk about between us except the books we have read. And we can chat to the people in the library, they are very helpful about recommending books. I gave them my new list, they always keep particular books I am interested in. I always know they will have something I will appreciate.

"You might be interested in *Rebecca* by Daphne Du Maurier, Miss Jones the librarian suggested to me today." So here I am with a copy of it to read at my leisure.

I tell Fanny she should read more serious books sometimes. Those superficial romances she reads seem very trivial stories.

"Those shallow romantic novels are not really meant for octogenarians like us" I point out, "they are for the young and ignorant".

"That's all very well for you to say," she protests "but I never got married, and I like to read about the romances and happy marriages I never had."

"Marriage is not all that romantic" I retort. "People don't just fall in love and marry and live happily ever after you know. Besides in real life there are all the hazards of childbirth, and the worry and grief that children bring. Perhaps you should think yourself lucky you have led such a sheltered life."

"At least you have lived, experienced what life has to offer. I have to live my experiences through reading about them."

"One struggles to support children, get them an education, help them to a happy life. But things never turn out as one would like."

"Well you've got Mollie and Teddie, and all those grandchildren, what more could you want?"

We are startled by the doorbell ringing. It couldn't be Joan, from along the road, we had met her in the library and she said she was going straight home. Helen we know isn't well, and there is no one else likely to call at this time of day.

"Perhaps it's one of those returning soldiers looking for work, wanting to dig the garden or something," Fanny says, as she goes to answer the door. I get out my purse. We can't afford to give them very much, but every little helps. Through the window I notice a car standing at the curb.

I hear a man's voice,

"Can we come in?" It is somehow familiar, and then a woman's voice,

"A pleasant day, don't you think?" It is my son Francis, who has driven over from his seaside retreat with his actress wife.

"How are you?" I ask, as we give each other a perfunctory kiss. I am not sure whether his wife would welcome a kiss or not, I've met her only once or twice before. I decide against it. I am trying desperately to remember her name. "And how are you, and your mother?" I enquire. Francis has to support his widowed mother-in-law, he has made a nice home for her.

"She's doing very well, thank you," is the reply. Somehow she makes her mother sound impersonal, as if she is talking about a pet dog or cat.

We get them tea of course, but I wish he had let me know, we have nothing in the house but bread and butter, and some rather indifferent jam. Fanny bustles off to make the tea, and we sit down together. Elaine, yes that's her name, Elaine sits decorously on the edge of the sofa.

"What brings you over here?" I enquire.

"We just thought we would like to see for ourselves that you are all right," Elaine says. "Living on your own like this. We have been wondering how you are getting on."

We talk about the weather, and the health service. After all Francis is a doctor, and it seems to be the one subject he is really interested in.

"No good will come of it," he says. "If you take away the administration from the doctors, stupid medical mistakes will be made. Besides people will demand attention for all kinds of trivial ailments. You'll have people coming to a surgery to have a dressing put on a simple cut, you mark my words, and they'll be demanding an X-ray for things like a sprained ankle. Almost all the medical profession is against the idea. The country can't afford it anyway. There'll be no time left to treat those who are really ill. Of course medical care had to be extended, but it could perfectly well be done by improving the old system."

He did ask about my grandson Harold, who is his godson, who had had a room at his house for a while before the war. But he wasn't really interested.

"Nice garden you have," says Elaine, as the conversation grinds to a halt. I stare bleakly out at our small uncut grass plot with its encroaching weeds.

I look at Francis and try to imagine the rather solemn little redheaded boy he used to be, or even the attractive ladies man he later became. But all I see is a balding, tired, middle aged man with a self-satisfied false smile.

Fanny had managed the jam sandwiches quite well, lucky we had some butter left over from the rations. She had even hurried round to the corner shop and bought a packet of some kind of biscuits. Well, they weren't too bad. It was all they had she explained later.

I suppose one shouldn't be relieved at the departure of one's own son, but talking to him was like talking to a stranger. I always felt he treated his first wife Connie and their only son very badly. Connie might have her faults, but this Elaine was such a silly shallow kind of woman. Perhaps all actresses are like that. Connie is ten times better then her.

When they have gone I tell Fanny, "I'm glad that's over."

"You should be ashamed of yourself," says Fanny, "it was nice of them to come."   .

I know she is right, I'm glad they came. But I wish I could feel comfortable with them.

"All, all is vanity" I find I am muttering to myself. I am not sure if I am thinking of Francis and Elaine, or the difficulties of falling in love.

A New Life

'Goodbye,' we said to Grandmama and Aunt and Dickinson that September long ago. It felt strange, all three of us sisters starting out on a new career. 'Nothing of us but doth change, into something rich and strange,' I repeated to myself as we set off on our long train journey down to the South of England.

We were full of excitement, eager to explore the world but I must admit that as we sped across the countryside the world seemed rather a dismal place. I hadn't realised before just how many northern towns appeared as replicas of each other. Those streets and streets of houses, as if huddled together for comfort, those chimneys on the skyline with their smoke floating skywards in gentle supplication, or so it seemed to me that day, the people waiting below perhaps for divine intervention on their behalf. I was prone to such fantasies in those days. Buildings were being pulled down or built up, with those inevitable patches of waste ground and dirty puddles. Dirty those places looked, all of them looked so dirty and mean.

I suppose, I thought, that's what Huddersfield must look like to other people. I realised how perspectives can change quite abruptly. One minute you are part of something, like the place you grew up in, the next you review everything from a critical distance. I remember something I read somewhere, about not being able to see the wood for the trees, or alternatively not being able to see the trees for the wood, something like that, as if you could never make sense of the whole thing altogether, never being able to see the wood and the trees at the same time. There were coal towns, steel towns, railway towns, cotton towns. But all the workers must feel just the same, whatever factory they happen to be working in, I thought. All those armies of workers trying to escape. No wonder people have been afraid of revolutions.

Further on it was the woods and trees and green fields, the sheep and cattle, and people bringing in the harvest, those trim fields with corn stooks drying in the sun. Women with bonnets to protect them from the sunlight, men with their caps and scythes, bending as they made their rhythmic movements cutting and harvesting the growing corn, miniature people they seemed as we flashed by them. 'It doesn't look real, does it,' Fanny said suddenly. I thought she had fallen asleep.

Some gentlemen had got into the carriage at the last stop and Ada was looking at them in a much too interested way. I asked her about the book she was supposed to be reading. Fortunately the men get out at the next stop. 'You should be ashamed,' I said to Ada, 'to be so free with your glances at those men. You should always ignore men unless you have been properly introduced to them.' 'I thought we had left all those instructions of Aunt's far behind in Huddersfield,' Ada said petulantly. 'When has following Aunt's rules ever got us anywhere in the past. We never had a chance in Huddersfield to meet anyone at all.' 'Some of the girls at school had brothers,' Fanny says. 'There was one...' 'That's not the same at all,' Ada answered, 'besides they were all so dumb.' Fanny blushed. Ada could be very unkind sometimes. 'I never wanted to get to know any of them,' Ada continued. 'Now those men in the carriage, I expect they were really rich, and interesting,' she added as an afterthought.

Arriving in London was quite an experience. For one thing it was such an enormous place, the streets seemed to go on for ever and ever. When we did eventually arrive at the station there was such hustle and bustle, such noise and shouting, ten times more than there had ever been at Huddersfield. I was frightened I might lose Fanny and Ada in the crush. I knew we were to be met, but suppose no one came. We did manage to get a porter, who got all our luggage down for us. I hope I gave him a big enough tip, he was very helpful.

We stood there on the platform, feeling quite deserted. What, I wondered, hesitant for the first time, could we do if no one came. 'Pull yourself together, Minnie,' I can remember scolding myself under my breath, as my sisters began to look a little worried. 'Get a horse cab and just arrive,' I told myself. I wondered if we should have enough money to pay for so long a journey through London.

'Excuse me, young ladies, are you the party for Forest Hill School,' a gentleman's voice asked politely. 'Let me introduce myself, my name is Edward Allen, a cousin of Miss Haines, the headmistress who is to employ you. She has asked me to fetch you as she was unable to come herself. Let me present you with a letter of introduction.' I duly inspected it.

What a pleasant, good-looking young man, I thought. We were soon packed aboard a horse bus, and as we struggled through the London traffic, narrowly missing carts and people, coach horses and cabs, he regaled us by pointing out landmarks, telling us amusing stories, and generally making the time pass pleasantly. What an agreeable companion, I thought. Fanny and Ada couldn't keep their eyes off him.

We had to change buses several times, and we realised we could not well have managed without our companion. He was most solicitous in managing our luggage and seeing we were comfortably seated. He had to ride upstairs on his own on one of the buses. Since ladies are not allowed upstairs, and there being no room for him downstairs, we were left to our own devices. But we managed very well, considering.

We took a four wheeler for the last part of the journey through what seemed like a park, an oasis in all that turmoil of traffic, and arrived at a large house with a green lawn in front of it. Edward Allen deposited us at the entrance door, exchanging brief greetings with several people, then making his excuses to depart, saying he was overdue at home, but hoped he would see us again one day soon. We thanked him heartily for his help and kindness as he set off and left us standing there in front of the house surrounded by our luggage.

The whole school seemed to be waiting for us, so many girls crowded onto the lawn, chatting excitedly, looking so very fresh and clean and pretty, so happy and untroubled. Nor could one have failed to recognise that Miss Haines was the headmistress standing there by the door, surrounded by a little group of teachers. She was very tall and very thin, her hair pulled back in a tight bun. She was dressed severely with a high collar to her lace embroidered blouse, such delicate embroidery on the collar and double cuffs that the workmanship made me wonder if the girls made it for her themselves. Not even a headmistress, I thought, could have afforded such luxury. Her eyes looked straight at you, with a penetrating gaze, but they were not unkind. 'There's not much Miss Haines doesn't notice around the school,' I thought. She greeted us kindly in a most dignified manner. She had our luggage taken to our rooms by Mr Jones the school porter.

There were introductions, to Miss Purdy, the home economics mistress, to Miss Shelley in charge of English, and Miss Brightside in charge of Needlework. 'You will meet other teaches later,' we were told. 'As you know we do have a few boarders at this school. We have no male staff, except for the dancing master Mr Dando who comes in once a week on Friday afternoons, and of course Mr Jones the porter, whose wife is our housekeeper. Dinner is in half an hour in the big hall. Elisia,' Miss Haines said, beckoning to one of the girls, 'please take the Misses Winder up to their rooms.'

She had managed to convey to us, in those few short sentences, which teaching subjects she considered most important, that good manners and household management were part of the training for her pupils, that male staff were excluded unless considered indispensable, and that we were to be treated with respect. We had indeed arrived.

We changed for dinner as we inspected our rooms. Ada was to be a pupil still for the time being, until she was sixteen and was to sleep in a dormitory with the girls. I thought she might mind being there with strangers on her own, but I realised she was really quite pleased that it was so. Fanny had a small room next to mine. We had always slept together in the same room in Huddersfield, except of course when I was ill. I was quite pleased to find myself alone for once but I think Fanny would have preferred it if we had still been together.

There was no more chattering as we entered the big hall, but a row of silent faces, the girls all standing up as we and other teachers followed Miss Haines in a procession to the top of the table. Miss Haines said grace and indicated where each teacher was to sit among the girls. Everyone sat down to the scraping of chairs, and the beginning of murmured conversation. 'We think it important for the girls to learn the art of polite mealtime conversation,' explained Miss Haines.

We soon realised that we were expected to memorise each name on first introduction. I got a most reproving look for calling Miss Brightside Miss Shelley as I struggled to join in the conversation. 'Memorising names is part of the social training that we insist upon,' Miss Haines said. 'Everyone should instantly remember all those to whom they have been introduced, it is one of the basic rules of polite society.'

I noticed Miss Haines ate hardly anything at all, whether it was because she was so busy noticing all that went on around her, or because she didn't like the food, or that she thought hearty eating impolite I couldn't tell. 'No wonder she is so thin,' I thought. I didn't eat much either, despite the fact I felt so hungry after the journey. I spent most of that meal repeating names to myself, over and over, in the hope that I would still remember them in the morning. There must have been all of twenty girls, and about twelve teachers there, and of course by the morning there would be all the day girls to remember too. Recalling people's names was one of the things I learnt at Forest Hill School, it is an art that can easily be learnt by practice, and I have always found it useful all through my life. Just one of the little things for which I have always been grateful. Aunt had always insisted we should behave like young ladies. Now we were being introduced into the ways of polite society.

*

I am staying for the week-end at my granddaughter's. She and her husband David have just moved to Oxford. Now that they are so much nearer, and they have so often asked me to come and stay with them, I decided to hire a car to drive me here. I shan't stay more than a couple of days, the car will pick me up on Monday. I like to have a picture in my mind of where those I am fond of happen to live, I like to picture them in their proper surroundings. When I am home again I will feel much more comfortable thinking of them here.

Sometimes one feels one needs a break from one's usual surroundings. Fanny and I had words the other day and we are not best pleased with each other. 'I do my best to run the house properly, old as I am,' I told Fanny. I wish Fanny wouldn't interfere, it makes for so much confusion if two people think they are both in charge. It is not that I am not fond of my sisters, but the best of company can sometimes seem oppressive. People need a change sometimes.

Since we have had such excellent daily help for the past months, I see no reason to think my two sisters will not be well looked after while I am away. After all there are two of them, and they can summon help for each other should the need arise. I left the doctor's number by the phone.

Our quarrel was all on account of our daily help, our treasure Mrs Burton who has been 'doing' for us. She reminds me of Mrs Mop in *Itma* that radio programme that kept us all laughing through the war.

She doesn't actually say, 'shall I do you now, Ma'am', but I wouldn't be the least surprised were she to do so.

Mrs Burton has been so very satisfactory that it would be madness to upset her. But what does Fanny do but try and interfere with her normal routine. I happened to overhear her saying, 'do you think, Mrs Burton, you could take down the curtains today and send them to the laundry.' I can't think what possessed Fanny, Friday would have done just as well, though for myself I can't see they need cleaning for at least another month. In any case it was Wednesday not Friday, and Mrs Burton does extra jobs on Fridays. On Wednesdays she cleans the bedrooms including mine. At any rate Fanny and I had words.

This is a strange house my grandchildren live in. It was much neglected when they bought it, that was why they could afford it I suppose. It certainly needs a lot of money spending on it. But then so many properties were neglected during the war years. At least this house has not suffered from any bomb damage. Poor dears, they are still in the process of redecorating it themselves. It's never the same is it, doing such things for oneself. After all it would be strange if they could do it as well as a trained decorator could. I must admit they are making a much better job of it than I ever thought they could. I suppose nowadays everyone has to be able to turn their hand to anything. Of course the furniture and curtains and carpets have had to be purchased on dockets so most of their furniture is second-hand. They have obviously worked hard, putting the garden to rights, cleaning up the place as best they can. It's hard on the young folks these days.

The best room in the house is the study, where David's students will come for their tutorials next week. It looks quite professional, with book shelves lining the walls, a desk and a carpet of sorts. The long corridor leading into it still smells of paint. They have a pre-war car, a baby Austin, I think they call them. They are very kind, drive me round to see the Oxford colleges, but I could hardly say the car is comfortable, I felt so cramped, like a sardine in a tin as they say. They don't seem to be so badly off for food, and the garden is full of fruit trees and David has many of his meals in College. Still I do think young people these days have a hard time of it. Mary gave me several jars of fruit she had bottled, and some jam she had made. I remember she was quite good at cooking even when she was quite young. I enjoyed my visit, it was a nice break, but I could see how busy they were, and I was quite glad to get home again.

I am back in Worthing; Fanny and I are friends again. "We missed you," she says. They had gone to all the trouble of making a celebration tea on my account, the best china, the silver teapot, a cake, quite like old times except our visitors were missing. I was glad to be back. I think Fanny and Ada were glad to see me again. They seem to have managed quite well without me.

I have decided to turn out some of my drawers, I tell Fanny and Ada we should be more particular about what we keep, and throw away things we no longer need. I have discovered at the bottom of one of them, where I keep the cards and presents people send me, some old letters of times past. Some of the writing is faded, but I can just make some of them out. It's a strange feeling to read letters from those you knew so well, but are now long gone.

Even now I feel it is impossible to write about some of the letters, they would bring back such a storm of emotional memories, of friends, husband, children, that I know I would be overwhelmed. They say a drowning man sees his whole life pass before him. Perhaps I shall before I die, but not yet, not yet. I put the letters away.

*

Minnie as an infant in the arms of her mother, Margaret – 1861.

Minnie with her granddaughter – 1919.

Grandmama at Huddersfield – 1882.

Minnie's brother Arthur Winder – 1917.

Minnie's husband Frank Allen – 1917.

Minnie's son Harold killed in active service – 1917.

Minnie's son Arthur died in active service – 1944.

Minnie's daughter Mollie and her husband Teddy with their
children Harold and Mary – 1919.

Five of Minnie's grandchildren: Anne, Harold, John, Mary and Ruth – 1928

London Life

I remember teaching my first lesson at Forest Hill School. 'You are to teach English and science to our senior girls,' Miss Haines explained. 'You will be responsible as the science teacher for teaching human physiology and hygiene. We leave such lessons until the girls are fifteen. Parents expect the girls who leave here to understand the facts of life, and become responsible wives and mothers.'

I did have illustrations and diagrams I had brought with me from Huddersfield, but as yet I didn't know the girls, nor they me. One feels very isolated being so small, many of the girls were already much taller than me. It is so much easier for teachers like Miss Haines to look down at their charges, not up to them as I must. I feared disciplinary problems with such a subject to teach, confronted by girls whose reactions I could not possibly foresee. 'Be dignified,' I told myself, 'don't forget how important it is to have a "presence".' One finds out much about one's pupils in such a class; some giggled with embarrassment; one girl even fainted, and had to be revived with smelling salts; some smirked, obviously knowing as much if not more than they should. 'If I survive this,' I thought, 'I shall survive the rest of my teaching career.' I suspected Miss Haines too looked upon this first lesson as a test of my teaching abilities. But I must have passed the test since there were no complaints.

Fanny taught English to the ten to twelve year olds. I knew she wasn't very happy. Not that anyone complained, and she seemed to get on well enough with teachers and pupils alike. It was just that increasingly she seemed to feel less at home at the school. She was restless, and sometimes I had to admit she lacked the necessary concentration. Sometimes she would give me summaries of her lessons to check, and she often made careless and unnecessary mistakes.

Ada became friendly with one of the newer teachers. Miss Haines called me into her room one day, and said she was worried that this might lead to disciplinary problems. 'It will be different in a few months time, when she takes up her position as a pupil teacher, but meanwhile I would be grateful if you would advise her to be careful. I am most pleased with her progress, I wouldn't want her prospects to be jeopardised in any way.'

We had company always on Sunday afternoons when Miss Haines' cousins and other friends were invited to tea. I had been well prepared by Miss Purdy before the guests arrived the very next Sunday. There were six brothers, Frank, Tom, Charles, William, Edward, and Walter, all quite good looking in their way, Miss Purdy said. Sometimes another cousin Hugh would come, a musical genius we were led to believe. Such a talented family, the Allens, she explained. It was Charles and Walter and especially Hugh who were so interested in music, William was a wood carver and painter. Tom liked to write poetry, and he and his mother published a book of poems called *Poems by Mother and Son*. Frank was manager of a haberdashery firm. I felt sorry for Frank, dismissed rather as an inferior being for not having the artistic aspirations of his brothers. A very kind and self-effacing sort of man he seemed when I was introduced. Tom was a bank employee and Edward, the one who had fetched us from the station, a civil servant. I soon learned that should I want to know details about the school Miss Purdy was always ready to supply it. I had learnt much about the Allens by the time Frank and Edward arrived for tea that very next Sunday.

Miss Purdy also gave me a few homilies on what one should expect on making arrangements for a happy marriage.

'It doesn't do for a man to marry a girl without a settlement from her father,' she said.

'That puts me in my place,' I thought. 'In such circumstances I am destined never to marry at all.'

'If a women is more intelligent than her husband she should conceal it.'

That is something I thought that I could never do, I replied.

'All that is needed is a good hand in writing and good connections will do the rest.'

'I may have a good hand in writing,' I thought, 'but good connections are a different matter. Here in London I have no connections at all.'

'Women's feelings are more general before they become focused on marriage duties, while men are more interested in physical attraction, and only later become more generally affectionate.'

'Marriage postponed brings greater pleasure.' These last two I hotly contested.

They were very pleasant, those Sunday tea parties. So much interesting conversation from those who actually were able to demonstrate their expertise. Music was played, pictures examined and criticised. We played a game called the poetry game, invented I think by Thomas. You have to write a question on a piece of paper, fold it back out of sight and pass it to your neighbour. He or she in turn must write a 'difficult' word, hippopotamus perhaps or exomorphic, for example. It is then passed on again, and each recipient on opening his paper must write a short poem, bringing in the word and answering the question asked. The first question I ever got was 'Why do men hate women?' The word was 'impenetrable'. I thought I acquitted myself rather well, though Fanny said I was becoming cynical.

> Men love a woman's lovely face
> Of cleverness they want no trace
> But 'neath the glamour all they find
> Is an impenetrable mind.

At least it made everyone laugh. Fanny always hated that game, and seldom joined in, but sometimes she would provide a most perceptive poem concerning people's feelings.

Ada on the other hand provided amusing answers, often with a macabre twist or spiteful implication. Yes, those were pleasant enough afternoons. One somehow felt one was part of an intellectual and artistic group. Sometimes other visitors came, friends of one or other of the cousins. There was George, over six foot tall, thin and rather pale, and a most amusing talker whom I noticed with particular interest one day.

After a while I began to have strange feelings when George visited us. Even before I was actually in his presence, I would hear his voice as he arrived and it would be a kind of shock to the system like a nerve exposed, half pleasure, and almost, I thought, half pain. I began to experience that sinking feeling that I had been told comes upon one as you watch the one you love look towards you. You spend time waiting for the next glance, the next recognition in the other's eyes. There is that pride I had in everything he said, that protective urge I felt whenever he was subjected to any kind of worry or of criticism. It is a weird state to be in, so disconcerting, so unexpected, so impossible to control, so unlike any feelings that have gone before that I was left defenceless. This I thought is what the poets write about, this extraordinary response to a particular person. I would find my thoughts wandering in the middle of a lesson.

I would forget prudence in making opportunities to meet him, be alone with him: I would want to hold his hand: I would see a crease in his shirt and feel that I should remedy even such a small defect. I even thought, despite the fact I do hate sewing so, that I should like to sew on a button that was coming loose. I felt as if some alien force had taken control of me. I was a silly love struck girl, old enough to know much better, but quite incapable of doing anything about it. Fanny called me moody, Ada said I was making a spectacle of myself, Miss Haines inquired kindly if I had been feeling unwell lately.

George was always kind, always thoughtful, always amusing. There was no one like him for seeing the funny side of every situation. Perhaps those intellectual afternoons would have seemed oppressive without his being there to make everyone laugh at themselves. He was a little apart from the others, did not join in everything they did. I thought he might not be so strong as some of them as he seemed pale and listless sometimes, tired, not like his usual self. He worked long hours and I inquired if fresh air was available in the office where he worked. I even asked Edward about it since they both worked together in the same office. Aunt had always said fresh air was what was needed. There is too much illness about for you to take risks I told him. Once he had a sudden coughing fit. Sometimes I seem to manage to get dust stuck in my throat, he said, it's nothing really.

I soon became accustomed to the teaching programme. The emphasis was always on good manners, and some required accomplishments like piano playing and drawing, and especially good handwriting and orthography. We often had spelling bees for the girls, which they seemed to enjoy very much. For those who were

more intelligent extra classes were provided in languages for the sake
of interest. But unlike Huddersfield High School, no one had any
pretensions to go to university, or to provide themselves with any kind
of professional qualification. They had no need, since their fathers
could always provide a settlement for marriage.

I received a letter from Aunt.

> *Greenbank*
> *Gledhill Road*
> *Huddersfield*

Dear Niece,

*I am writing to tell you we have now moved house.
Please note the change of address.*

*(As far as I could picture it Gledhill Road was about
half a mile from our old house at Brunswick Terrace up
by the station. I seemed to recall trees and grass about
where new modern houses, quite large as I recall, were
being built.)*

*It is a near a pleasant park. You will appreciate that
it is better for Grandmama, less noisy, much pleasanter
surroundings, and the house is easier to manage. Your
Uncle Dickinson has been doing very well lately in his
business.*

*(I could see the logic of such a move but I felt it as a
kind of personal loss, one can become attached to
places, houses, I realised. I had always hated Brunswick
Terrace, but now in retrospect I would regret never
going back there again. Besides Mama and Papa at
least knew where we were to be found at that old
address, should they ever come to look for us. Now they
would never know how to find us. I suppose I had
always hoped that one day we might see either one or
both of my parents again.)*

*I hope you are continuing to say your prayers each
day, we all need guidance in these difficult times. Do
not stray from righteousness in that wicked city of
London. Such dreadful things we read about it in the
papers. I also hope you have found my training in
ladylike behaviour to your advantage. Letters from all of*

*you would be much appreciated. I will say no more,
except that we all wish you well.*
> *Your loving Aunt,*
> *Fanny Dickinson*

Loving, I thought, that's the last thing she would ever be. But I wrote back, and found that correspondence was a better channel of communication than speech had ever been. Writing only of practical matters seemed to suit us both.

Arthur wrote enthusiastically from Edinburgh university. It was the first letter I had had in answer to mine telling him of our move to London.

Dear Min, [I hated being called Min, as well he knew]

> *Thank you for your letter, and the news of your move to London. At first I must admit I thought it very foolish of you, sneaking off like that, but now I have found my freedom here, and I have heard from Aunt I think it was the best thing you could have done. You know I suppose they have moved house.*

> *Edinburgh is a wonderful place to be. Such a grand place with its grey stone Crescents and the Castle and the Royal Mile leading up to Holyrood Palace and that hill called Arthur's Seat. Arthur's seat, you note. This is a place full of legends, you would like it here I know. By the way, it is just as well you didn't go to college, you would never have kept up with the work. I find it very tiring being a student. It is very hard being short of money, I suppose you couldn't send me some of your earnings to help me out. When I make my fortune I will be able to repay you then. There are a lost of pretty girls here, but I am holding back until I meet my rich princess. Have you found a rich young man yet?*

> *Perhaps I will get the chance to come and visit sometime.*
>> *Give my love to the girls.*
>> *Your affectionate brother*
>> *Arthur Winder*

Perhaps Arthur and I had less in common now or perhaps I felt this way because of my growing attachment to George. At any rate Arthur seemed more distant to me now. I felt George respected me in a way Arthur never could, for George never made fun of me, nor made those disparaging remarks I had always hated so. Arthur could never really take me seriously, while George encouraged me in everything I did. I sent Arthur some money though I couldn't afford very much, saying to myself, 'I shall see to it he pays me back one day.'

Parties consisting of various teachers and the Allen brothers and their friends often made excursions exploring parts of London together, such as visiting the Houses of Parliament, or the zoo in Regent's Park. This latter was of particular interest to me, looking at animals as they actually exist is a very different matter than just studying them from drawings. No amount of illustrations can convey the sinuous movement of a tiger or the size of an elephant. George and Thomas frequently took Fanny and myself, we were often together on these expeditions. We were often joined by Frank, a most dependable escort. Ada refused to come with us, being too busy with her new found friend Marjorie.

Thomas and his brothers were brought up in the environs of St Paul's, and Thomas often took us to St Paul's Cathedral, 'such an inspiring building,' he would say, and we often went there on Sundays to a service. I had to agree with him, that there is something in the architecture of Wren's building which it seems only God could have inspired. It isn't just the feeling one has concerning the countless number of people who have worshipped there over the years, whose thoughts seem somehow to have permeated the very walls themselves. It is also that one cannot but have uplifting thoughts in such a beautiful and well proportioned building.

And there was the picture, the original picture of Jesus knocking on a door, the same picture a reproduction of which had made me feel so guilty and uncomfortable in the church at home. Those same eyes that seemed to follow me wherever the picture was in sight. How strange to find the picture here. I recalled the days of our Sunday visits to the congregational church in Huddersfield, my trying to avoid those eyes, and my guilty feelings as if I were being watched by God. But this was altogether a different experience of what one might call, I suppose, a feeling of the presence of God. Not guilt, but tranquillity.

Thomas was a religious man, I think he felt he had some experience of God he would like to impart to his fellow men, either through poetry or through earnest discussions with others on the subject. He said he had thought of being ordained in the faith of the Church of England but this was impossible as his mother, being a Quaker, opposed it. Besides he had to consider financial commitments and the loss of salary he would suffer while undergoing the required training. Also he said he might find he had to move away from home. 'You see,' he said, 'that would be quite impossible.' I thought of asking him why, but hesitated, after all it was none of my business. Later on I wished that I had pursued the subject for Fanny's sake, but it didn't seem important at the time. But Thomas was good company despite his earnestness and I could see that Fanny felt at home with him.

The house where the Allen family were brought up was adjacent to the Dowgate Wharf. Thomas's father worked as manager for the railway company there. The wharf seemed to have been the brothers' playground when the boys were young, and it was here we often strolled now watching those graceful sailing ships as they came in. There were steam ships too. I was reminded of Huddersfield, and the Ramsden canal with all the bustling transfer of goods from one place to another. Tom's brother William, I thought later, did some of his best pictures of the waterfront there, the water and the boats and the beauty of the sails when they catch the wind.

One of their childish games, Tom told us, had been to hoist each other out over the water on the huge cranes which lined the water side. I think it must have been rather a dangerous game. It sounded as if all that family of boys had little supervision outside their home when they were young. Perhaps, I thought a bit later when I knew them better, that they were rather wild because they were so dominated at home. Besides I suspected their father was too busy working, and their mother too busy reading, to know what wild games they got up to sometimes on their own.

We were once invited to visit the house where Tom's parents still lived, in St Paul's Mews. His father, who was in charge of the loading and unloading on the railway wharf there, was a hard working man whom I was told was seldom at home. His mother was a most domineering woman, so fiercely intellectual, and so strict with all her sons. I think she was particularly attached to Tom, after all they had published that book of poems together, and Tom like her had deep religious feelings. She was a very devout lady, a Quaker, with strong principles and an inflexible will. All her sons were scared of her. That first visit was a formidable experience. Fanny and I felt as if we were there to be vetted, the old lady wanted to see what kind of company her sons were keeping. But one of the first things she said was that none of her sons had time for taking up with young girls like us. We were not so much being vetted we realised as being warned off. 'You see,' said the old lady, 'my sons have intellectual gifts they are expected to develop, and they cannot afford such trivial distractions.'

As it happened it was the first time that we met Charles, another of Tom's brothers. The bell rang, as we sat drinking tea and feeling uncomfortable. The door opened and in walked a rather jovial looking kind of man holding a book in his hand. 'Mother,' he said, walking across the room, and ignoring all else, 'here are some poems I think you should read, I find them most interesting.' He walked up to her presenting her with the book, which she took from him in silence. There was no other greeting. She put the book down reluctantly as Tom introduced us to his brother. 'I will need a detailed account of your studies of course, the sooner the better,' she said to Charles, ignoring us as we sat uncomfortably there. Seeing that we were intruders we made our excuses and left as soon as possible.

Tom explained later that Charles had on that very day and at that very moment returned from abroad, having been away over a year studying music. 'Do you mean to say', we said, 'that this was the first time he and your mother had met for over a year?' Tom nodded. I had found the old lady most intimidating and hoped it would be a long time before I met Mrs Allen again.

Charles came to parties at our school quite often now. I remember the Christmas party we had, it must have been the second year that we were there. It wasn't on Christmas day of course, Mrs Allen saw to it that all her sons spent that day as Christians should, celebrating the birth of Christ. I suppose it must have been Boxing day. We played charades, acting out the syllables of words in a most hilarious fashion. One can play fictitious characters with obvious likenesses to those one knows, and say things one could never say in ordinary conversation. Of course it behoves one to be careful not to hurt another's feelings. But it does no harm, I thought, joining in with enthusiasm, to see oneself on occasion as others see us. I had a particular penchant for playing the part of a witch. I have often wondered why.

*

It is Christmas 1948. We are sad that we have lost the company of our good friends, Philip Harpenden and John Maurice. We haven't heard how Philip is since he went to live with his daughter in Brighton. It is difficult to communicate since he can neither see to read and write, nor hear over the telephone. We sent him a Christmas card but we haven't heard from him. It is perturbing, missing one's friends and not knowing whether they are alive or dead. As for John, we were sad to hear he died a month or two after we last saw him. A heart attack, they said when we inquired. So now we three old ladies, we realise, are in danger of being sad and on our own for what should be a joyful occasion.

We bought each other several little presents, a piece of soap, a handkerchief, a few sweets, anything that isn't on the ration at the moment. We opened them this morning, it was like pretending we had been visited by father Christmas. Perhaps it is true what they say, that old folk live a second childhood. It is the old folk's choice, being old inclines one to want to relive the past whenever possible. So many people have nothing but memories to help them through the years.

We have invited two old ladies from the house along the road to join us for supper and charades. It is only a simple supper, but we begged a chicken from the butcher on our saved up coupons, and have managed to make a small trifle. No Christmas pudding as it gives us old folk indigestion, besides rations would not allow it. But we have made pastry for our mince pies with a reduced fat content recipe, quite palatable really. We have made things look quite festive, the fire is burning well with the coal we have saved, and we are waiting for our guests.

The meal is a great success. We regale each other with tales of past Christmases enjoyed, and tell each other about our families, and show each other photographs. It is very sad for the old ladies. The older one Helen lost her husband in the first World War at Ypres, her son at sea during this second war, and her grandson at Dunkirk. "What a very handsome boy your grandson was," we say kindly, "you must be very proud of him." She just sighs. "All gone", she murmurs, "all gone." Her only sister died a few years ago she says. As for Joan, her whole family disappeared with the German bomb which reduced their house to rubble.

"We never thought, living in the country, that bombs would be dropped there," she said. "I think the damaged German plane was just unloading its bombs to make it safely home."

We felt the need for some light relief, so we play charades. We act out the syllables of our chosen word, COVENANT. Three syllables we say, but we'll act the first two syllables together. We three sisters act a 'coven', a witches' dance, and then 'ant'. The whole word covenant was soon guessed. At least we all had a good laugh together. It was past ten by the time the ladies left. I expect we shall meet again soon.

I thought how lucky I had been. True I had one son killed in the first World War, a son and son-in-law badly wounded. Another son lost in this war too, so sad and depressed that he was to be sent abroad again. But then I have my grandchildren, all of my daughter's seven children home again, and settling down. My other grandchild went to Canada as an evacuee, and now I doubt if I shall ever see him or his mother ever again. Poor young Francis. And I am almost ashamed to be so happy, how lucky I have really been. The past is so much more interesting than the present.

*

Falling In Love

We were all so happy and light-headed for those first eighteen months at Forest Hill. Or at least I thought we were. Then Fanny said to me one day that she had decided to become a nurse. 'Have you thought,' I said, 'of the risks you will be taking?' I didn't want to lose her company, naturally. 'I have thought about it for quite some time,' she continued, 'and I am not going change my mind. I have enrolled at Barts Hospital, and I start next month.' I was taken aback. Never before had Fanny done anything without consulting me first. 'It is one of the hospitals where Florence Nightingale's ideas have had some influence, a very ancient and respectable hospital, and it is quite nearby,' she said to placate my obvious concern. I suppose I realised she had always wanted to be a nurse, ever since she was quite small, and I thought by temperament she was probably quite fitted for it.

I pointed out to her that any nurse has to have a very strong constitution, because of both the heavy lifting and the long hours of work required. Most of all I told her I was worried because of a need to be able to resist the various infections that are inevitably found in a hospital environment. But she was not to be deterred. I wished her luck, what else could I do. But I wasn't very happy. However she left the school a few weeks later.

Ada became more than ever attached to her friend Marjorie, and there began to be talk of she and Marjorie setting up a school together. 'Ada is such an excellent teacher,' Marjorie said, 'and since I now find myself with a not insubstantial legacy, we would like to set up a new school together. It will inevitably have to be some distance from Forest Hill, we have no intention of competing with Forest Hill School for pupils from this area.'

While I saw less and less of my sisters, I saw more and more of George. I was glad not to have the restrictions of a chaperon imposed on me which would have been considered necessary were I, for instance, one of my own pupils. Miss Haines always said that what teachers did in their own time was their own affair, provided the school was never brought into disrepute.

George and I went for long walks together, we walked over Hillie Fields and across to Sidenham and explored the riverside. His touch sometimes sent me nearly swooning as he helped me into a bus or hansom cab, such an extraordinary feeling would come over me, and I tried in vain to control it. George became ever more attentive. Sometimes we held hands as we crossed the fields together. He often brought me little presents. We held earnest conversations about the Reform Bill and a democratic right for everyone including women to have the vote. 'It was all very well,' George said, 'for only men to have the vote when men's and women's interests were mostly centred on farming. But in an industrial world, and with such an expansion in population, the needs of men and women are often diametrically opposed.' We talked about the problems of South Africa, the Irish question. Like all young people everywhere we thought we could set the world to rights. We began to talk as if marriage were inevitable.

He brought me a silver bracelet one day. It was a beautiful day, I remember. One of those days that bring in the spring, when the wind is light and fresh and the sun first feels warm on one's back after the winter has passed. We went to Hillie Fields, where the primroses were beginning to display their soft yellow presence, the birds were singing a hallelujah chorus, and the bees were busy buzzing to and fro over the short grass where we sat together. Such a lovely bracelet, so prettily decorated, and he fastened it round my wrist for me. 'I'll never take it off,' I said. 'You can't sleep in it', he said laughing, 'you would injure that very pretty wrist of yours. Let this', he said, 'be a token between us.' It was the first time we kissed. All the sweeter for being so long delayed, I thought, as I trembled in his arms. That wonderful afternoon, such perfect happiness, such great accord between us. He so attentive, so responsive to my feelings, and I so ready to enjoy whatever was on offer. I don't suppose it is given to many to live even for a few brief hours in such great happiness and harmony. We both took it for granted that one day soon we would become officially engaged.

Fanny and Tom had become good friends, I could see it in their eyes. Not that I saw them very often, for Fanny was working in the hospital, and I was far too engrossed with my feelings for George to take much note of other things. But there were still the school Sunday afternoons, and Tom and sometimes Fanny, when her work allowed, would join the party. I was glad to see Tom and Fanny so happy together.

Ada was seldom seen at all, since she and Marjorie were busy setting up their new school. I can't say I much approved of their deepening friendship, not now that it seemed to exclude all other types of contact. Not that I had anything against Marjorie. I have always thought what a nice person she was. But Ada was so pretty, she could have made a good match for herself if she hadn't become so increasingly uninterested in male company.

Fanny sometimes brought a nurse friend of hers called Annie to our gatherings. I have always admired the way Miss Haines encouraged so many people to meet together at the school. But Annie, now Annie didn't fit in with everyone at all. She was domineering, rough in a rather masculine kind of way. I felt embarrassed by the way she expected Fanny to agree with everything she said. Fanny was such a kind young girl, so easily persuaded, I felt protective towards her. But any interference on my part only made matters worse. But I knew Fanny was fond of Tom, and if they should marry, I expected Annie would soon find herself alone again.

One day Fanny came to tell me everything was arranged, that she and Annie were going to take up a post together in Wales in the employ of Philip Lort Phillips as district nurses. I was appalled. 'What about Tom,' I asked. 'What about him,' she said in a guarded tone. 'But I'll miss you,' I said. 'No you won't,' she retorted, 'you've got George, and Ada has Marjorie. It's too late now anyway, all the arrangements have been made. We leave next week.' So that was that, it was no use trying to persuade her otherwise. 'I suppose you know what you are doing,' I said, but I doubted it.

It was a long time later that I learned the real truth. It seems that one day Tom had taken Fanny to see his mother. 'Fanny and I would like to get married,' he explained to the old lady, 'and we would like your blessing.' It was a painful occasion by all accounts, the old lady said not a word the whole time they were there. Tom tried to smooth things down, tried to explain, to make conversation. At last he said that with or without her blessing they would soon be married. 'You had better leave,' was all the old lady said. They left, Tom still protesting he would marry her whatever his mother might say. 'My father is pleased at the idea', he said, 'we will have his support. We will just have to be patient and wait for mother to get used to the idea.'

That was the last poor Fanny saw of Tom for many, many years. Old Mrs Allen appeared one day at Barts hospital and insisted on talking to Fanny. Fanny wasn't allowed to say a word. 'You will know', the old lady said, 'that all my sons have intellectual capacities I wish them to develop. I know you would not stand in their way. It is Frank and Tom who support their brothers in their studies since it is they who pay for musical education and art training. You understand that should you marry my son Thomas you would be curtailing the endeavours and ambitions of his brothers. How do you think that would make him feel, each time he looked at you he would feel the pricking of his conscience. Nor can I foresee that there would be happiness in such a match. Thomas has gifts as a writer, as you no doubt have discovered, and we hope that one day he will become well known in his own chosen field. The kind of companion he needs is one who can match his intellect, help him in his work, not some well-meaning little nurse like you. Think how he will feel towards you in a few years time, his ambition thwarted, with you and perhaps a family to support. You would be like a millstone round his neck. What chance of happiness would you have then, I'd like to know. If you love him, which I suppose in your own small way you must, then you must see the only course to take is to refuse to see him ever again.'

Fanny said she wrote to Tom. She showed me a copy of the letter later. I thought it most thoughtfully penned.

Dear Tom,

Your mother came to see me yesterday. She pointed out most forcefully to me all the drawbacks of the marriage contemplated between you and myself and the financial, intellectual, and emotional stress that this would put upon you. I would not wish to hold you to an agreement which you may have made in haste and which would result in your repenting at leisure later on.

I realise how difficult it might be for you to marry me knowing the antagonism your mother feels towards me. However I am sure that I at any rate would be able to discount such feelings should the need arise, and would

*hope to persuade her in time that we are well suited to
each other.*
*I shall anxiously await a reply from you within the
week so that we both can know where our future may lie.*
As always with my love.
Your very affectionate
Fanny Winder

She never had an answer to her letter. She waited in vain for two
weeks for a reply, but heard nothing. She went once more to the
Allen house to be told Tom was away, and would be away for some
time, and would appreciate her not calling again.

She waited another fifty years before she really heard what
happened. Not only had her letter to Tom been intercepted so that it
never reached him, but a letter from Tom to her had also never been
delivered. Mrs Allen had sent him off on an urgent errand, and by
the time he came back Fanny was in Wales. She told Tom when he
came back that Fanny had left a message to say she was more
interested in her vocation as a nurse than in the prospect of marriage.
I suppose Tom never dreamt his beloved mother could stoop to such
deceit, even if she had thought she was doing it for his own good.
Poor Fanny.

*

We decided to go to the cinema today, at last we had a chance to see
that film called *Brief Encounter*. It's about ordinary people with
ordinary lives, a change from all those films that either set out to be
comic, or on the other hand are all about wars and battles and heroic
deeds. So we went to see *Brief Encounter*, the tale of love lost to the
imperatives of other obligations.

It is a strange thing that one can read a book, or see a play, or
watch a film and get emotionally involved. Laughter or tears come
easily in sympathy with any such story well produced. At the same
time one knows the whole thing is unreal. Dreams on the other hand
seem more real, yet even nightmares seldom produce either laughter
or tears. When it comes to one's own circumstances, to one's own
tragedies, it is sometimes much later, or perhaps not ever that one can

express emotions in such a physical way. I suppose it is a psychological protection of some kind.

Take the news reels of those dreadful Nazi camps, where such horrors are impossible to understand. One sees the pictures on the screen and treats them like a play. How else could one stand one's own emotions in reacting to them. I don't know how my second granddaughter will live with her experiences having been sent out with the red cross unit as soon as the camps were opened up. Her experiences are real. Perhaps she treats them as some kind of nightmare. It is emotional sentimentality some would say, when one can react to something, even be moved to give charity funds to something, provided one can distance oneself as if one were experiencing a play.

The dilemma of a love that for some reason can never be fulfilled, which is what the film is all about, brought back to me my youthful feelings, when love was denied to me and my dear George. I never cried then, my feelings were far too deep for tears. Perhaps this film has made me cry at last concerning my own loss, who knows. I felt a fool sitting there, dabbing my eyes, hoping my sisters wouldn't notice me. They said they enjoyed the film but neither of them cried.

*

Life Is Never Fair

That had been such a perfect afternoon, I supposed that nothing could ever surpass it, nothing could destroy our happiness. George and I parted with such hopes for the future, such plans, so much to look forward to. We had decided to keep our feelings to ourselves for the time being, until we announced our official engagement when everything had been properly arranged. Had I told Grandmama or Aunt, George inquired. I had not thought of it before but I assumed Dickinson must be my official guardian, and I would need to notify him of our plans. I lived in a dream, and waited impatiently until we should meet again. George would call next evening, he said.

It is curious that the absence of someone you love can make life such a misery, even if it is only for a few short hours. I longed for the touch of his hand, the look in his eyes, his quiet voice, anything to make him feel near. Then instead of his coming next evening a short note arrived, such a formal little note, that I started to worry about what could possibly be the matter.

'Dear Minnie,' the note said, 'I am afraid I shall not be able to visit you for the next few days. I have to put my finances and other matters in order. I will come and see you and explain the situation as soon as I am able.

Yours affectionately, George.'

What could it mean, I thought. Such a formal little note after that wonderful afternoon we had spent together on the primrose hillside. Primroses. I had planted a primrose, hadn't I, on Betsy's grave all those years ago when we had left her there in that churchyard. I felt cold. What could have made me think of that. I shivered despite myself. 'What will married life be like,' I thought, 'if each time we are apart for a few days I begin to imagine such ridiculous things.'

George had mentioned finances. Perhaps it had taken him longer to sort out his affairs than had been anticipated. It might be that he was negotiating about renting a house where we might live. There would surely be a perfectly reasonable explanation.

Another message arrived to say his presence would be further delayed. I sent a note back saying nothing could be so important that it kept him from me for so long. A further note proclaimed another delay. I began to fret. I was beginning to imagine all kinds of things. Perhaps he had a relative whose affairs he had to settle. He had never mentioned anyone, he always said he had no family at all. But relatives did sometimes appear of whom one had no knowledge. Perhaps there had been a hurried message and he had had to go and make arrangements in some distant part of the country. He must have left in a hurry, that was it, no time to write a proper letter. There would be something in the post tomorrow.

Perhaps he had been dismissed from his civil service job, and had had to go to seek new employment elsewhere. Civil servants, I understood, like bank clerks, were supposed to tell their employer that they wished to get married so that provision could be made for the support of a wife. That certainly would be something that would need his immediate attention if he were thinking of marriage arrangements. Perhaps he had been promoted, and was even now making proper arrangements. Perhaps, perhaps.

Gloomier thoughts came to me. Perhaps he had had to arrange to borrow money. Perhaps even now he was trying to escape arrest because he couldn't pay back what he already owed. None of these ideas seemed very plausible but uncertainty and worry does stimulate the imagination in the most ridiculous way.

I began to imagine all kinds of stupid things. Had I been too anxious to please, had he found that my compliance lessened his affection for me? Had he found an old acquaintance he had once been fond of, I speculated, and now he finds her company preferable to mine. I wouldn't blame him. Me with my scarred shoulder and my small stature. I supposed George and I did look rather ridiculous together, me so small and he so tall, and he being such a very handsome man.

I took out my bracelet time and time again. I fell to rubbing it as if, as when Aladdin rubbed his magic lamp, my love would come swiftly back to me. I stroked the bright smooth silver. Silver has a wonderful glow hidden in its depths, a smoothness that seemed the only soothing presence in my agitated state of mind. Had I not suggested he should go and see his doctor? Suppose that that was what was wrong. It was a possibility I didn't dare to admit to myself.

Miss Haines said I looked pale and should take a holiday when term was over. I concentrated on teaching to keep my mind off other things. Alice Purdy came frequently to my room and brought me cups of tea and inconsequential gossip that nearly drove me mad. The girls looked askance at me, or so I thought, as if they knew of my worries. Perhaps it was just my imagination. Sitting through the next Sunday tea party was a kind of purgatory. I left as soon as politeness allowed it.

I searched the post box every morning, started at each sound of the doorbell. Any time I heard a man's voice my ears pricked up in case it might be him. Even footsteps on the path attracted my undivided attention. I couldn't sleep, I couldn't read, I couldn't eat. I was in such a state of apprehension that I could think of nothing else but George. I pictured his face, imagined the feel of his hands, inhaled his imagined scent, heard his imagined voice.

Somehow days passed slowly by and at last I heard from him again. 'I will call on you', he wrote, 'on Saturday afternoon next at three o'clock.' Now I was really alarmed and apprehensive at the continued formality of communications. What had happened, what was the meaning of this now obviously altered relationship? What had I done, or what had he done, that had brought about this sudden change? It was cruel of him to leave me in this state of agitation.

That Saturday I sat alone in what the school chose to call the interview room, where parents came to discuss their daughters, or prospective teachers were assessed for their suitability. Most often it was used as a kind of teachers' extra common room. That afternoon no one else was there, everyone seemed to have quietly faded into the background over the last half hour, not even Alice Purdy was there to regale me with her gossip, nor Miss Haines seeking to give me sound advice.

George was five minutes late. The relief when I saw him overwhelmed me and I hastened to greet him with a demonstration of affection, with a hug and a kiss to demonstrate how much I cared for him. I thought after our experiences on the Hillie Fields the last time we met entitled me to proffer such a greeting to a man to whom I was soon likely to be married. He gently held me off, and he indicated we should both sit down. My heart beat fast with agitation. What could all this mean, he must have something portentous to impart to me. I could hear my heart thumping so. He sat a little way apart from me, but reached for my hand and kissed it with a kind of reverence. He looked pale and drawn I noticed, with dark circles beneath his eyes. He coughed, a long, choking cough.

When he had at last recovered his breath he said in a strained voice that he knew no way of speaking gently to me. He paused as if to gather his strength of purpose. 'The truth is I cannot marry you now, the doctor has confirmed that I have tuberculosis. There is no way now that we can ever marry.' There was a long pause, a long silence while I tried to understand what it was that he was saying. 'It can be cured,' I said at last, hurrying over my words, refusing to believe such finality. 'You can get treatment, I know it can be cured. I'll wait until you have recovered. There is no need to be in such despair. Our marriage will only be postponed.'

I was not sure which of my feelings were uppermost at that moment, relief that he still loved me, or concern for his obvious ill health. I suppose I had been worried for some time about that cough of his. 'People can be cured', I repeated, 'you haven't had it long, and nowadays so much more can be done for anyone with that complaint. Why, I've met lots of people who have had it and recovered. Why even Miss Haines says she had it as a girl, but you would never think so now. You'll see, in a month or two you will be well on the way to recovery. Doctors nowadays so often exaggerate a problem.' He shook his head, sadly, slowly, but with great finality.

'My dear Minnie, my dear dear Minnie, he said, I really haven't much to hope for. We both have to be realistic, don't we. My case is one of virulent, of galloping consumption and the doctors hold out little hope for any kind of recovery.' I wished to kiss him, to comfort him in any way I could, but he coughed again. When he had recovered his breath he told me he had been warned that his type of tuberculosis was highly contagious. 'I cannot even kiss you without fearing I might contaminate you, my darling Minnie, and that is the last thing I would wish for.'

What could I say, what could I do. I pressed his hand, such a formal inadequate gesture in the circumstances. 'I am sure you can be treated,' I repeated in a hopeless kind of way, realising all certainty had left my voice. 'Of course I'll try,' he said. 'I am going away tomorrow for the best treatment I can afford. But no one holds out much hope.'

It was a bright and sunny day, I remember, and we decided to walk quietly together through the nearby park. We held hands, that at least we could do, and caring not at all what people might make of it we lingered until after dark, wanting never to have to part. But the air was getting cooler, and that made George cough in great paroxysms which left him quite exhausted. I realised how tired he was becoming. We found ourselves outside the school again. 'I won't come in,' he said. He kissed my hand, a long lingering kiss which brought the tears running down my cheeks. 'Goodbye', he said, 'goodbye', as we turned away from each other. And that was the last I ever saw of him.

We wrote to each other every day of course. 'My dear dear little Minnie,' he would begin his letters, and I would write back to 'my darling daddy long legs.' Lengthy letters they were about our love, about life and death, about trivialities, about religion, amusing incidents, anything and everything that we could enjoy together in our correspondence. He wrote back to me, long letters every day at first but soon becoming shorter and less frequent, and then no letter for a week. It was as if we·had to crowd what would have been a whole lifetime together into that brief period, a whole lifetime crowded into what could be but a few months or even weeks of correspondence, exchanging ideas and expressing our pent up emotions.

I became two people, one the teacher, an automaton that carried on as if she were a creature unrelated to myself, someone I was observing, a shadow, rather than someone who was a living human being. I neglected everything else, I answered no letters from Arthur, Aunt, nor even my best friend Kate from school in Huddersfield. One half of me was a teacher, only a teacher, performing a routine task in a most routine manner, the other half an intensely emotional being living an existence of frustration and apprehension.

This other half of me thought only of the love of my life, my George. Waking, sleeping, eating, my real thoughts were now only of him. What was he doing at this moment, what was he thinking, perhaps against all odds his health might be improving. I refused to admit to myself at first that it might be deteriorating. I thought only of my darling George. Who was looking after him, was he comfortable, was he getting the best treatment. What was he thinking, how could I help him, should I go and see him. This last he had begged me not to do, one goodbye was enough he had said. I missed him so, I dreamt of him, I loved him so, I fretted as the days past without a letter.

An official envelope arrived. It was a kind letter, written by the nurse who had looked after him. I thought how grateful I was that he had been looked after by someone who could write so kindly and sympathetically to me. 'A very peaceful death', the writer said, 'and till the last he talked of you.'

I thought I might will his spirit back to me, as if his ghost might appear at any moment in the room beside me where we had often sat together. I could almost see him, feel him sitting there, so that we were together once again. Strange fancies one has at such traumatic times. Reading that letter now I can see myself, with this very letter in my hand, staring at it in an unbelieving way.

There was a letter too from a lawyer, telling me where George had been buried a few days ago, about the service, about the people there. I was glad there had been people there, some cousins and some friends from work, the letter said. But that had been nearly a week ago. It was never explained to me why I was never told in time about the funeral. Perhaps it was George's idea. The letter said George had left me all he possessed. He was a careful man, it said.

I have no recollection whatsoever of the next few days, even the next few weeks. Ada came to see me, I remember that. 'You will recover,' she said, when I explained how empty life had now become. Life goes on. 'Recover,' I thought, what does that mean. 'I will never recover, never be the same again.'

What was it, I thought about myself, that brought tragedy each time I became fond of someone. There had been Betsy my favourite sister, Jane my best friend, and now the love of my life, my George, they all had died. I think it was then I decided that I would never let myself become really fond of anyone again.

There were a few weeks to the end of term and the automaton part of me carried on efficiently I suppose, because no one complained. I wrote to my friend from school, Kate Pearson, who still lived in Wakefield. The school summer break was imminent and I was desperate to get away. Kate and I decided to go away together on a short holiday. 'You realise I am very low', I wrote to Kate, 'I may not be very good company.' She wrote back and told me not to be such a goose as to think that would deter her. I wrote to Aunt and said I thought of coming on a short visit, if it were convenient. I had never mentioned George to her of course. Her answering letter sounded quite welcoming.

Kate when she wrote asked me about George. 'I do not wish to speak about him,' I insisted. 'Everything to do with George is in the past and I do not want to hear him mentioned ever again.' His life I felt had become part of me, a secret life that belonged to me alone. I didn't even wish to go and see his grave. It seemed that to go and see where he was buried would only in a curious way distance him from me, as if to be able to picture him there would take away something from our closeness. I can't explain it, I just wished to keep him to myself. For in a strange way now his personality seemed to have become mine, as if we two were now one. 'I don't want to talk about him, ever again,' I repeated.

*

Ada isn't well. We know she hasn't being doing much lately, she has seemed increasingly tired over the last few weeks. She hardly eats a thing. Fanny and I have both remarked on it. But then at our age we all get tired, don't we, age is such a tiresome thing. We all look pale. Walking to the corner store for example, especially in bad weather has become more of an effort for all of us lately. These days Ada often stays late in bed. To give her her due she always used to be the one to get up first.

"I am arranging to go to my nursing home tomorrow," she says after breakfast in a matter of fact voice. We know she sometimes visits a friend there, so we are not unduly surprised. "The time has come," she says, "to move in there." We feel we have been knocked down by a bus. "I'll still be able to enjoy my little pleasures when I'm there," she says defensively, "Matron quite understands."

Pleasures indeed, Fanny and I look at each other. For little pleasures you could read more drinks of whisky and gin. But why not, I think to myself on reflection, if that is what comforts her, then so much the better. The nursing home is about three miles away.

"I've ordered a taxi," she says "for half past nine. I've packed all I need to take with me."

"I don't know if we can come to visit you very often," I say, hoping she will change her mind. "It is quite a way, even by taxi."

"I'd rather you didn't come at all," she says, defensively. "I feel I want to be on my own. Dying is a tedious business, I know because I looked after Marjorie for all those months before she died years ago. Now mind, I don't want visitors, just to be left alone, to be looked after, and not to be deprived of my little comforts."

I hadn't felt sorry for Ada for a long time. Of course now I feel guilty for all my unkind thoughts. Not only that but one has to have a respect, an admiration, for someone who has made such quiet and convenient arrangements to die. Not a word has she said over the last few months about the fact that she knew she was so ill, dying in fact. She is rather a difficult person to feel sorry for.

"I'll be glad to die," she says, "since Marjorie deserted me there really has been nothing I really wanted to live for any more."

"What about us?" I ask. "We'll miss you, and so will our friends."

"Don't be so hypocritical," she says, " you always were a bit of a hypocrite, Minnie." Ada has always been honest in what she says, even if not so honest in what she does. But of course we will miss her, how could it be otherwise.

We go with her in a hired car to the Home, and watch her slow progress along the corridor as she walks, almost creeps to her room. I really hadn't noticed quite how frail she has become these last few weeks. One doesn't notice such things day by day, but now as she walks down that long corridor I realise what a struggle it is for her.

"I'll do very well" she says, as she sinks thankfully onto the bed. How tiny she is. "I won't be any trouble to anyone. The funeral arrangements have all been made long ago." Fanny had brought the bed jacket she had been knitting for me to give to Ada. I gave her a bar of my best soap, I'd nothing else available.

The Matron is cheerful and matter of fact.

"Let us know," I suggest to Ada, "if there is anything else you want, perhaps some of the things from your room?"

"I told you, I've got everything I need," is her irritable reply. I don't want to ask her what to do with her things, but as she so often has in the past, she reads my thoughts. "Give them all to the church jumble sale."

We find there's nothing more to say when it comes to wishing her goodbye. I look at her there, and wonder if she ever thinks of God. I wonder to myself if it ever could be possible to meet someone again after they are dead. It would be very devastating to think someone could read the thoughts you had about them while they were alive. How could one recognise anyone, would I for instance want to meet people I knew long ago if I am trapped in this ancient, feeble body of mine. I dare not ask her what she thinks about it all. It's a lot of rubbish, she would probably say, to make people feel better.

"After all I shan't know that I am dead, only that I am dying," she says, "and that's not so bad when it comes down to it." We exchange kisses as we say our farewells, but it is as if she has already left us, and was thinking now of dying rather than of us.

Our little house is strangely empty without her when we get back. Fanny and I do not look at each other for the next few days, we pretend to be busy in the house. We don't go out, we wait for news.

We get a taxi and go to visit her one day, we feel we must do something, not just creep around the house waiting, and waiting. When we get there she doesn't want to see us. To our surprise we see her friend Andrew Patey the retired vicar emerging from her room. He greets us affably.

"You mustn't mind," he says "that she doesn't want to see you. She is quite content, but very tired. But she says give you both her love."

I think about Ada all the way home in the taxi, such a contradictory person. Marjorie was the only person she ever really cared for the whole of her life. There was the time Ada taught in the same school as myself, and she still had to be watched in case she helped herself to little things. There was the time she looked after my little daughter when we were all at our wits' end. Most of all there was the time when she and Marjorie became partners in their own school. Ada was an exceptionally good teacher, perhaps her sometimes sarcastic manner was what children most needed to learn well. And then she went and helped herself to all the school money.

I don't believe in all these newfangled psychological theories myself, expounded by such writers as Freud and Jung. Kleptomania they may call it, as if it were an illness, but it is just something that has to be dealt with one way or another.

Giving it a fancy name doesn't alter anything. Marjorie forgave Ada and kept her on, and Ada never stole again, at least to my knowledge.

It was if Ada had been waiting all her life to find someone she could test to the limit, and once tested and found still to be a real friend, there was no more need to steal. She was indeed lucky to have someone like Marjorie as her friend.

I think perhaps when we were children I could have done the same for Ada, had I had the kind of feeling for her that was needed then. I think she had a happy life with Marjorie, she always said she did. It is Andrew Patey who brings us the news of her death two weeks later. "Very peaceful," he says, "She was happy I think."

The four of us go to her funeral – Fanny and me, Joan and Helen. Andrew conducts the service. Perhaps funerals are irrelevant for people as old as we are. There is nothing more to be said or done. Except to give the contents of her unoccupied room to the church bazaar.

*

Exploring The Past

We planned it together, Kate and I, for us to go and visit Chorlton in Manchester to see if there was any way I could make contact with my mother and her family there. 'I will know if it is either possible or impossible ever to find her again,' I said, 'and one way or another it will set my mind at rest. We can meet in Huddersfield, and travel on from there.'

I had the strangest experience at the station as I set out. George seemed to be standing there along the platform as large as life. Despite the fact I knew of course that he was dead, my heart began to thump in the most uncontrollable way. Of course it wasn't George; I could see that plainly enough when he turned round. But for a wild second, time seemed to have reversed itself. The stranger was tall, and had a certain air about him that had somehow seemed familiar.

I went first to see Grandmama and Aunt. They greeted me warmly, at least Aunt greeted me as warmly as she was able. 'I do not really approve of your attire,' she said, holding me from her so as to examine me. 'Your dress is not suitable for someone in your position as a teacher. You should take more care with your appearance. Besides, you are far too pale.' She gave me a peck on my cheek, as if it cost some tremendous effort on her part. 'I can see something has been troubling you', she continued, 'but we all have our troubles, and moping about the place does no one any good. You must pull yourself together.' If only she knew the real depths of my despair. Dickinson was cordial if distant, murmuring that he was sorry to hear that I was not so well. Grandmama gave me a hug as she always did and that brought tears to my eyes for the first time since I had left home. But her memory was confused now about many things. She spoke as if she thought I was still recovering from the smallpox. Then she too scolded me for not looking after myself properly.

I stayed in that new house, which seemed not the least like home. I had to admit the house was much more convenient than the one we had been brought up in at Brunswick Place. Grandmama's chair had been placed for her in the parlour, but she didn't look at home there, even though her table was beside her as before. Elisa had left sometime ago to get married, and the new servant was prim and proper, a shadow in the background, not like the kind and overflowing Elisa who had been so good to all of us. I asked where she had gone but no one seemed to know.

Although Grandmama now remembered so little about the present she fortunately still remembered things a long way back. Kate came visiting and we obtained what information we could from her and Aunt and Dickinson about Chorlton where I had once lived with my mother and father. We asked about Lorton too where my grandfather came from. This holiday, I explained, had been planned as an exploration into the past, and we would be grateful for any information that might help. Aunt handed over some papers she had kept, an old address, the note from my father which my mother had brought with her to Huddersfield. But that was all. As for Grandmama she was able to explain where Lorton was, where my grandfather's cousins supposedly still lived. We still had not much information on which to base our search but I had to hope it would be sufficient.

My brother Arthur appeared, on vacation from Edinburgh University. He had nearly completed his studies and would soon be qualified. I was glad to see him, and he was full of energy and enthusiasm for his medical studies. One thing I noticed as soon as he looked at me was that the glazed look he had had in his eyes for so many years had gone. 'University life obviously suits you,' I said. 'It is just as well girls can't be doctors because they would all be fainting in the lecture theatres,' he retorted. 'Imagine what it would be like when dissections are done. I wouldn't want any wife of mine to have to undergo such an ordeal. Familiarity with such scenes would make any woman hard and unfeminine. No you are much better off, Min, with your teaching.' He asked about the school, and what I was doing, but he wasn't really interested. He had grown away from me, become more distant, a man about town, a young man with prospects. I teased him that he used to boast about a plan to marry a rich wife. 'You never know,' he said, 'don't I usually manage to get what I feel

I want?' 'Who is she,' I asked, realising he had someone now in mind. But he wouldn't say. 'First I have to be properly qualified,' he insisted, 'before I start thinking of a wife.' I suppose I couldn't blame him for his reticence, after all I'd told him very little about George. I asked him if he wanted to come with us to Chorlton and to Lorton. He shook his head. 'Why bring up the past', he said, 'it is the present we should be concerned about. Women are always too sentimental about such things.'

He gave me a book to read by Jules Verne, about travelling under the sea. 'I've read it', I said, pleased to think I could hold my own in a scientific conversation, 'I found it a most exciting fantasy.' 'My friend Peter', Arthur continued, 'has decided to join a regiment as soon as he has his degree. He is very interested in war and war machines. He wants, he says, to be a hero. I would like to introduce you to him sometime, you'd get on well together. I rather fancy him as a brother-in-law. If you won't have him perhaps Ada or Fanny will. He's very rich you know.'

'There is a book everyone has been reading,' Arthur continued, 'called *The Battle of Dorking*. It is the account of an imaginary war when England is successfully invaded by a foreign power. It could happen, so all the experts say. Here are we British with our science, our inventions and our Empire, the leaders of the world, you might say, and we are so stupid as to leave ourselves a sitting target because we don't bother about our armed defence. The French and Germans are developing their balloons and their submarines and their firepower in a way that should scare us into doing something about it now. It is no good thinking we are still in the age of Trafalgar and Waterloo. Progress and modern science has changed all that.'

'Whatever use would balloons and submarines be in a war,' I asked. Arthur disdainfully ignored this remark. 'The French haven't forgiven us yet for the defeat of Napoleon, and the Germans, who envy us our trade and colonies, are flush with their success against the French in 1870. Of course the French hate the Germans, and it is possible if we are lucky they will fight each other instead of turning on us.' 'I didn't know,' I said, 'that you were so enthusiastic about war. I thought you were supposed to be learning to heal people, not kill them.' 'That just proves my point', he went on, 'women never understand about war. Do you really want to be ruled by the French or Germans?' 'No,' I said, 'of course not.' 'Well thank God then, that you will have men to defend you.' 'But can't people prevent wars', I suggested, 'there is enough sickness and injury everywhere without adding to it.' 'That's just like a woman, to think you can prevent men trying their luck against each other. That's the way the game is played. All you have to do is to keep one step ahead of your enemies. Once you are perceived to be weak you invite a war. Being prepared prevents wars, it doesn't encourage them, silly. At the university they all talk about a coming war, as if it is inevitable. I don't agree with that, but to stop one we must be properly prepared with the latest inventions and equipment. Peter can explain it better than I can, you'll see.'

We started out on our journey two days later. Kate having become a district nurse like Fanny, looked after me like one of her most precious patients. I was grateful for the way she entertained me, kept me warm, saw to it that I was fed, made sure I didn't tire myself too much. For myself I didn't really care whether I ate or slept. No one could have been more solicitous. We went first to Lorton, because the trains fitted better that way. We would go on the Penrith line and alight at Cockermouth where we could hire a trap to take us further. I had written to my distant cousins who now lived there, and they had invited us to stay. I must admit I found the journey tiring, but it was well worth it.

The Cumbrian hills are most friendly and spectacular at the same time, both welcoming and also forbidding. They have a character all of their own, the browns and greens and greys of the fells with their tumbling escarpments seemed somehow familiar and reassuring. I had never been in such wild country before and I felt like a traveller coming home. It was a soothing experience, and a kind of calm descended on my mind. It was as if as in a plant some root of mine began to grow again. I tried to explain to Kate but in her common sense way she just thought I was being fanciful. 'You do tend to make everything so personal', she teased me, 'even the scenery has to have a special meaning just for you.' 'Well, it does', I said, 'I can't explain it, that is just how it is.'

We arrived at Lorton as the sun was setting, being driven in the pony trap down such a steep and winding road that I feared the pony's feet would slip on the stony surface. The village there, with its little church and the few scattered houses along the short main street are very picturesque. It really was like being in some secret valley, enclosed as we were on all sides by the towering hills around.

Lorton Hall was just as I had imagined it to be from Grandmama's description, long and low and grey, looking as if it had been there for ever. The Winder crest was carved on the wall by the gate. There stood the huge beech tree in whose branches King Charles was supposed to have sheltered. When we were ushered into the house they were rather aloof, my distant cousins, as if our company was not what they were used to. We only stayed one night.

We were shown round the house, which I must confess seemed somewhat neglected. It had a gloomy entrance hall and disused little chapel. The best room is a beautiful panelled drawing room. Its meandering staircase led to a large number of bedrooms on the upper landing. I wasn't sure that I would ever like to live there.

We went for a walk the next morning, climbing the nearby hills, then wandering along the shores of Loweswater. We had been shown how far the Winder lands had once extended with the fells and the lead mines, the pastures in the bottom of the valley, where the quiet sheep and the sleek cows still grazed. I stood on a little hillock, feeling like a Lord of the Manor, surveying all my possessions, thinking 'this is where my ancestors once lived. This is the land they owned, this was part of their heritage'. It did feel somehow like coming home, despite Kate's teasing.

We said our goodbyes and set off once more to cross the Pennine Hills, reminding me of that journey long ago when we arrived at Huddersfield. A reverse journey this one, since now I was retracing my steps, going back to beginnings, not setting out for new unknown and unimaginable places. To explore one's own history, I was finding, was a somewhat unnerving experience.

Chorlton when we arrived looked very small and mean, I had to admit, I hadn't remembered how crowded everything had been. We searched for a whole day to find where I had lived, but either my memory was at fault or the house must have been demolished. We went to the cotton mill, that was still standing, and we inquired was there anyone called Jolly still working there. Surely, with all my mother's brothers, sisters, cousins, there would be someone there who remembered my mother.

We did find one old lady, bent and wizened, who said Margaret Jolly was her cousin. 'Where does Margaret live now,' I asked, my hopes at last rising. 'She moved away many years ago,' I was told. 'I'm beginning to remember', she continued, let me see, 'she was the one whose husband deserted her, poor lass, and she was forced to abandon her bairns. The children went to live with distant relatives of her husband you know, we always thought he was too grand for her in any case, it doesn't do you know for the gentry to mix with the workers. When she came home again all on her own poor girl, she soon found another fellow for herself. She had a lot more children, five I think it was.'

It felt strange that I should have had five half brothers and sisters growing up, and I had known nothing of them. I inquired what my mother's new name might be, when she remarried. 'Well, she couldn't remarry could she with her first husband still alive, that's why they moved away so no questions would be asked.' 'What was his name,' I asked, 'the father of her children I mean.' The old lady couldn't remember. 'Evans it might of been, but then again it might be Smith, or Jones, or any other name you care to mention.' 'What about the rest of the Jolly family,' I asked, my awakened hopes fading rapidly. It seemed my mother's brothers, sisters, cousins were all dead or had moved away, no further information was forthcoming.

We tried the registers of course, what a weary day that was spent looking at long lists of names in the record books, looking for the union of Jolly, or Winder with some other likely name. I acknowledged at last there was nothing more that could be done, except to put an advertisement in the local newspaper. But nothing came of that either and I was forced reluctantly to abandon the search altogether. At least I now knew there was no hope of my ever seeing Mama again.

*

My daughter Mollie and her husband Teddy came to visit us today. I had written to tell them about Ada's death.

"Why didn't you let us know before, we would have liked to have come to the funeral" my daughter says.

"Ada particularly asked that none of the family should be told about the funeral," I tell her defensively. "I can't please all of the people all of the time."

'That's all very well," says Mollie, "but I feel I should have been there."

"All the same," says my son-in-law, "it doesn't really seem right, not being there." They look a little bewildered, sitting there in front of me, and I feel guilty. But what else could I have done.

Despite their displeasure we have an agreeable afternoon. The wind is far too strong for us to go for a stroll along the front, so we chat about the family over tea. Mollie does have rather a lot of children and I get a little forgetful about what they are doing just now. There were too many of them for their parents to manage them very well, I used to think when they were small.

I enquire about Harold, he is the eldest, a handsome young man if not very tall, and I have always thought he had a difficult childhood.

"He is doing well as an accountant, now that he has his qualification," Teddy says. I feel relieved. I have always thought Teddy didn't understand his eldest son. Not surprising when you think the poor boy was born in the middle of the first World War, and Teddy came home soon after having been so badly wounded that he wasn't expected to live. It took a long time for anyone who had been fighting in those awful trenches to get back to normal. In any case it often happens that a father does not get on with a first born son. Harold should have been a botanist, or a musician, an academic, not an accountant like his father. But you can't tell parents these things.

Then we talk about Mary, I often think she is a bit like me in many ways. "She writes me long amusing letters," I tell them. "She started writing to me when she was being bombed in that hospital in London, you know, and she still writes quite regularly."

"We go over to their house in Oxford to play bridge almost every week," Teddy says.

"She seems to be enjoying her extramural course at the university" Fanny interrupts in a proprietorial tone. She likes to make the point that she is particularly interested in Mary because she used to have her to stay sometimes when she was small.

"And to think," Mollie says, "that when Mary was little I was afraid she was mentally retarded. She didn't start to talk until she was nearly three, you remember."

I reel off the names of the rest of those children in my head, hoping I have got them in the right order. Nancy, John, Ruth, Sylvia, Anthea, they all seem to have turned out to be quite enterprising, I have to admit. I think perhaps I was getting too old to enjoy my younger grandchildren by the time they came along. They seemed so noisy and unruly and bad mannered when they were growing up. After all I was seventy by the time the youngest, the twins, were born.

We have some business to transact about Ada's estate. Teddy has always been so helpful in sorting out our affairs. All these rules and regulations make my head spin. Not that there was that much to sort out. Ada left no will as she always said she had nothing to leave, she merely lived off her annuity.

Teddy says it will be getting dark soon, and he doesn't want to drive too far after lighting up time. Mollie doesn't drive. I am glad really, driving is a man's job I always think. We reluctantly say goodbye, and they promise to come again soon.

"They look tired," I say to Fanny, as the car disappears round the corner.

"No more than anyone else these days," says Fanny. "You always fuss so."

*

What Do I Do Next?

I started what I like to think of as my fifth life all at sea. It really felt as if I were a ship adrift in the midst of an endless sea, with no sail, nor engine, nor rudder, nor anchor, not even a star to guide myself by. I remember when I wrote that sentence down all those years ago thinking at the time what an apt analogy it was. I had written off the past, and yet had no idea of what I really wanted from life, except that I wanted something other than what I was doing at the present time. I would never get married now, I was too old I supposed, after all I was twenty-four, so I must occupy myself with what would bring some satisfaction to what now seemed such a very empty life.

I returned to Forest Hill School and to my teaching. I did manage to institute some high grade classes for the best of my pupils. Fond as I was of the girls, teaching can sometimes become a bit monotonous without some extra stimulus. Of course it gave a certain amount of satisfaction to learn that one girl had become engaged to a Duke. 'Partly because of her good handwriting, for which you were responsible,' Miss Haines said when she told me the news. Another girl to whom I had given extra French lessons was now married to a diplomat. But all teaching seemed to have become a routine from which some real satisfaction seemed missing.

There was a lot of talk about the Reform Bill. At last it seemed women were to get the vote, along with agricultural workers. Now that would be something to feel proud of, to be part of an historic event such as the emancipation of women. In Huddersfield I had met Miss Lydia Becker 'that champion of women's rights' as I have heard her called so often. It was largely her energy that had been responsible for the granting of the franchise to propertied women in the municipal elections, and to appointments to the School Boards. It was through her that I and Alice Purdy now joined a London suffragette group. I began to feel I was engaged in doing something more worthwhile for a change. I spoke at meetings, helped produce and deliver pamphlets, lobbied members of Parliament. It was exhilarating for a while. This was the real world.

Then Mr Gladstone had the question of women's franchise dropped from the Reform Bill of 1884. I had never thought of the Prime Minister before as being opposed to Women's rights. You never can rely on politicians. It was then that I and many of my new found friends gave up the struggle. It was obvious men were not lightly going to relinquish their privileged position, however good the arguments might be against them.

In one of my letters to Arthur I had complained about the way men treated women. 'Just like a woman', he had replied, 'to bother about such inconsequential things as women's rights. It was much more important to make sure the agricultural workers got their vote, they at least contributed to the country's economy. And there were many other decisions that shortly would have to be made', he declared. 'Politics is for men,' he said. 'There are so many important matters to debate.'

'Like the Irish question, you mean', I suggested, 'why doesn't Parliament pass the Home Rule Bill and settle the matter once and for all, I can't see why they shouldn't govern themselves if that is what they want.' 'Just like a woman to be so credulous' he answered, 'there has always been the Irish question, and there always will be. Home Rule would not be the end of the question, mark my words, but just the beginning. If there were nothing to complain about, the Irish would soon invent something, that's what my friend Peter always says, anyway, and he ought to know, being Irish.'

'Why did the politicians make such a muddle over Khartoum, then, if they are all so clever,' I wanted to know. 'If they had sent General Gordon extra troops in time he would never have been killed. What a terrible waste of a brave man's life.' I got the kind of scornful answer I deserved, I suppose. 'Women know absolutely nothing about fighting', he said, 'so what gives you the right to make pronouncements about troop movements and the conduct of a war. Imagine what would happen if women actually tried to run the country', he scoffed. 'Then every general's life would be at risk.'

'The papers say there will be a war soon, do you think there will be,' I asked. 'Yes,' he said. I hoped he was wrong, but I could quite see we had to defend ourselves against the Germans and the French. I knew his friend Peter was in the army now. 'Provided we are properly armed', Arthur said, 'any war will be over in our favour in a few months. First we will have to fight in Africa, the Boers will break the treaty agreement with the Zulus and then the Germans will seize their chance. All of them, France, Russia, Germany, Turkey, they all want our markets, sooner or later there will be a war. But I don't suppose you can understand that.'

With so very little encouragement I gave up trying to be interested in politics. Besides, my life was changing. A new friendship was developing which I never would have considered possible, even a few months ago. The Sunday tea parties at the school had continued, and often I would find Frank Allen sitting next to me. He was such a kind, unobtrusive man, so quiet and helpful, and when one got to know him he had a quiet humour all his own. When London sight seeing trips were planned he would often be at my side. He had sometimes come to franchise meetings with me. I found when I needed advice or when I was angry or frustrated it was to him I turned for comfort. I found I was beginning to rely upon him.

It was on a September day that he asked me to marry him. I was taken aback, I had never even thought of marriage since George died. There we were, standing by the river, quite a party of us, admiring a steam boat coming in. We were momentarily separated from the others, and he took my hand, turned me round to face him, and said in his matter of fact way, 'I would like to marry you if you will have me.'

I stammered out that I didn't know, that I had never thought of him like that, that my feelings were still numb after George's death, that I needed time to think it over, that... I am not sure what I said in my agitation. And then I looked into his face. Such a hurt look in his eyes, such a crestfallen look, such a look of despair. 'You know, I suppose', he said, 'that I have loved you ever since we first met that Sunday after you first arrived at school.'

I don't know what came over me. A great wave of emotion seemed to well up from within. I couldn't tell if it were affection for Frank, or gratitude for his patience; if it were pity for myself, or for a sudden end to my loneliness; I really didn't know. I only know I felt his arms round me as great floods of tears engulfed me, and I cried like a child. I was embarrassed, but there was no way I could stop my tears for quite a while. By the time we rejoined the rest of the party we were engaged to be married.

We planned to have the wedding as soon as we possibly could. I would give in my notice to the school straight away, so I could leave at the end of term. 'What about your mother,' I asked in some trepidation. I told him about Fanny, and how his mother had been so opposed to Tom's marriage to her. 'You should have told me,' he said, angry in his own quiet way. 'I would have put a stop to such interference. It's too late now, I am afraid, I know he is courting someone else. One thing is for certain, we will not allow any interference in making our own arrangements.' 'What are we going to do,' I asked. 'Leave it to me,' he said. 'Meanwhile you had better get in touch with your guardians, I hope your Aunt and Uncle will be pleased.' 'Of course they will,' I said.

*

It is Fanny's birthday today. Since Ada died we haven't been out for a treat, and I have decided we need something to cheer us up. I think Fanny had forgotten it was today she is eighty-seven, and that is a considerable age by any standard.

I bought her a little present, only a new purse, but the one she has is falling to pieces. I think she is really quite pleased with it, but all she says is what a waste of money buying something that she will not be able to make sufficient use of.

'I'll not need it for more than two or three years, I don't suppose," she grumbles, "The old one would have done very well."

"It wasn't very expensive, besides I am tired of seeing coins falling out of your old one all over the place," I say, "It was only last week in the corner shop that people had to help you pick up coins from all over the floor. It was most embarrassing."

"That was my fault," she says, "my clumsy hands, nothing to do with my purse." I let that pass, but I know her old purse has had a large hole in it for quite some time.

"I have booked matinee tickets for the Black and White minstrel show," I tell her. It is quite nice to have an occasion when we dress up a little bit. All we do normally is to put on a hat and a coat over our everyday clothes to go to the corner shop, or the library perhaps.

I always enjoy the Black and White Minstrels. I like the songs they sing, such a polished performance they give, they are always so entertaining. Sometimes I suspect that one or other of them is a real Negro, someone who can sing those Negro spirituals with such understanding must, I think, have a talent of native origin. I amuse myself trying to figure out which of them could possibly be a genuine African.

"Black people do not seem quite so foreign any more, not now when one realises how musical they can be," I say to Fanny, "and underneath their coloured skin they are just the same as we are."

"What strange fancies you sometimes have," Fanny says. "Africans will never think the same way as Europeans."

I think Fanny enjoyed herself. After the show we had a cup of tea at the Pavilion. I had asked Helen and Joan, the two old ladies from along the road to come and join us for supper, just a few sandwiches and a cake, I had explained to them. They arrive soon after we return home, each with a little present, a box of chocolates and some talcum powder. Fanny looks embarrassed.

"Don't be ridiculous," Fanny complains, when we get home again, but is pleased none the less. I produce the cake with fifteen candles on it.

"Eight candles to count for eighty years," I explain, "and seven for the years since you were eighty."

"How childish," she mutters. We all blow out the candles together, and laugh as if we were children. Fanny enjoys her piece of cake even if she disapproves of the candles. But I know she has really quite enjoyed her birthday celebration.

*

Next time Frank and I saw each other he explained about his family situation. 'Now that we are to be married I think I should tell you all about our financial arrangements,' he said. 'First I have to tell my mother that I can no longer contribute to her family expenses. We have always been very close, my brothers and I, we have always got on well together, and I have done my best for them. But now Charlie is musically qualified, and married, and has decided to go to Australia, he no longer needs our support. William has finished his art training to his own satisfaction now, and there is no need for me to help him either. I can be independent. Mother will not like the idea, of that you can be sure, and she is likely to find some good excuse against our plans. I will not risk her interference. I don't like deceit, but I see no other way but to make our arrangements and tell her of our plans only when she realises opposition would be futile.'

Frank's cousin lived at Alton, and we arranged to get married there. 'As soon as you are free from school you can go and stay with my Aunt, she'll welcome your company, she's a widow now. There is a pretty little congregational church there, and I am acquainted with the incumbent. I know you will like to be married there. In any case I will take you on a visit soon and you can make up your mind about it then.'

We rented a house in Devonshire Road, not so far from the school and set about furnishing it to our liking. Ada came and helped me choose the pattern for my wedding gown. Uncle Dickinson was to give me away. It was to be a quiet wedding. Fanny couldn't get away, she said, from what I called her hideout in the wilds of Wales, but Ada would be there. Aunt would not be coming as she said she couldn't very well leave Grandmama. She sent me a long letter instead explaining the duties of a wife. Why are wives always supposed to have duties rather than pleasures, I wondered. Arthur would come. Frank's brothers Tom and William too. Kate Pearson would be my bridesmaid. There is always so much to do before a wedding that no one has time to stop and reconsider, weddings have an excitement of their own that carries everyone along on a predetermined path.

Mr and Mrs Allen got their invitation two weeks before the wedding, but neither of them came. He said he was too busy, and she just sent a curt note demanding Frank go and see her straight away, and of course she would refuse to give her permission for any such contemplated marriage. Frank ignored the letter. I asked him if he minded such a break with his family, especially as they seemed so close. 'Don't you worry', he said, 'as soon as we are married you will be accepted, mark my words, and then they will both start regretting they didn't come. Don't fret, I know them both well enough.'

Frank's cousin was very kind, I felt at home with her from the moment that we met. She would take care of everything, she said, including all the arrangements for the wedding breakfast, and she would provide the wedding cake as well. 'You are not to worry about a thing', she said, 'you will soon be one of the family, and we are only too pleased to do what we can.'

The wedding itself was wonderful. I felt I looked my best, at least Frank said he thought how beautiful I looked. And so did Kate, she said she had never seen me look so happy. Frank was right about the little chapel, so pretty and everyone so kind. A spring day, with all its April freshness. A bright day, so full of sunshine. There seemed to be flowers everywhere. So much goodwill, so many good wishes. We set off on our honeymoon in a cloud of love, or so it seemed.

Family Matters

We settled down, Frank and I, to what is so often referred to I believe as married bliss. I couldn't wish for a kinder or more considerate husband. Frank was right about his parents, I was grudgingly accepted, and sometimes even invited to visit their house. Edward, who had met us so charmingly when we first arrived in London, always seemed to be there, and that helped to make things easier. He had worked as George had done as a civil servant, and he too suffered from tuberculosis. He had contracted it at the same time as George, but unlike George his treatment had proved successful. 'I didn't mention it before', Frank said, 'but I think in some odd kind of way my parents blamed you for Edward's infection. After all he and George did work together in the same office. Nonsense, of course, but she insists it is a contagion that you and George passed on to Edward.'

I was soon pregnant. It somehow comforted me to think I could create life as well as seemingly destroy it. I still at times, despite Frank's admonitions, recounted to myself the death of the various dear ones I had lost, Betsy, and Jane, and George, as if somehow I had been responsible for their early demise. But I gradually forgot the past, and we were very happy, Frank and I.

Aunt wrote to say Grandmama was very ill, so I travelled up by train to Huddersfield. Arthur met me at the station. I don't think Grandmama was really conscious of who we were, but I tried to explain that I was pregnant. 'Minnie will soon be needing a baby's cradle,' Aunt said. The old lady's eyes flickered as if she understood, and a fleeting smile seemed to appear on that careworn face. I hope she understood. It would please her to know that life was starting for another generation.

She died a few days later, and we buried her in the cemetery next to the high school I used to attend. I always think of her now sitting by the fire in that chair of hers at Brunswick Place, with the lamp shining, and the welcoming arms she always extended to us children.

Arthur was now a junior partner in a practice at Honley on the outskirts of Huddersfield. He talked much about the girl he meant to marry. 'Her name is Penelope France,' he told us, 'and she is the only child of a rich woollen merchant from Manchester. I'm not marrying her for her money,' he said, 'but it is a great convenience that she will not be penniless.' He introduced me at last to his friend Peter. 'You should have married my friend Peter instead of your dull Frank', he teased me later, 'he is very rich you know.' I hope I looked as scornful as I felt, even though I knew he was only teasing me.

I went back again to Huddersfield a year later to be at Arthur's wedding. It was at Honley church. It was the first time I had met Penelope France, tall, and a bit gaunt, with a very decided personality. I wondered how Arthur could get on with someone with such a strong character. I liked her father, and his many business friends, burly and down to earth. He was a walking advertisement for the woollen cloth he manufactured. Very Yorkshire, and very hospitable. I was sorry when I heard a year later that he had suddenly died.

My first son was born a few months before, such a helpless little creature, only six pounds in weight. He had such bright eyes, such dark hair, and a kind of amused look on his face as if the world he found himself in was a huge joke. There is something so endearing about a helpless baby. He was no trouble, a bit stubborn perhaps, Frank and I thought the world of him as you can imagine. As he grew into a toddler his eyes seemed to become brighter, his smile more mischievous, and the antics he performed to gain our attention quite hilarious.

Tom got married to a girl called Dorcas. I liked her well enough, but I think he would have been much better off with Fanny. He just brought his new bride home one day, without a previous word to anyone. They settled down quite close to us in Forest Hill, and she was soon expecting her first child.

We were all frightened by the news headlines concerning a man in London they called Jack the Ripper, and the particularly horrendous fashion in which he murdered his women victims. No woman dared go out on a foggy night by herself near Whitechapel, and no one felt safe anywhere else either. It would be almost impossible when the fog is really thick to see who might be following behind one. I would look from the window at the dim smoky air outside, and shiver to myself, thinking of some dark man who might be lurking somewhere out there unknown to any of us. I wouldn't let Maria our maid go out of the door when the fog came down, even if it was her day off. He was never caught, that awful man. Although the killings stopped, it took a long time before any one woman would feel safe again.

Mollie, my dear and only daughter was born. She was not a bit like her brother Harold, but pudgy, with lots of auburn hair. She had a slightly elfin look, despite her pudginess. Tom and Dorcas had a baby daughter about the same time, a pretty little thing but not as pretty as my little Mollie with her auburn hair and funny little smile. They named their daughter Christine.

Frank and I were content. The children quarrelled sometimes as children will, Mollie could be stubborn too, but her brother had only to play some silly prank in front of her and she would forget her peevishness to laugh at him. Their games of pretence had to be seen to be believed, such imagination they both showed. We were so happy, Frank and I. We loved our house in Devonshire Road, we had our friends, and the family, and most of all we had our children. I still think of those few years as the most content of all my life.

Arthur was right about the war in Africa. He wrote to say how upset he was at the death of his soldier friend Peter who had been killed at Mafeking. Peter had written several letters to him before he died saying how much all the soldiers thought of Baden Powell, the commander of the garrison, who had stood out so long against the Boers until the town was at last relieved. Arthur sounded quite inconsolable about the death of his friend. A man to be greatly admired, he said. It is always difficult to say what one feels at such times, and even harder to make sense of the world in which we live.

'Your Peter was a great man, too,' I wrote back to Arthur, 'your accounts of him have always shown him to have such a kind and upright character.' Quotations always seem to come into my mind at stressful times. 'Faith, hope and charity, these three, St Paul says,' I wrote, 'and the greatest of these is charity'. Didn't Jesus himself say, 'Greater love hath no man than this, that a man lay down his life for his friends.' Peter died for all of us, just as Jesus did, and his place in heaven is assured, I am certain of that. Those who die in battle we are told go straight to heaven. I don't know if what I was able to say was any comfort to Arthur, what can one do to soften the loss of a friend? I don't think Arthur ever really got over Peter's death. He has always seemed more remote, aloof, since then.

Our great Queen Victoria died. A sad life she lived after Prince Albert died all those years ago, as any widow can appreciate. Just as well the Prince of Wales took so much interest in affairs of state. So many tours and official engagements he has always undertaken. If anyone can prevent a war, Frank says, it will be His Majesty, King Edward VII.

It was a great occasion, the Queen's funeral. Frank and I went to watch the procession through London. I felt proud to be British, all those foreign and colonial Heads of State, come to pay her homage, walking behind her coffin as it passed slowly by to the sound of the funeral music, a very solemn occasion.

Another pregnancy, and I was beginning to find I was overtired so very often. Of course I had Maria our maid to help me, but Maria was only young and rather inexperienced. Frank, dear Frank, was always so considerate whenever he was there. But this pregnancy wasn't so easy as the others. I was clumsy sometimes, I might feel giddy, sometimes things seemed such an effort. I would be so glad when the nine months were up, another three months was beginning to seem a long time to wait for this next baby's arrival. I had got so large by six months that Frank teased me and called me the bus.

Not being very tall has always seemed a handicap. I was always being caught out because I was so small. Houses and kitchens are always built for those with average height. Shelves and the tops of things have always been just out of my reach. One has to stand on a chair or steps so very often when it comes to organising a household. One can't just ignore the jobs that have to be done. Everything, especially when one is pregnant, seems to be just out of reach.

It wasn't their fault, poor little things, on that dreadful day when I fell. They were merely playing a kind of hide and seek, laughing and shouting, running round the steps I stood upon. I suppose it was my own silliness, standing up there putting things back on that high shelf that was to blame, I should not have done such a foolish thing. But shelves get so dirty with all the smoke and grime of London, I felt I couldn't stand the thought of them a moment longer. Maria, the girl, had quite enough to do without bothering with the shelves. The two of them, Harold and Mollie, bumped into the steps once too often and down I came and everything went black.

The next few months are a kind of blank in my mind. Of course I had a miscarriage after that horrendous fall, twin boys, I was told later. A miscarriage at so late a date can be a most dangerous event. It left me with an infection that made me very ill for what seemed like a very very long time. 'We thought you were going to die', Frank told me later, 'the doctor didn't hold out much hope.'

*

Worthing has been invaded, we have had a continental cloud of ladybirds, blown over in swarms by the prevailing winds, or so we are told. Everywhere you walk there are heaps of them, on the roads, on the beach, everywhere. They fly in through windows, jam the doors as you try to open them, get blown into your face as you walk along the pavements, and most unpleasantly scrunch under your feet as you walk, since there is no hope of avoiding them as they swarm on the pavements.

I have always thought of ladybirds as friendly creatures, eating up pests like unwanted green fly. 'Ladybird, ladybird fly away home, your house is on fire and your children have gone,' is what we used to sing, as we held out our hand to the sun to see them fly off.

Why that line should still bring tears to my eyes, I don't know, but it always has, 'your house is on fire and your children have gone.' Perhaps it was to do with my own childhood, and thinking we had flown away from our parents' home. Now it also brings back memories of my own children, and the way they flew away too. Life is never simple, nothing ever stays the way you would like it to be.

*

By the time the infection was cleared a dark despondency had descended on me that was like the heaviness of death. I can't really describe it, no one who is not a woman can understand the dreadful cloud of depression that takes away one's will at such a time, a dark brooding physical inertia that is terrible to feel. I didn't want to see the children, I didn't even want to know about them. In my strange state I blamed them for the catastrophe, for their unheeding play around me, as if they had deliberately injured me and killed the twins. It was quite irrational of course, but one doesn't know that at the time. In that state of mind one believes the most ridiculous and impossible things. Half of me told me that it was not their fault, was nothing to do with them, the other half couldn't face them without feeling a deep and angry resentment. It was a struggle to get by, day by day. One is thankful that another day has passed. The leaden cloud hangs there like an enemy one cannot fight.

Why in despair some lines of an almost forgotten poem should come to mind I cannot think. The lines brought a kind of comfort, as if I were not alone in my wilderness, others had been there too.

> Dark, deep, and cold the current flows
> Unto the sea where no wind blows,
> Seeking the land which no one knows.
>
> O'er its sad gloom still comes and goes
> The mingled wails of friends and foes,
> Borne to the land which no one knows.
>
> Why shrieks for help yon wretch, who goes
> With millions from a world of woes,
> Unto the land which no one knows.

I could remember only a few lines. It was written by someone called Ebenezer Elliott. Ebenezer, that name made me suddenly laugh. Frank's startled face seemed a great distance away as uncontrolled mirthless laughter unexpectedly enveloped me.

Frank did his best to meet the situation. The doctors thought I might never recover. I refused to have the children near me, indeed the very sound of their voices seemed to make me worse. I was glad when I could hear them no more. Frank told me he had arranged for them to be looked after elsewhere. He was even afraid, he said at the time, that I might harm them, so disturbed did I become even at the sound of their voices, even though they were nowhere near me.

Later on I could appreciate the help the family gave us then. It was much better that the poor little mites should not be sent away to strangers. I have always thought children can stand changes regarding those who care for them, provided they remain in familiar surroundings, or alternatively they can manage strange places if they are with those they already know. To have changed both place and faces would have been an even more frightening experience for them.

Arthur and Penelope were pleased to have Harold to stay with them, for they didn't expect to have any children of their own. Ada said she would take care of little Mollie for the time being. 'It will be no trouble,' she promised Frank, 'because she can be in school with me during the day, and she can sleep with me at night.' Frank tried, I know, to get Kate to come and look after all of us, but unfortunately she was already committed to another case she couldn't leave, so he had to make the arrangements for the children, and hire a nurse to care for me.

That was a difficult time for all of us. I was in no state to know how long matters rested so. Day was night and night was day, a twilight world: I was myself and not myself, I watched my own behaviour and knew that it was strange, but no way could I do any thing to prevent myself from continuing so. I ranted at poor dear Frank, and shouted at the nurse. An evil self seemed to have taken possession of me. No wonder reference is made in the Bible to possession by a devil. It was a long, dark evil struggle that left me weak and changed. My only consolation was the constancy of Frank's unfailing support. No matter how difficult I was, how abusive even, he would always be there to help and soothe me.

It was six months before the doctor decided I was fit to have the children home again, but that was not as easy as it sounded. Arthur and Penelope had grown so fond, they said, of Harold that they wished to adopt him, and have him live with them permanently. 'We can help him such a lot, send him to a good school, and when the time comes pay for his university education,' Arthur said. 'We have grown so fond of him, and he seems quite settled with us.' Penelope said it would be a shame to uproot him once again. 'Besides, you will find the strain of looking after children quite considerable after all you have gone through. Why don't you have Mollie home, and see how that works out, and we can consider Harold's future later?'

It sounded like common sense. Frank and I were both reluctant to have it so, but we agreed to see how things worked out. Ada brought Mollie home. Ada always did make a great fuss of her niece, she had bought her clothes, done her hair differently, and was busy telling her to mind her manners. Despite all Ada's coaxing, Mollie pointedly ignored her. When Ada left to go back to her school, Mollie wouldn't even kiss her Aunt goodbye. I never have discovered why Mollie disliked her Aunt so much after that enforced visit to the school. But she has refused to have anything to do with her ever since.

At first poor little Mollie didn't seem to recognise us at all. How painful that is to parents, to feel they are so estranged that any bond between them and their child has been broken for good. We coaxed, she turned her back, we joked, she scowled, she hid in a corner and wouldn't come to us. At the end of that long day she fell asleep exhausted, while Frank and I spent most of that night discussing what we could do.

Apart from seeing that she was dressed and fed, we decided to ignore her unless she approached us. I went about the daily tasks of housekeeping and cooking. I hummed little tunes to her, I kept an eye on what she did, but that was all. A few days later while I was making pastry a little person pulled up a chair and started helping me. I gave her her own pastry to make, and in almost complete silence we cooked it for her daddy. When he came home that evening he ate the rather sticky greyish 'tart' she presented to him as if it were the greatest feast in all the world. Suddenly she burst into tears and flung her arms around his neck. I have been rather fond of pastry ever since.

We said we would like Harold to come home. He seemed pleased to see his sister, and they romped together once again. He showed off frequently to gain our attention, but that was understandable under the circumstances. He still had those dancing eyes, that roguish smile, but unlike Molly's emotional reaction to us, he never seemed to get over the kind of coolness he displayed towards us after he had been away. That made me feel uneasy. But we all settled down once more to live together.

Arthur, having got his MD, had moved to Blackpool, and with the help of Penelope's money set up his own practice at Southshore. He wrote to say he had an excellent arrangement with the local hospital where from time to time he would carry out minor operations on his patients, or make provision for those needing proper nursing care. He was obviously enjoying his work and rapidly becoming a most successful doctor. Harold often asked to go and stay with his Uncle and Aunt at Blackpool. It was more fun, he said, so we often let him have his way.

Fanny and her friend Annie made a new life for themselves. We were not told who, but they had come to know a rich man who had a daughter who needed constant supervision. He bought a house in Sanderstead, Surrey, and there he installed the three of them, making provision for Fanny and Annie to look after his daughter Josey for the rest of her life. It was a comfortable arrangement, Josey was little trouble, and they were all provided for. Fanny took to breeding yappy little Pekingese dogs, which I could never abide. But Frank and I did manage to go and visit them at intervals.

Right And Wrong Choices

I have been looking over some more old letters I have kept all these years. They say fact is stranger than fiction, but as I read Arthur's letter once again it seems the strangest tale. It is the kind of story one would automatically dismiss as too far fetched to be the truth.

> *Dear Minnie,* [the letter read]
> *Prepare yourself for a great shock.*
> *I am writing to tell you of the strangest circumstance. You know at the Infirmary we care for all kinds of patients, rich and poor alike. One of my colleagues came to me last night and told me there was a destitute old man who had been admitted, but his speech and especially his handwriting would indicate he had seen much better days. 'He is asking for you, but he won't give any reason. His handwriting is the best copperplate I've ever seen, he's a real artist,' said my friend. 'He's dying, I'm afraid, and I thought he might like another educated man to talk to. I thought you wouldn't mind my asking if you could have a word or two with him, I know he would appreciate it.'*
> *I must admit I was reluctant to oblige. Penelope I knew would be anxiously waiting for me at home. He was not my patient. What prompted me to go and see the old man I'll never know, but thank goodness that I did.*
> *Well, the long and the short of it, (now prepare yourself for an unbelievable circumstance,) is that as we chatted I discovered his name was Frank Winder, yes, it was true, don't turn your unbelieving mind away, it was Papa. He had come back from America a month ago, knowing how sick he was. He had been trying to find us.*

He was so anxious to know all about the family, and I told him all I could. He was especially pleased to know he had a grandson and a granddaughter, sister dear, you should rest content that you gave the old man a few moments' real pleasure as I described them to him. He made me promise to look out for them. He was getting weaker by the minute as we spoke. He murmured answers to my questions about his life since he had left Rochdale, but I couldn't by this time hear what he was saying. He died in my arms a few minutes later.

You can imagine my agitation, sister, a father found and lost again within the space of half an hour. I am still stunned.

The funeral will be next Thursday, which should give you and everyone else time to attend if they so wish, I do hope you can get away. I am writing to Fanny and Ada, and to Aunt. I am exhausted, and my mind as you can imagine is in a turmoil. I hope to see you in the next day or two.

Your affectionate brother
Arthur Winder.

We went to the funeral, Arthur, Ada, Aunt and Dickinson and Frank and myself. There was a strange feeling of unreality about the service. We all agreed we were glad my father had come home, but there was sadness that he had been unable to find us soon enough for all of us to talk to him. We wept for a father we could scarce remember, and for our lost childhood. I was thankful that Frank and I were still able to be parents to our own children, despite our problems.

My married life now proceeded quietly enough, even humdrum some people might call it. I had two more children, Francis born in 1894 and Arthur in 1899. They made up a little for the boys I had lost, although I still grieved sometimes for those twins. What would they have become, I often wondered. I still do, all these years later. Harold became more of a stranger to us as he spent more and more time in Blackpool at his own request, it was more fun he said, especially when Mollie stayed there with him. Mollie often didn't want to go, but a request from Harold himself would always end in her joining him there.

Frank's father retired, and he and his wife moved nearer to us to a house in Devonshire Road. William the painter got married to a woman called Adelaide. They had followed our example, and as we had found to be expedient, arrangements were made and the marriages took place without his parents being present.

I felt sorry for old Mrs Allen. One always does feel sorry for someone who is their own worst enemy. I do believe she enjoyed having grandchildren round her though she would never admit that it was so. 'It would be a pity,' we said 'for all the talent that your family has shown, that it should not be passed onto another generation.' She had six grandchildren by now, four of ours and two of Tom's, Christine and Steven. Mrs Allen would never admit to any affection for any of us, but often asked to see us. She was particularly interested in Mollie because now she had started music lessons she was beginning to show considerable aptitude.

Arthur and Penelope wanted to adopt Harold, and bring him up as their own son. 'We have a proposition for you,' they wrote. 'I promised Papa that I would look out for your children, and we have been thinking of the best way that this could be done. You arrange for the adoption and we will pay for the education of all your three boys at Arnold House School in Blackpool.' Frank was rather against the plan. 'It is blackmail', he said, 'offering to help us with school fees knowing our financial difficulties, and then saying this is on the condition of an adoption having been arranged.' Harold seemed quite pleased at the prospect when we asked him. He had always seemed fond of his uncle and aunt ever since he had stayed there when he was small. It wasn't as if he didn't know them. Frank waived his objection with some trepidation, and so it was decided. Harold went to live at Blackpool, and all the boys in turn had their education paid for at Arnold House.

Despite all Harold had said, I think he missed his sister more than he admitted, his letters sounded as if he were feeling lonely, although he never complained. School was great he said. He did ask quite often if Mollie could go and stay. Penelope was always delighted at the idea. She wrote me a somewhat strange letter, but that was just her way, I thought, of saying how much she enjoyed Mollie's company

Dear Sister-in-law,
It is Arthur who has always wanted a son, and I am delighted that he has his wish now we have adopted Harold. I on the other hand have always wanted a daughter. We could provide a good settlement for Mollie when she gets married, as I am sure she will one day. In return when she comes to stay with us she can play the piano for me, I've heard her play very well, and her voice will be very pleasant to listen to when she reads to me. I will be able to buy her some good clothes and introduce her to some good society. I expect you realise we will do all we can for her. I hope you will allow her to join her brother.

I wrote back.

Dear Sister-in-law,
There can be no question that we would allow Mollie to be brought up as your own child. We wonder sometimes if we made the right decision regarding Harold. He is always such good company whenever we see him, amusing and lively, but there is something about his restless behaviour when he is with us that still makes me feel uneasy. However we are very grateful for all you have done for him.
I am sure Mollie will like to join her brother for a visit from time to time, but we feel one adoption in the family is quite sufficient.

It was arranged at Harold's urgent request that Mollie should join him for a holiday. The holiday passed, and still she wasn't home. She was missing attendance at Forest Hill School; her music teacher was saying it would be a pity if she should not be able to make the best of her musical talents. Francis and especially little Arthur kept asking where she was. Frank travelled up to Blackpool to fetch her home. We would only allow her to come and visit again, we insisted, if she was brought home when requested.

Mollie and her cousin Christine became great friends. They were always up to mischief, playing pranks and getting into scrapes. I discovered one day that they had borrowed some of my clothes, and dressed themselves up with hats with veils, and gone visiting a nearby school pretending they were parents of a prospective pupil. Naughty little things, they were only thirteen at the time. They must have had quite a talent for acting, I thought, to have got away with it.

Francis went to school in Blackpool with his brother Harold. Mollie had already missed a lot of school because of her visits to Blackpool, but that didn't seem to matter so much for a girl. She had become a really competent pianist, and spent hours trying to teach Arthur to play, so, she said, they could play duets together. I was delighted to feel we had such talent in the family. Arthur seemed somewhat backward, after all he couldn't read until he was eight. Mollie taught him that too.

Mollie started getting into trouble at school. Not to mention the pranks she got up to with her cousin, she was also said to be inattentive, rude, and difficult. 'She is very obstinate,' we were told, 'and not always to be relied upon. We think the influence of her cousin is not good for her.' When asked about it she said she missed her brothers, now they were in Blackpool.

Parents always seem to make mistakes, no matter what they do, or however good their intentions may be. Life is always a matter of choosing the lesser of two evils, or rather that you hope that is what you have done. We said Mollie could go to Blackpool for a while to see how she got on. Of course Penelope was delighted.

Where Did We Go Wrong?

It is a bright and sunny day, and I can hear the gulls down by the shore. I can't see the sea from our bungalow, but I imagine to myself the sparkling sea, and the gentle waves and then far out all the mysterious depths. I think I know why men want to be sailors, I think they want to be part of the great oceans, to tame the storms, and feel at one with the world. I would never express such ideas to Fanny, she would call it romantic nonsense, but John would have known what I was talking about. It is sad I can no longer talk to him. I always felt more cheerful when he was about.

There is a picture hanging in my room which has the same kind of calming effect on me as does the sea. I often sit and look at it, and I feel I know every detail, each leaf on the trees, and each reed by the water side. It is of a lake, with autumn trees, and a sunset, and it was painted by my daughter Mollie. It is like the calm after a storm, so that everything feels as if it has returned to its natural state. Such talent she has, but she has never really made use of her gifts, not made the most of them I mean. I think she could have been an artist as talented as her Uncle William, or a musician nearly, if not quite as good as her cousin, Sir Hugh Allen.

They say children first love you, then judge you, then hate you. They don't add the further stage of just tolerating you, which is even more uncomfortable for the parents. Looking back on it I think Mollie must have been in the phase of hating us, and her Uncle and Aunt, particularly her Aunt, and all the world as well, I suppose, to behave as she next did. It was dreadful to find out that a child of mine was so unhappy, yet I never knew it at the time.

It is so difficult to know what goes on in children's minds. I think by nature they are secretive as they grow up, they need to be to assert their independence, as we all know. After all I had insisted on my independence on leaving home when I came to London with my sisters, a lifetime ago. I was much older at the time, and more capable of looking after myself. I had had more time to learn about the world. Poor little Mollie. She always made a joke of everything. I had no idea how unhappy she had become.

I was blind, I can see that now. One letter she wrote described in most amusing terms her abortive efforts to play tennis. She seemed to spend so much time reading and playing music for her aunt, she said, that she never got any exercise. 'I persuaded Aunt to let me join the tennis club,' her letter said triumphantly. The next letter described how she was fitted out with the latest tennis clothes and racquet, and deposited at the club one Saturday afternoon. No introductions, no indication to Aunt's friends that this was her niece looking for a game. There the poor little thing sat, waiting to be asked for a game, but nobody came forward, neither that first day nor any other. Mollie not surprisingly abandoned tennis and then got into trouble for having wasted money on clothes she didn't really need. Mollie told it so amusingly I was stupid enough not to see how lonely she must feel, with no companions of her own age to mix with. Of course Harold should have looked after his sister better, he must have been aware of what was going on.

A letter came from Penelope, I have it here, a strange letter, as all Penelope's letters seemed to be.

Dear Sister-in-law [it reads]
Mollie has run away. We feel it may be partly the result of Harold's influence, for his behaviour has been giving us some cause for concern over recent years.

I can still conjure up the feeling of isolation that statement brought me, as if I had had no right to be told of problems concerning my own children. Neither Arthur nor Penelope had given Frank and myself the slightest hint that any problem had ever existed, not with Harold or his sister.

She did leave a note, saying she had gone touring with a band who had recently been entertaining the crowds on Blackpool pier. She says she plays the piano for them, and she is in love with the band leader.

Gran Minnie lives again in n

A story to tell: Mary Williams with her husband Professor David Williams.

GORING village hall hosted a sparkling evening for the glitterati of the literary world last Friday evening as local author Mary Williams launched her second novel.

More than 150 people assembled in the hall to celebrate the launch of *The Nine Lives of Minnie Winder*, inspired by Mrs Williams' grandmother, a Victorian woman whose life was full of hardship.

Mrs Williams said: "I was very fond of my grandmother and I had some information about her.

"She just seemed to me to be an interesting character."

The 78-year-old had to travel to Huddersfield to research information from records offices about her grandmother, who was abandoned by her parents when she was a young child and brought up by "a horrid aunt".

She was beset by tragedy, including the fact that her sweetheart died of TB. Two of her children also died young.

Mrs Williams r Goring 17 years a decided to take u recently when ill prevented her fr her former hobb tiles.

She said: "I ha wanted to have s expressing what

● The book is Minerva Press a at The Arcade G Westholme Store £9.99.

ovel

● Seventies star
es a comeback:
Page 10

ers to complement it.

"So if there's someone out there with gardening skills we'd be happy to hear from them for the best way to go about it."

Any green-fingered folk who can advise blue watch on doing up their pond should contact the station on 0118 932 2901.

Pond appeal: Jo
Picture: John Ha

● 'Not enough' warning

Cash b
for loca

moved to
ago. She
p writing
-health
m continuing
y of painting

e always
ome way of
I am doing."

published by
d is available
allery and
s, priced

THE £761,000 handout for Berkshire schools announced this week by education secretary David Blunkett won't be enough to cure all Reading's classroom maintenance problems, say councillors.

Opposition leaders on Reading Borough Council welcomed the county's cut of the £2 billion allocated for urgent repairs to the nation's schools.

But they warned that Berkshire's share would not stretch very far over the 118 schools on the list - and they noted that many more in need have been overlooked.

Conservative leader, Fred Pugh, said: "I'm absolutely delighted. Reading will be taking over the schools next April in far better fettle than they otherwise would have been.

By
Ed

"But
enough.
over plac
roofs w
replaced

"Ther
schools
building
That's n
in the 2

Readi
Fenwick
welcome

"But
require
absolute
in the v
resourc

One

Four injured as ca

FOUR people were injured, two seriously, when the car they were

The Pe
lost contr
tion, stru
a parked

The news could not have been much worse. What could Arthur and Penelope have been thinking of, not to have known of such a liaison before such disaster struck? I had trusted Arthur and Penelope to look after my children properly. I had always thought Arthur owed me something for the fact he was provided for at university and I was denied it.

'The band has left Blackpool and is now touring in Belgium we have discovered. Arthur and I will have left for Belgium by the time this letter reaches you. We will forward an address when we have found her.'

At the time I felt deeply shocked, afraid for Mollie, and irritated by her stupidity. But now I can only feel sorrow at a situation which had driven the poor girl to such strange behaviour. Frank and I have often blamed ourselves. We should have kept her at home, realised what was going on.

The frantic efforts we made all those years ago to rescue Mollie. The worst time was the first few days after we had been told of her escapade, wondering, speculating, sitting up half the night discussing what was to be done. The prospect of her wandering round Europe as the mistress of a third rate band leader was too terrible to contemplate. Such a life could not be anything but dreary, no money, no marriage, no status, she could starve for all we knew. I thought of my father, that down and out old man who had come back to England, dying and destitute, without family or friends.

Penelope had left no address as yet at which to reach her and Arthur while they were in Belgium. We had no idea where they might be. Mollie was only fifteen, far too young for such an adventure. She had proved a difficult child at school, but partly we had blamed the influence of her cousin Christine, hence our decision to let her stay for a while in Blackpool. We should never have let her go; the road to hell is paved with good intentions, so they say.

It had been easy, while the boys were away at boarding school at Arnold House, and Mollie was staying with Penelope, to become involved in public affairs once more. With hindsight one can always wish one had behaved differently, but at the time I was content. I had begun to feel I belonged once more to some wider part of society, that I was doing something worthwhile again in working for the suffragette movement, with all those meetings, pamphlets and demonstrations. There had been the match girls' strike, with which I and most of the country I think had great sympathy. There was far too little notice taken of the hazards of the use of chemicals and other substances in the manufacturing industry, especially where women were concerned. It was only by women being given the vote that such wrongs could ever properly be prevented. But now I began to feel I had bought such satisfaction at the expense of my own children's happiness. I remembered Dickens' character, Mrs Jellybub, who neglected her own children while she wrote letters about heathen Africans.

While we waited for news we had a postcard from my young son Arthur from Arnold House, it was his first term at the Blackpool school where he had joined his brother Francis. It was addressed to Mollie Winder, (why Winder, not Allen, we wondered). We supposed Mollie must have told her little brother she would be away, and he had taken it for granted that when she left Blackpool she would come straight back to us in London. Mollie was always very fond of little Arthur.

'I hope you are very well', it said, 'keep all my toys. Where is Auntie? Please send 1/6 for sports entrance. Thanks for dressing gown and post cards. No more time.'

I felt I wanted to cry. All I could do was send a non committal message and enclose 1/6.

Arthur and Penelope returned, but with no news. 'We have left instructions', they wrote, 'for the Belgium police, in case anything is heard of her. They are very sympathetic, but say there is no more they can do, since the band leader moves around so often he is almost impossible to trace.'

That was a terrible year, yes a year, a whole year, when we heard nothing. Frank went about with a defeated look, almost a shadow of himself. He was such a kind man, so fond of Mollie. Being at a loss to know what could be done, he seemed to turn his worry in upon himself. I was distraught, but could only find respite in becoming more involved in the suffragette movement. Frank's business suffered. My fellow workers found me often less than helpful.

Harold, we found on enquiry, was behaving more badly than ever, debts and wild behaviour now seemed the order of the day. Little Arthur pined for his sister: when the two boys came home from school on holiday I could see the look on the face of Francis that I had used to observe on that of my brother Arthur when we were children and lived in that cellar in Rochdale. Arthur seemed quite lost without his sister. It was a truly terrible year. Not knowing about a lost child I think, is almost as bad as knowing of a death. One has such wild speculations about their suffering, their loneliness. One lives in a kind of limbo, waiting and hoping. It brought back all those memories and emotions of the loss of my parents, and the years of hoping and searching, but never being able to give oneself any real hope.

Rescue

About a year later we had a communication from the police, saying they thought Mollie had been found at last. She was staying at a convent at a small Belgian village and she was being well looked after there by the nuns who were quite used, the police said, to looking after girls in this kind of situation.

Frank and I departed for Belgium immediately. It took us some hours after the crossing to find the convent, it was quite late by the time we arrived. The nuns were very kind, and said Mollie had been brought there by a man who had asked them to look after her. 'And he paid us handsomely,' they said.

We talked late into the night, trying to understand the situation. The nuns were most helpful. It was decided if Mollie wished it so she should stay at the convent for the time being. There was a good school provided and the nuns would be very happy to have her there. 'No one will ever know from us of her recent history,' they suggested, 'no one in England need know of her difficulties. She can return to England in due course and start her life again.'

In return for our promise not to tell anyone of her escapade, Mollie promised to stay at the convent for at least a year. She kept saying how kind Harry, the band leader had been to her. 'Is he likely to come back?' we asked. She shook her head. However we took the precaution of asking the convent for the information to be sent to us immediately if he ever reappeared. Mollie seemed content enough. She showed us that picture of the sunset she had finished painting just weeks ago. It seemed a kind of talisman, an indication of a brighter future. She promised to write to her Uncle and Aunt. Now more than ever she would need some kind of financial settlement if in the future she were ever to want to get married; she couldn't afford to ignore them. We came back to England, much happier of course, but still very worried about her future.

We wrote to her often, consoling her, hoping she was happy, wondering how she was. All we got in return were amusing little notes about her painting lessons, about her fellow pupils, about the nuns, about the countryside, anything in effect but information regarding herself and what she really felt.

'There's a fat girl here,' she wrote, 'who is always hungry, and buttons are always popping off the front of her bodice. Whenever we have a meal, she takes it upon herself to pass round any left over items, "Do have some more," she says, and everyone, looking at her anxious eyes, says no thank you. We all watch with a certain amount of fascination as she consumes it all.'

'You wouldn't believe,' she wrote another time, 'that nuns can be so quarrelsome, self-centred, so petty. Being religious makes them more contentious it seems than other people, not less. Whose turn is it to light the candles, why is the nun who provided the food today so bad at cooking, who has lost the visiting Father's special cup. Why did Mother Superior give a special privilege to a comparative new comer to the convent.' Mollie was always a keen observer.

Was it my fault, I wondered, that things had gone so astray. Harold never wrote, but was always affectionate and amusing whenever he came to see us, which was quite often now, about once a month I suppose. He was seventeen by now, and an independent young man. He worked for the civil service, having said he had no wish to go to university. I wasn't sure whether this was because his examination result would not have allowed it, or if he merely felt he needed his independence.

'He has a bad reputation as far as girls are concerned,' my brother wrote. 'I have spoken with him, but he still goes his own way. He has considerable expenses, and his salary doesn't seem to cover what he needs. We are not surprised that girls take to him, he is so amusing, so attractive. But perhaps it would be better for him if it were not so.' Francis and Arthur away at school, were not causing us any anxiety, thank goodness. Francis was doing well at his studies, and knew he wanted to be a doctor: Arthur had at last learnt to read and was rapidly catching up in his work. All parents seem to have problems with their growing children. Perhaps we were exaggerating our difficulties. Perhaps things would be better now.

The suffragette movement, Frank and I both agreed, was getting out of hand, too militant in the conduct of its affairs. Of course I still agreed with the objectives, but such unfeminine behaviour could only act against the cause, not for it. Prison sentences, hunger strikes and the horror of force feeding might provoke some public sympathy, but would bring the granting of women's franchise no closer to acceptance, might even impede it. Besides, Frank said, if I were seen to be too closely associated with such extremism it might be bad for trade, and things were difficult enough already, we had responsibilities towards our children after all. But I needed something to distract me from my constant worrying.

I became gradually more interested in an organisation called the Band of Hope, which had been set up to look after pregnant women who had been abandoned on the streets. Funds were raised to provide a hostel, a refuge other than the harsh interior of the workhouse. There seemed so many young girls who through no fault of their own, except perhaps too great a trust in men, found themselves destitute and alone. They provide better care for such unfortunates on the continent through the help of the catholic church there, I had come to realise. I would often visit the hostel, I enjoyed the company of the little children. I used my contacts with Forest Hill School and the Suffragette movement to raise a considerable amount of money for them.

I was now becoming wary of the behaviour of women in a variety of ways. Penny Farthing bicycles , the 'ordinary' and then the new smaller models are all very well for men, but they necessitate riding astride, something no decent woman should ever contemplate. Besides, to make it possible women have to wear those dreadful ugly garments called bloomers which they wear in such defiance of their sex. William, Frank's brother, has a bicycle on which he tours the countryside with his painting apparatus. I can see the advantage for him. I entirely agree with old Mrs Allen's shocked response to the suggestion that the new bride he had recently brought home should also get herself a machine and accompany him.

Mollie came home at last. We had left her in Belgium a young unsophisticated girl, despite her adventures. A young lady came home, a young lady with a rather wistful look perhaps, but that only added to her charm. She had such lovely hair, such a rich auburn colour, no one could deny how attractive she had become. Her brothers were quite overcome by her metamorphosis. 'She's like a butterfly,' Arthur said in admiration.

We didn't want to lose her company again so soon, but when Penelope offered to take her on a grand tour we would not stand in her way. We felt that Mollie needed some gaiety in her life. She said she would like to go. She was bought sophisticated clothes. Her hair was such a lovely colour, shown off by her new sophisticated hairstyle, and we felt really proud of her.

Her letters were enthusiastic, full of news of places visited and people met. She was in demand for parties, where she played for the company gaining high praise for her musical talent. She enjoyed herself. She danced, she sparkled, she was happy.

We went to the funerals in Blackpool, first of Dickinson and then a few months later of Aunt. They had enjoyed their retirement, plenty of concerts to attend, choirs to join, and above all no responsibilities concerning us children, whom they had worked so hard to bring up properly. Aunt was never the same after Dickinson died. She seemed lost and uninterested in all that was going on round her. Neither of them had taken much interest in our children, it was if they wanted to escape from anything to do with us, once we had left home.

I asked Arthur what he thought of the latest inventions: Zeppelins could drop things on us in a war, I suggested and so could aeroplanes. 'Bleriot has just flown a plane across the English channel. We are no longer an island protected by our ships. In any case the Germans are building submarines to sink the navy. It sounds quite terrifying.' I was only repeating what I had read.

'There won't be a war,' Arthur had said, 'not a full scale one anyway. The King has seen to that', he said, 'on his visit to the Kaiser. Blood is thicker than water you know and the Kaiser and the King are cousins after all. Besides there are so many alliances now, with France, with Russia, the Germans wouldn't dare. No one wants a war anyway, it wouldn't solve anything.' I sincerely hoped he was right. Nonetheless there did seem to be a general feeling, difficult to know how anyone came by it, that a war was coming. It was nothing anyone particularly said, it was just a feeling. 'Unscientific', Arthur said, 'that stupid thing called women's intuition I suppose, and who ever could rely on that.'

Edward VII died, and the 'intuition' became stronger. Frank said I was becoming morbid. We went to see the King's funeral procession. Despite his short reign he had done a lot for his country, and he would be much missed. George V the new King was an unknown quantity.

Francis my son went up to Trinity College, Cambridge, to study medicine. Mollie visited him there, met some of his friends. One of these was Maggie, a woman with an ambition to go to the university. Nothing would deflect her, and she wanted to know why Mollie couldn't come too. 'She's clever, you know', Maggie said to me one day, 'I'm sure she could get accepted if she wanted to.' Mollie said she would think about it. She had another friend Joe, a young man getting his medical qualification there.

It would be nice if politics could proceed without such drama. Poor George V, he had to cope with the House of Lords crisis almost as soon as he became King. I think there might have been a revolution if the Liberals hadn't managed to pass their welfare legislation. Something had to be done to help the poor. The House of Lords was very foolish to vote against it, for now their powers have been much reduced.

There was the terrible news about the Titanic. I went round the house thinking of the hymn with those lines 'Oh hear us when we cry to thee, for those in peril on the sea.' I was suspicious myself that it might have been the Germans practising with their submarines rather than an iceberg which had sunk her. How else could one account for the sinking of an unsinkable ship. No one but the Germans would think of using a passenger ship as a practice target. Everyone was talking about it, the drowning women and children, the band playing as the boat sank, the terrible loss of life. It is sometimes difficult to have faith in the goodness of providence, for how could any God who cared for people allow such a monstrous thing to happen.

It seems that I am destined to write my thoughts in rhyme. I didn't wish the words to come, they just appeared one morning as I stood looking out of the window.

> Shadows, dark shadows, the shadow of my dreams,
> Flickering in my half awakened mind
> Some hidden fear, imagined dread, it seems
> Would overwhelm me should it be defined

I think it is better to ignore such thoughts, it only brings on worry and depression. 'Sufficient unto the day is the evil thereof.'

We had a hurried postcard from Mollie today, with a photograph of her and Francis and their friends watching the Cambridge boat races – a sunny scene, bright happy faces.

This is us watching the races. I go to London tomorrow to meet Marjorie on her way through and we are going to the January Exhibition. Learnt to punt yesterday, and I am quite good really. Joe has got through his exams, 3rd class, very delighted. It is lovely Maggie and I are going up to Newnham next term.

How thankful we were that after all the troubles, things were working out well for the family.

Part Three

The Beginning Of War

Life during wartime is a unique experience, it is a life on its own, nothing that happened before, and nothing that follows can ever be remotely comparable. The war lasted four years. This was another life, my seventh life. In wartime there is no past and no future, just today, how to struggle on from one day to the next. Things happen, people get maimed, people get killed on so grand a scale that normal feelings are left numb, emotions buried. To let one's feelings loose on so great a scale would I sincerely believe send one mad, indifference becomes an anaesthetic.

Who would have thought that the murder of Archduke Franz Ferdinand of Austria would have resulted in the death of millions and almost ended the ordered life of our quiet civilisation. Big trees from little acorns grow, so the saying goes. Such a small event in itself, that murder, aristocrats were always being murdered, one way or another. After all even our own Queen had once nearly been assassinated.

After the Archduke was shot one could begin to feel the tension in the air heighten, as if everyone was waiting for something, though no one knew exactly what. The papers were full of praise for our army, the need to be patriotic, the competence of our commanders, particularly General Kitchener. There was little talk of diplomacy any more. If Germans wanted a fight the English were ready and able to retaliate. Perhaps the only way to solve the problems of a restless Europe was after all to fight it out. Why wait for Germany to get stronger?

Every one knew as soon as the Germans marched into Belgium that war was inevitable. I can remember that feeling, the morning the news broke, almost a feeling of relief that now at last the Germans had shown their real intentions. It was true then that the Germans had all along wanted war. Their invasion of Belgium showed they had been secretly preparing for it for many years.

Everything seemed to change overnight, even one's feelings. It must be right, we women felt, that men should fight to protect their women folk, and the lives of their children. They urged their men folk to fight now, whereas only a few weeks ago they might have done just the opposite. Men began to talk more about the glory of fighting, of excitement and adventure, but above all of one's duty towards one's country. No longer did men seem to dread death, but almost gloried in such a prospect.

> Happy are they that die for they return
> Into the primeval clay and the primeval earth
> Happy are they who die in a just war
> Happy as the ripe corn and the harvested grain.

Charles Peguy wrote that poem, so apt, so inspired by the relevant mood of the time.

Everything changed in such a short time. Mollie came home from Blackpool and began working in an office, there could be no more talk of her going to university. My brother Arthur joined the army as a medical officer despite his age, he was after all fifty-six by now. However he remained stationed in Blackpool. Penelope was put in charge of the red cross nurses, who were recruited to look after the wounded in the various premises made available as temporary hospitals in Lancashire.

My son Harold joined up. I can scarce bring myself to mention even now what followed. At first he was not accepted, Arthur told us, not at least until he had had treatment for what the war office named as syphilis, but the young soldiers called the pox. We could hardly take it in, that a son of ours could... well, least said the better. It was just as well his condition had been diagnosed and treated. When and where he had picked it up no one knew. We had learned from my brother that his conduct had been somewhat wild in recent years, and the company he kept not that of the best. But this... How life changes. There were no more certainties for any of us, no more reliance on past standards, of proper conduct.

We saw many of our brave soldiers come and go. Harold would bring his friends, always laughing and joking, as if war and death were normal occurrences. We met men from Australia and New

Zealand and Canada with their strange drawls, and listened to the ugly accent of the South Africans. I was proud to be British, to think we had kept the loyalty of all our various overseas dominions, whose men now volunteered to come to our aid. We all felt part of a wider family, as if we were fighting, not just for Britain alone, but for the survival of our civilised world.

Then the Belgians arrived. I opened the door one morning to find a middle aged couple with a battered looking suitcase standing on the doorstep. They looked scared and dishevelled, two strangers, no one we had ever met before as far as I could recollect. They handed me a letter. 'Please,' they said, with a foreign accent. I asked them to come in. I read the letter. It was from the Mother Superior of the convent where Mollie had been at school.

> *Dear Mrs Allen, [it said in perfect English]*
> *As you know our poor country has been invaded and we are all fearful for our lives. There are already reports of beatings and rapes and even murders, atrocities perpetrated against our innocent people. The bearers of this letter are Menheer and Vru Louvein who have fled before the German advance. We would be grateful if you could do what you can for them.*
> *I doubt our convent will survive the war.*

I gave the two strangers a meal, they seemed very hungry. The fact I knew a little German helped with our communication problem, since they were of Flemish origin. They had fled to the channel coast it seems, and been able to find a boat to bring them across to England. They had left everything behind except what they carried with them. He was, or I suppose to be correct had been, a merchant banker, but of course he had now lost all his money. They had three sons and a daughter, but hadn't heard from them since the Germans came. They had that defeated look that one soon learns to associate with refugees, a baffled look of disbelief.

What could we do? Frank and I and Mollie agreed that they should stay, at least for the time being. We fed them as best we could though we got no allowances for them from the shops as food got scarcer and scarcer. We provided them with clothes, we taught them some English, we accepted their help in the house. Our own little maid soon left us to work in a munitions factory with better wages given. It was out of the question, we were told, that Belgians should be given work to do in England, in case they turned out to be German spies. Or even, the official said, had been sent over here to sabotage our industries. Other people were curious, wary, of our visitors. They in their turn kept themselves to themselves. It wasn't a very comfortable arrangement, how could it be? Belgians are rather dour people.

I decided the best thing I could do to help would be to support the House of Hope – that refuge for unmarried mothers. There are so many young mothers in wartime with their babies, their men killed before a marriage is arranged, so many sorrowful women with no means of support. I badgered my suffragette friends, ex-pupils, fellow teachers, anyone whom I could persuade to support us. Somehow we kept going.

Mollie's friend Joe joined up. He had originally decided to stay and look after those who might need medical help at home but something had happened to make him change his mind. Mollie was quite upset, after all they had been friends for quite some time now, and he had led her to believe he cared for her. He said, she reported, that he wouldn't contemplate marrying anyone until after the war was over. 'It's not fair', he had said, 'to expect a wife to wait at home and worry all the time.' They had quarrelled and he had left. Mollie said she suspected he had been sent a white feather, as so many men had been, to persuade them to join up whether they were fit to fight or not. We kept expecting to hear that there was an end to the fighting, that a treaty had been arranged. All this fighting and killing seemed to be getting out of hand.

The only people to whom the war seemed to make little difference were my two sisters and their two friends. Ada and Marjorie went on teaching, and as far as I know they did no voluntary work to help the war effort. I don't suppose Ada would have told me if they had. Fanny, rightly I suppose, said she had a duty to Josey, her patient, and she and Annie must see that she was properly looked after twenty-four hours a day, as they had promised her father. There was therefore little opportunity for them to do anything else.

*

Fanny is not well. I found her this morning rolling in agony on the floor. The doctor came promptly when I summoned him.

"Inflammation of the gall bladder," he proclaims, "a very painful and sometimes very serious condition. It may mean there has to be an operation but we'll see. At her age that could be very dangerous. We'll prescribe some treatment and then see how it goes."

"What about the pain?" I ask, "you must be able to give her something for the pain." He gave her an injection, and I could see immediately that she felt better. I thought of Aunt, and the laudanum that would immediately have been provided in those days gone past.

"Will the pain come back," I ask anxiously.

"Probably," he says, "but I'll prescribe some tablets for when it does." I realise everything has to be on prescription these days, one can't go to the chemist and just get what one wants.

My mind then began to calculate the expense. Of course we would find the money for an operation should this prove necessary, but it would make things quite difficult. We are not paupers after all, dependent on charity, we can always pay our way. But it would be a bit of a struggle.

"Don't worry," he said as if he could read my thoughts, "I will do my best to make sure no operation will be needed. Your sister, however, will have to be on a very strict diet, the cause of the complaint is the inability of the gall bladder to digest the fat that is eaten. No fats, no butter, no cream, no fried food, that is the order of the day. I will prescribe something called slippery eel, to be eaten instead of an evening meal. With luck it will resolve the problem altogether."

"How much do we owe you for this visit?" I ask.

"Nothing, nothing at all," he says, "when you are ill these days everything is taken care of, prescriptions, attendance, hospital, operations, the lot."

"We don't want charity," I explain.

"It's not charity," he says, "It's your entitlement. You've paid taxes, and that is what pays for the medical service." Of course I felt relieved. The part of my mind that worried about paying for medical treatment had now stopped worrying. But I felt slightly bewildered, there was a kind of vacuum in my mind, as if nonetheless I ought somehow to be financially responsible for my own health.

Poor Fanny had a dreadful time. I would quite often find her writhing in agony, but fortunately the spasms never lasted too long. Slippery eel seemed to be having its effect, as the pain gradually abated in both length and severity.

I couldn't bear to be left on my own. If anything happened to Fanny what would I do. No one I could talk with about the past, no one I could grumble about, no one whom I cared for as I do my sister. Of course there is my family, but they have their own lives to live, and I would never think of living with any of them. I'm sure Mollie would be quite pleased to have me stay, but no way would I be persuaded. One should never permanently inflict one's presence on the next generation, however kind and thoughtful they may be.

Fanny gradually improved. Of course it was difficult providing fatless meals all the time, there wasn't that much available to eat in any case. But old fogies like us don't require all that much.

Fanny and I have been talking again of those war years. I bring out my souvenirs, including such a very pretty French glove.

*

Stalemate

The war dragged on. There was the offensive at Gallipoli, with so many of the young men we had met as friends of Harold who would never return after that disastrous offensive against the Turks. Russians retreated, then advanced. Italy declared war on Austria. Those despicable Germans launched those terrible poison gas attacks, served them right we all said when the wind blew clouds of it back onto their own troops. A submarine sank the liner *Lusitania*. Were no civilians to be safe, people said fearfully to one another. It was becoming clear that this was to be not just a war fought between armies, but against civilians. If Germans could leave women and children to drown, then what would they not do if we lost the war and they occupied our country. The Americans we were told were outraged, nearly two hundred of their citizens had thus been murdered. Germany could be seen in her true colours by the whole world.

The fighting had reached a kind of stalemate, the German advance towards Paris had been halted with considerable loss of men. The soldiers on both sides had dug themselves into those infamous trenches. Food began to get more scarce, but at least the harvest had been gathered in, thanks to help from anyone able-bodied lending a helpful hand. They were much worse off in Germany we were told. Whether this was said to keep our spirits up or because it happened to be true no one really seemed to know. People still held their breath, waiting for something to happen, for some decisive action to be taken, for the war to end.

Mollie announced one day she was going to get married to someone called Herbert, 'or rather Teddy', she said, 'that is what I am going to call him, I refuse to get married to someone called Herbert.' We had been introduced to this rather dour young man a few months ago. 'He will be old enough to join up soon, so we will get married straight away. We plan a very quiet wedding.'

Frank and I were not very happy at the prospect. He was so young, a few years younger than Mollie, no profession, and not many social graces either. They had become acquainted as Mollie passed by the house where he lived on her way back from the office, and they had started chatting together. Then he had asked her in, and they started playing together, he on the clarinet, she on the piano. I could see they had fun together. There was little enough fun to be had during the war years.

Then Joe came back on leave, and asked her to marry him instead. To our surprise she had refused him, saying she preferred Teddy. 'Well', she said, 'I couldn't let Teddy down, could I, he would be so terribly upset. Joe can soon find someone else, but Teddy would be heartbroken.' I could see what she meant, Teddy was such an intense young man.

Teddy asked Frank formally for her hand in marriage. We warned them both that we felt we would have to tell Teddy's parents about her Belgian escapade. It wouldn't be right, Frank said, to leave a respectable family like his in ignorance. Teddy was furious. 'It is between Mollie and me', he said, 'and nothing to do with anyone else. With or without yours or my parents' consent we intend to get married. Your interference will only make family relationships more difficult, they have said already I am too young to take on such a responsibility.' I began to see why Mollie had chosen him. He was obviously deeply in love with her. I admired the way he wished to protect her.

It was a painful interview, what else could it have been? Mr and Mrs Davis refused permission for the marriage. 'It will bring disgrace on the whole family,' they said. 'Not if you don't tell anyone,' we said. 'What we have disclosed has been in the strictest confidence.' To do them justice I don't think they ever discussed the matter, even among the rest of their own family.

Teddy and Mollie got married regardless, and Teddy said he didn't get on with his family anyway. 'If I am old enough to fight for my country, then I'm old enough to make up my own mind as to whom I choose to marry,' he proclaimed. They found themselves a small flat. They seemed very happy.

Mollie and Teddy were always trying things out on each other. Mollie told us how she had had a brain wave because of the food shortage, she would try mixing cheese with porridge to create a more nourishing breakfast. Teddy walked out. He could stand most of her experiments he said, but not that.

One day he told us he had come home to find Mollie was not there. She had left a note for him in the hall. 'Have gone away', it said, 'and taken the piano with me.' When he opened the sitting room door he was met by her uncontrollable peals of laughter. It was their way I supposed of relieving the tensions of the war.

Teddy joined up and was sent for military training. Francis finished his medical training and he too joined up. Two of Teddy's brothers joined up. More and more women seemed to be taking over the men's jobs as they went off to fight. Food got shorter. Those great German flying balloons, the Zeppelins, dropped some explosives in London, but they did little damage we were told. But everyone became frightened as to what they might be capable of in the future. People went about looking at the sky, looking for the first sign of one of those flying machines approaching.

Trying to remember what fighting went on during the war is very difficult. Distant names like Verdun or the Somme, or Ypres began to sound familiar. There were long lists of casualties, those awful telegrams that seemed to be delivered to so many of one's friends. Troops from round the world were seen more often on the streets. There were events like the Easter uprising in Ireland, I remembered what Arthur had said about there always being an Irish problem. I didn't like to hear of the rebels being shot but then in wartime what else can you do? No one could afford to let Germany take Ireland. General Kitchener was drowned, there was the Battle of Jutland which kept the German navy at bay.

Mollie had a miscarriage. She was very distressed. 'I want children above everything' she said. I could well understand how anxious she felt.

Teddy came home badly wounded. We went to see him in a London hospital. The doctors said he had been hit by a sniper's bullet near his heart and was not expected to live. 'He's strong,' I told Mollie, 'don't give up hope.' Hope was the name of the ward he was in. 'It's a good omen,' I said, 'there is always hope. He has the best of care, you can see that.' We waited for anxious weeks until he was out of danger. He still has a fragment of metal lodged near his lung, but it would be more dangerous to operate than to leave it where it is.

Francis came home with a wound to his head. 'We cannot guarantee,' the doctors said, 'that his mind will not be affected. he has a hole in his skull, to which a metal plate has been affixed to protect his brain. It will be some time before we know if he can lead a normal life again.' A longer wait this time, a full year, before we were sure he could carry on his life as a medical practitioner.

1917 was a terrible year. Harold, my laughing soldier son was killed fighting at Arras. I had always feared to hear such news. With so many young men losing their lives it might seem surprising if one or other of my family were not to suffer the same fate. But then of course one always hopes against hope. Part of the gaiety of life went with him.

The way I heard about his death has always upset me, as if I had been deprived of my rightful place in his life. It wasn't any one's fault that the fateful telegram had been sent to my brother Arthur, after all we had consented to his being Harold's legal guardian years ago. But Arthur was away when it arrived, and we were not told until three weeks later. Somehow I felt we had let my son down, as if we had demonstrated that we didn't care. Of course nothing was further from the truth. We were proud to have a hero son, fallen protecting his country. As I had written once to Arthur, those who die fighting for their fellow citizens will assuredly find their place in heaven. He is buried somewhere in France with his fellow soldiers and there may he rest in peace. We put a tribute to him in the Times, about our dear laughing soldier.

We were sent the few belongings found in his possession, the usual papers, his army book, a few French coins, and that was all. All that is except a pretty woman's glove, which smelled of a lovely perfume, and with it a faded red rose. I often imagine to myself to whom it could have once belonged. Perhaps some beautiful French girl to whom he had become really attached. So many girls he had had in his short life, but none of them the kind he wished to settle down with. Perhaps this unknown lady was one for whom he had had a real affection.

My son Arthur joined the army. He was eager to go – 'not to let the side down' he said. He was so young for his age, trusting in the goodness of life, in the goodness of people. We feared he would find the army very rough. We had letters from him. They said nothing about army life, no complaints, no real messages. The less he said, the more we feared he suffered. The only complaint he ever made was that he missed the cold baths they had had at school every morning. He had always been fastidious about his appearance. He said would we write and tell him about ordinary little things. 'You are always writing little poems yourself mother, so I thought I would too, just to show what I mean.

> Are you sitting by the fire having tea?
> Are you looking at the sunset down the street?
> Are the blackbirds singing in our tree?
> Are you listening to those sounds of passing feet?
> Mother dear.
> Have the Spring flowers turned their faces to the sun?
> Have the blackbirds built their little home?
> Are the children laughing as they run?
> Or are you sitting in the dark alone?
> Mother dear.

I read a poem called the 'Fountain of Tears', by someone I had never heard of called O'Shaughnessy. I suppose there are some good Irish things. They certainly know how to write.

> If you go over desert and mountain,
> Far into the country of sorrow,
> Today and tonight and tomorrow,
> And maybe for months and for years;
> You shall come with a heart that is bursting
> For trouble and toil and for thirsting,
> You shall certainly come to the fountain
> At length, – to the Fountain of tears.

Very peaceful the place is, and solely
For piteous lamenting and sighing,
And those who come, living or dying
Alike from their hopes and their fears;
Full of cypress like shadows the place is,
And statues that cover their faces:
But out of the gloom springs the holy
And beautiful Fountain of tears.

And it flows and it flows with a motion
So gentle and lovely and listless,
And murmurs a tune so resist less
To him who has suffer'd and hears –
You shall surely – without a word spoken,
Kneel down there and know your heart broken,
And yield to the long-curb'd emotion
That day by the Fountain of tears.

But none of us could cry, not yet, if ever.

Things changed.   There was the Russian Revolution and the monstrous murder of the Tzar and his entire family.   Russia left the war.   America joined in.   Americans had suffered too many civilian casualties at sea to stay neutral any longer.   Besides, we were told, the Germans were now supporting America's enemies in Mexico. American troops started arriving.   Teddy's brother Harold was killed, his brother George wounded.

Teddy had recovered sufficiently to be posted to Aldershot in an administrative job.   He and Mollie settled in a little cottage in a nearby village.   Mollie was pregnant.   Our Belgian visitors began to say they would soon be going home.   We didn't feel we knew them any better than the day they arrived.   At least food was becoming a little more available as the convoy system began to protect our shipping from those dreadful submarines.   We waited for peace to come at last.

Mollie had a son, a dear little fair haired boy.   They christened him Harold after his two lost uncles.   He was proving a difficult child, but then many war babies were found to be difficult to rear. You could tell even when he was only a few months old that he had a terrible temper, when he would almost turn blue as he held his breath in a great rage.

There was another German offensive. War weary as our soldiers were by then they held out, but with yet more casualties reported. It couldn't go on.

When peace came it seemed so sudden no one really believed it at first. The Kaiser abdicated, the Germans surrendered, an armistice was signed and peace treaties began to be organised. Normal life would begin again we at last began to hope.

Armistice Day was a release of emotion no one can imagine who wasn't there. People screamed, cried, cheered, shouted, danced: everywhere arms waved people embraced friends and strangers alike. They threw each other into fountains, climbed statues, cheered the King until their throats were sore. Many got drunk, but who could blame them.

There was a film with the actor Charlie Chaplin in it called *Shoulder Arms* which everyone went to see. It is amazing how much can be conveyed by actors even when there are no spoken words. It was hilarious, such a clever exaggeration of the way military minds seem to work, that we were all sitting there wiping tears of laughter from our eyes. 'Not such an exaggeration, neither,' said a man sitting next to us.

The Aftermath Of War

The war was over, or at least the fighting was. It had been a war to end all wars, so we told ourselves. Now things would get back to normal. Everyone wanted a new life, a new start. We wanted to forget the war, to blot it out as if it had never been. What was done, was done. The politicians seemed to be still negotiating treaties all over Europe, it was several years before everything was settled. And as soon as anything was settled it started to become once more unsettled. Uprisings, strikes, all Europe seemed unsettled. Even the Americans, who had had the imaginative idea of a League of Nations to help prevent future conflicts turned tail and now refused to support it. There was still the Irish question. America seemed to have become the dictator of policy, now the richest and most powerful country in the world.

Menheer and Vru Louvein returned to Belgium. I still have the letter they sent, but that was the last we ever heard of them.

Dear Mrs Allen and Mrs Davis,
   We are very sorry we couldn't see you before we returned to Belgium, we are so much indebted to both of you.
   We left on Friday morning, a car man took our luggage. We reached Dover. Several of our oak wooden homes were damaged there. The weather was fine, no one was sick on sea. We reached Ostend, everybody cheered your glorious Vindictive, which is half out of the water.
   Between Ostend and Ghent a lot of damaged houses, bridges and burnt churches. No light in the carriages, which are all German.

Mother came to meet us, other relations followed, everybody wept.
When we came home we were sleeping as soon as we got a chair, our beds will come later.
We are anxious to know if Mrs Davis and the baby are all right.
We shall always remember both of you and your continuing kindness to
    Your grateful Belgians.
    Detney

Frank and I decided to move to a better part of London. Frank's business had done quite well during the war, he had made better money even though he would never stoop to profiteering. Soldiers of course had needed clothing, and he was able to see that contracts were fulfilled. He was not a rich man, but certainly better off than he had been before. Frewin Road in Wandsworth was a nice quiet road near the Common. We had good neighbours, it was a pleasant place to live. But no one could really forget the war. Nor did things return to normal, I don't think anyone knew what normal meant any more.

Teddy had been mentioned in dispatches and then had been awarded the Military Cross. I never really understood what constituted his outstanding acts of bravery mentioned in the citation. He would never talk about it, only said others deserved it much more than he did. He had dreams, sometimes, Mollie said, nightmares that left him sweating and exhausted, but they faded with time.

You would think, wouldn't you, that his family would be proud of him. I had come to realise how unhappy Teddy had always felt at home. Instead of showing how pleased they were, they said they thought his older brother should have had a medal, rather than him. You wouldn't think earning a prestigious award like that would lead to further family friction, but in this case it did. I never did understand the Davis family very well.

Teddy decided he would stay on in the army to get his accountancy qualification, he had found while working for the army that this was something he was good at. So he got his qualification coming second in all England when he took the national examinations. I had become very fond of him, and thought how lucky Mollie was to have found such a partner. Mollie loved the country, and insisted that was where she wished to be, the best place in which to bring up her family. Mary their first daughter was born the next year.

Penelope was awarded a CBE for her Red Cross work. Arthur retired from the army and from his medical practice. They were both somehow exhausted by the war. Arthur was not to live much longer, and Penelope's sometimes eccentric behaviour noted in the past became more bizarre as time passed. She had always been erratic in her decisions, but by now her behaviour had become totally unpredictable.

The streets seemed filled with ex-soldiers returned from the war, down and out a lot of them, selling goods no one wanted just so they could earn an honest penny. People bought all kinds of things they didn't want, just to save an ex-soldiers pride. I tried reselling such things in aid of the House of Hope.

We began to feel an unease everywhere. The fear of revolution that had haunted my childhood years seemed to be with us again. Who could blame men who had fought for their country, often wounded, gassed, their lives shattered, who could blame them for thinking those who had suffered less should make sure they now could lead a decent life. Life continued to be hard for so many people, war widows bringing up children on inadequate pensions, those chronically disabled men with missing limbs, the blind, the sick made ill by gas poisoning. It was a disgrace that there were no funds to help them, until General Haig founded the British Legion two years later in 1921.

But everyone was affected in one way or another. My son Francis was a changed man following his recovery from his head wound. Oh, yes, he could still practice medicine, he was a good doctor, with a charming manner. In Highgate where he settled in a handsome terraced house half way up the hill, he soon had many rich, even famous patients who had reason to be grateful to him. But his personality had changed. He was too easy going now, too easily persuaded into things. Gone was the meticulous keeper of records, who had once been the secretary of the Cambridge University Medical Society. He was a good doctor, no mistake, but no business man. Many of his patients were his friends.

And my poor Arthur. Gone was the childlike trusting youth we had seen off to the war. Instead there was a disillusioned and depressed young man who like his brother who had been killed, seemed incapable of making any lasting relationships. He was well qualified now, a well respected brilliant radiologist. But he was restless, unhappy, not knowing what he did or didn't want. At times he seemed to suffer from the most acute depression.

They say all things, however bad, produce at least some compensating good. In 1918 women got the vote, limited to women householders or wives of householders to be sure, and restricted to women over thirty, but at last the barrier had been broken. What is more women could now become members of Parliament and state their views officially to the government of the day. No man could possibly have had the face to deny women the vote after all they had proved they could do during the war. It was a lifetime away, before the war, that I had tried to do something about the 'subjection of women.' It wasn't the hard work of the suffragettes, their sufferings in prison, their later tendency to violent action nor that poor woman's act of heroism in throwing herself under a horse at a race meeting that had brought it all about, but the opportunities offered women by the war. The irony of things, I thought.

The papers all had long lists of commemorative messages for those who would never come home, many listed as dead, many listed only as missing, their fate unknown. We put a tribute to our 'laughing soldier' in the Times for several years. It was proposed that war memorials should be set up all over the country to commemorate the fallen. Every town, every organisation, every village even, had long lists of those who would thus be remembered. I shall never forget that first Armistice Day in 1919.

Such a profound silence as the guns went off in Hyde Park for the two minutes remembrance. The crowds round the cenotaph, the parades of soldiers all paying their respects to those who would never come back. It was an almost unbearably emotional experience.

The Next Generation

Life can be divided into two halves, I thought, one before the war, and one after the war. The past is the past, to be forgotten as soon as possible. After a tragedy one can only look to the future, to hope for the next generations. Mine was the outdated generation, I began to realise, still hoping to live in a world long gone. The present had been taken over by new feelings, new ideas, new inventions. My children belonged to the lost generation, reeling under the impact of a world war from which they would never really recover.

The economy, the papers said, would probably never recover. England would never again be the 'workshop of the world.' I read that our poor country was near bankruptcy, we had been ruined by the cost of curbing Germany's ambitions. Germany must pay reparations for all the damage she has caused the politicians agreed. But it was America who had stolen our trade, taking advantage of us during the long years of war, who was really responsible for most of our misery. How gloomy it all sounded.

But it wasn't only money that was in scarce supply now, but more importantly, I said to Frank, a lack of faith in the future. You could sense a kind of hopelessness all around you. All our best young men had been killed in the trenches. Faith in the miracles of science had been shattered. When I was young, I thought nostalgically, we had been convinced that the world of science would improve life for everyone throughout the world. Now no one was so sure. Science could also be devastatingly destructive. A feeling of direction seemed to be missing. If anyone had any energy it was frittered away. Nothing seemed to matter any more.

My brother Arthur died. In a way he was a war casualty too. He was ill for only a short time. Fanny and Ada and I did manage to go and visit him in response to Penelope's blunt message concerning his heart condition and we were there just before the end. Mollie refused to come, and said Penelope had made it quite clear she wasn't welcome. We three sisters travelled together on the train, as we did that day we left Huddersfield all those years ago, except that this time we had Frank with us to support us.

The train seemed to be full of men in army uniforms that had seen better days, or with medals displayed on the front of their worn civilian jackets. It was a depressing journey, a feeling of hopeless resignation seemed to be about. Everyone was tired. I suppose Arthur too, like everyone else, was tired. His heart had been affected, so they said, by the long hours he had worked in the hospital casualty wards.

I had never really understood Penelope. She greeted us very warmly when we arrived, and said how pleased she was to see us. Then she said brusquely she hoped we would not stay for long. She complained about expenses and then insisted a lot of unnecessary money should be spent on refreshments. 'How is dear Mollie,' she asked, but didn't want to be given any information. 'I have no intention of helping any of the family financially,' she pronounced. 'We must not bother Arthur with money matters, everything was settled years ago.' As if we were likely to start talking about money on such an occasion. She must have a very odd opinion of us.

Arthur was still his old ironic self, despite the fact he had but a few hours to live. 'You'll all pretend to miss me, no doubt', he said, 'but you forget how well I know the three of you. I held his hand, for a while, and he seemed pleased. 'We always did what we could, little sister, didn't we?' he said. He closed his tired eyes. 'Look after Penelope for me, won't you?' he asked. I could scarcely hear what he was saying. Penelope was hovering like a black shadow in the background, as if she wanted to prevent any conversation between us. I had never known her so suspicious, so unreasonable. She seemed to have altered much these last few years. She always was difficult, prone to sudden changes of mood, but now she seemed strange, so completely unpredictable, as if she belonged to a different world from ours.

There were a great many people at the funeral, army officers, local doctors, wealthy patients, and they all spoke so very highly of him. We all stood there shivering in the cold wind. We three sisters were glad when they had all gone at last from the house. Then the will was read. As I had suspected all along the money had been left in trust for Penelope. The executors were two lawyers I would never trust, not with my own or anyone else's money. There was something about them I didn't like. They certainly seemed to have great influence over Penelope. 'There is no need to have any worries, rest assured we will always be on hand to advise your sister-in-law on any money matters,' they almost seemed to gloat. I asked Frank if there was anything we could do to protect her from them, but he said of course there wasn't.

Poor Mollie, she deserved some help, after all those years at Penelope's beck and call, subject to her erratic demands, never knowing what to expect next. I'd only really realised years later what a tyrant Penelope had been when Mollie had been staying with her before the war. And now poor Mollie, with three small children, and a financial struggle to keep them all looked after, was not included in the will at all. And I was sure now that Penelope would never offer any help on her own account. Once she made up her mind she would never change it. She would never forgive what she considered Mollie's desertion when she had moved back to London and married Teddy at the beginning of the war. I could see that. Poor Mollie. Perhaps Arthur had never forgiven her either for her Belgian escapade. He was curiously conventional, Arthur, despite his irony, as if to live by convention was all that his childhood had left to him. We left after the funeral feeling somewhat uneasy. I sometimes wondered if women deserved to have been given the vote at all, when it seemed they could be so undependable.

And then the way the young things were starting to behave in a most inconsequential way. The papers were full of accounts of wild parties, and frivolous goings on, women were becoming so undignified it seemed. There was bobbed hair (if only girls realised men much preferred long hair) they wore short dresses now in the day, and long revealing dresses made of that new cloth called artificial silk, in the evening. I had to admit such materials could have a kind of glamour if they were worn with discretion. Women sometimes took to wearing trousers, if only they knew what men felt about that. (Frank says he thinks the glimpse of an ankle under a long skirt to be far more attractive than an uncovered length of leg). Trousers are so undignified. There was that most inelegant of dances, the Charleston, which no one could call graceful by any stretch of imagination (good exercise, some wag had said.) If only they would realise that one didn't have to ape men to seem emancipated. Quite the reverse, in fact, it only made them seem childish and immature. 'No good will come of it,' I said to Frank, 'women will lose the respect of their menfolk, and then where will we all be?'

Frank agreed with me. 'It's the way the Prince of Wales behaves,' he said, 'touring around the commonwealth, womanising, wild parties, encouraging the adoration of the ladies, and then treating them so badly. That young man will never make a good King, like George V his father, he'll never earn the people's respect.' Frank, like me, was beginning to feel that he lived in a world he could no longer understand. For a King to behave like that, it almost amounted to treason against the monarchy.

Frank teased me about my adamant opposition to the drinking of all alcohol. We had just been reading about prohibition and the development of gang warfare in America. I had always campaigned for total abolition as he well knew. Now I could see such a ban might produce worse evils than it tried to solve if the States was anything to go by. If only men, and women too for that matter, could be taught to have more self control.

Frank and I got tired of discussing a world which seemed to be so full of insoluble problems, and took refuge in the pleasure we felt in talking to our grandchildren. They called him Baba, I have no idea why, and me Banna, it's odd how such nicknames get invented by young children.

Poor Mollie, she was having bad luck with her children. Harold was an attractive little fair-haired boy, with the brightest of blue eyes, but, with such temper that his father was frightened for his health. Harold would sometimes turn blue with rage as he held his breath and wouldn't let go. Teddy said the only thing he could think of was to plunge him into a tub of cold water, for this at least made the boy take a deep breath. I said I thought this seemed a bit drastic but Teddy insisted he feared for the boy's life if something drastic wasn't done at such times.

Mary by now was over two, but had never said a word. 'I think perhaps she is very backward,' Mollie said, 'she is a dreamy kind of child, although she seems to understand perfectly well what is said to her.' I suggested she might be tongue-tied, and a doctor might be consulted. 'It's nothing physical, I don't think, but she was a breech baby, you remember, and she was turning blue under that cowl before it could be removed. But we'll wait and see. I don't believe in medical interference unless it is essential.'

They had bad luck with the house they lived in. 'Fancy all that fire from one match,' Harold said, as he held my hand and we surveyed the blackened trees around his woodland home. I had come down for the day on hearing of the recent forest fire that could have been the cause of a real tragedy. The burned trees were too close to the house for comfort. It is true the fire brigade had come promptly, when summoned, and the flames were soon under control.

'That does it,' said Teddy, as he joined us on our tour of inspection, 'we are moving somewhere safer as soon as possible. This place was getting a bit small for us anyway.' 'I was only trying to burn some of the rubbish out at the back,' Mollie said, 'it is the long hot summer that made everything so dry, that was the real cause of the fire. It's hardly likely to happen again. I like this house in the wood, I don't really want to move, we can manage perfectly well as we are.' 'I don't think the smoke will have done the baby any good,' said Teddy, 'we are moving, and that's that.'

The new house was called Woodland cottage, although thankfully there were no trees round the house this time. A pleasant enough place, closer to the village, with more rooms. By switching the beds round it looked as if Frank and I would sometimes be able to stay for a day or two without getting too much in the way. I was a bit worried about the canal which was nearby, water is always something to be wary of when there are small children to be considered. 'I'll see they learn to swim,' Mollie said.

They were delighted with their new neighbours, Mollie said it was nice not to feel as isolated as they had done in the middle of the wood. 'I was explaining to Mrs Noel who lives in the house at the end of the lane,' recounted Mollie, 'that Mary couldn't talk yet. 'I shouldn't worry,' Mrs Noel had replied, 'she has already introduced herself to me. "I'm Mary, and I'm two narf," she announced when I saw her this morning. A very self-possessed young lady. She can obviously talk if she has a mind to.'

The new baby was christened Anne at Crookham church. As a grandmother, I was delighted that my friend Kate Pearson was asked to be one of her godparents. It is a pretty little church, a very happy day. Kate is always so helpful. I asked her about Nancy's eyes, (for some strange reason she was always called Nancy, not Anne. I suppose Anne is rather a hard sounding name) I thought the poor little thing had trouble focusing her eyes properly. 'It is too soon to tell,' said Kate, 'but in a year or two it might be worth consulting an optician.'

'I don't think,' I said to Teddy, 'that it is quite safe to take Mollie and the children around in that red sidecar of yours any longer, they might easily fall out.' 'Don't worry', he said, 'they are quite safe strapped in.'

'Now that Mollie thinks she is pregnant again, she can hardly be expected in her condition to control three small children bouncing about in a sidecar.'

'It is what I need to get to Aldershot and back, I am still working for the army you know, and besides we couldn't possibly afford a car just yet.' I could say no more, but I was still worried about the way they dashed round the countryside in that ungainly contraption. 'I would prefer you not to interfere in our domestic arrangements,' Mollie said the next day. 'I was only...' I said. 'Well don't,' she answered.

Mary came to stay with us when John was born. I could manage quite well since we had a girl living in at the time. Frank and I found Mary delightful company. Not that she said much. 'Tado' she demanded one lunch time, which I interpreted as potato. 'Please,' I said. 'Please,' she copied me. At least, I thought, I can teach her some new words, and some manners. Frank played cooking with her, just as he had done with Mollie when she was small. Frank loved small children, he was so good with them. He had a magic lantern, with pictures of Egypt and Greece, he had a real interest in history. 'Magic, magic,' Mary said, delightedly, staring at the pictures with big eyes.

'I've a surprise for you,' I said to Mary one day, 'you just wait until teatime,' I had managed to have Nancy fetched by Kate to come and visit us just for a few hours. It would give Mollie a rest in any case. How she managed to cope with all those children, with only a daily help I can't imagine. However I could see by Mary's expression that the presence of Nancy was not a nice surprise at all. She scowled, and her face fell. It was stupid of me perhaps, I think Mary had come to regard Frank and me as her personal property, not to be shared by any other member of her family. One has to be so careful of a small child's feelings.

It was soon after that Nancy became seriously ill with an ear infection. A sheet soaked in disinfectant was hung across the bedroom door. The children were admonished to keep quiet and out of the way so as not to disturb their little sister. I came down to Crookham to see if there was anything I could do to help, but I felt I was only in the way. I went away thinking of hushed voices, long faces, unnatural quiet, and a feeling of admiration for the way those small children, usually so noisy and unruly, now took such careful note of what they had been told, and crept about the house as quietly as mice.

It took some weeks for her to recover, and then on the doctor's advice she had her tonsils taken out. Her eyes were tested, and she became less clumsy, much more aware of her surroundings once she had some proper glasses. She was a tubby little thing, with lovely curly hair, rather like her mother at that age. She had had quite a struggle, with one thing another so early in life. Perhaps that's why she was so prone to sudden wild tantrums.

Harold and Mary were attending the army children's school, with a splendid lady called Miss Seed in charge. It seemed a very good school, the children got on well, Teddy said. Teddy bought a car, a sunbeam, how proud he was of that car. Mollie soon learned to drive. 'You will be able to take the children to school,' Teddy said. The arrangement worked quite well for a while, but she soon gave up, because the car got stuck in the ditch while she was turning it in the road. Along came two young men in a large car who with the help of ropes, managed to pull the car out for her. They seemed to think it rather fun, she reported. 'They were very polite and helpful,' she said, considering they were the Prince of Wales and the Duke of York.' You never can be sure with Mollie, she loves jokes and fantasies. The two young men said perhaps she was finding driving rather difficult. She took their advice and never drove again. She never did get on very well with mechanical things. She is like Fanny in that she finds it difficult to make out how all these inventions are supposed to work. She is not nearly so clumsy as Fanny, however, in whose hands things always seem to come to pieces.

*

I turn my thoughts to the present once more, I discover Fanny has just burnt her hand making some toast, so I put on some cream and cover up the reddening blister.

"Don't make such a fuss," she says.

"You need to look after yourself," I say, "We all need to be more careful especially at our age."

"Well, I am less clumsy than I used to be aren't I?" she protests.

I am glad to say her gall bladder condition is improving. Slippery eel is a horrible concoction but it seems to be keeping the pain at bay. Of course it is difficult to tell, Fanny never was one for complaining. She does seem rather tired though sometimes.

We had a letter this morning from Teddy. 'Now that you say Fanny is better, why don't you both come and stay for a week,' he suggested. It is usually Teddy that writes their letters 'All the children are away one way and another, and we would welcome your company. I can easily come and fetch you now petrol rationing is ended, and the new car is very comfortable. The drive wouldn't take more than two hours at the most. It is a very pretty run, I think you would enjoy it,' Teddy always did have a nice way of putting things.

A PS was scribbled at the bottom in Mollie's writing. 'Bring your washing, we have one of these newfangled washing machines.'

"What do you think?" I ask Fanny

"You go," she says, "I'm sure they won't want me."

"Nonsense," I insist, "You know very well they wouldn't ask you unless they meant it."

"Well, they would have to ask me, wouldn't they? I don't want to be in the way."

"You know you like being in the country."

"They do have a very nice garden, I know. It looked so pretty that day we went to Mary's wedding. But Mollie is your daughter, not mine"

"And what has that got to do with it? It would be very inconsiderate of you not to accept such a kind invitation. I know how much you like sitting in that garden

"It'll be too cold at this time of year to sit out."

"Well come for my sake then, you know I couldn't leave you here on your own"

"I'm sure they don't want an old fogy like me to stay, I'd only be a nuisance."

"Well, I want you to come to keep me company"

"I've got no clothes I could wear"

"If you really think that, we'll go and buy some more." We looked at each other and suddenly laughed.

"You goose," I say, "You know you really want to come." And so it was decided.

A garden is a lovesome thing, God wot!

Rose plot,

Fringed pool,

Fern'd grot

The veriest school

Of peace; and yet the fool

Contends that God is not –

Not God! in gardens! when the eve is cool?

Nay, but I have a sign;

'Tis very sure God walks in mine.

Brown, I say, Thomas Edward Brown. I looked at Fanny in astonishment. All the years we have known each other, and she has never before quoted poetry at me.

"I didn't know you had such a poetic interest" I say.

"You don't know everything about me, do you?" she answered. It was quite perturbing to know she kept such a thing from me all these years. How do people ever know much about each other.

"I learned it years ago," she said, "It's the only poem I can still remember."

I wrote back accepting the invitation, and suggesting a date. My eyes are still quite good, but my hand is rather wobbly these days. I hope it can be read. We walked down the road to the post office, to make sure it got sent straight away. We felt quite light-hearted at the prospect. Mollie is such a dear, and Teddy always so kind. It would do Fanny the world of good.

"You know", said Fanny as we walked back "a holiday is just what you need. I've noticed you have been a bit off colour these last few weeks." I hoped some of the children would be at home.

*

London Life

I have always been proud of my grandchildren. I take out some photographs so I can look at them as I lie in bed. It is difficult to get to sleep sometimes. I go through the pictures I have of them when they were young. Frank at one time got all the children little sailor suits from his store, it was the fashion then, and they all looked so neat and happy as they stood there obediently while Teddy took their picture with his new camera. If only you could read the future of children – or perhaps it is better not to.

I have a photo taken one bright summer's day when we were enjoying a picnic with the children at Dogmasfield Lake, quite a big expanse of water beside the canal. There were two of us to keep an eye on the children, who seemed to be enjoying themselves immensely paddling about in the shallows. We were having a serious conversation, Mollie and I. Mollie didn't want to leave the countryside and move into town, and Teddy couldn't see how they could manage unless they did.

'There's the children's education to consider,' I pointed out, 'especially the boys. They will need a good prep school to start with, and then if they are any good, they can get a scholarship to one of the public schools.' 'They will have a much better education roaming around the countryside than the restrictions of streets in a London suburb could ever offer them,' she retorted. 'There's Teddy, too, you must see you need to consider him, now he has done so well in his accountancy examinations and become a partner in a firm in London. Just think of all the travelling he would be subjected to if he had to travel backwards and forwards from here everyday to the City.' 'It's a very good train service to Fleet', Mollie said. 'That's not the point', I argued, 'he would still have to get the two miles or so home from the station. Besides he will need your support, entertaining clients and so on. You can hardly do that, stuck out in the country all the time.' 'We will be much better off here, if all these threatened strikes come about,' she said. 'I have never liked living in a town. The most important thing,' she insisted, 'is that the children should be happy.' 'And what about their prospects when they are no longer children,' I pointed out. Mollie could be very obstinate.

Mollie rushed into the water to pull out Mary who had fallen in. She had just stumbled over, but she was very wet. We hung her clothes out to dry on the trees, I can see them here in this picture.' Just think what it would be like if one of them stumbled into the canal one day,' I said.

I was commissioned to find a suitable house for them all in London, close to Frank and me in Frewin Road at Wandsworth Common. Frank and I between us arranged to rent a big house in Nightingale Lane. I liked the sound of that, at least Mollie might find it reminded her of the country. It was a big house, three stories and a basement, we were lucky I thought to get it at such a reasonable rent. There would be room for some of the children to have their own rooms. The house reminded me a little of the Huddersfield house where I grew up.

They all moved in. Arrangements were made for Harold to go to a local prep school, from where he would be able to take the scholarship examinations to a public school. Mary and Nancy went to a private girls' school, very suitable I thought, and quite near home. I had been to one of their open school days, and watched the children with their singing and piano playing. They taught French too at an early age. Very suitable, we all agreed. John wasn't yet old enough for school, but he could later follow in his brother's footsteps.

'I told you it was a mistake to move into London,' Mollie said a few months later. A General Strike had been declared. 'I thought the idea of having that Labour Prime Minister Ramsey McDonald was to prevent such unrest,' I said to Frank. 'There's bound to be violence on the streets, now, and we shall be taken over by the communists any day now.' 'Don't be silly', Teddy said, 'it will all be over in a day or two if we keep our heads.'

There was violence of course, when there are strikes there always seems to be violence. Many people volunteered to take over the jobs of the strikers, especially the transport. Teddy volunteered among many others to drive a bus. I think he quite enjoyed the change, although he frightened us by stories of bricks being thrown, and bus windows broken as the strikers tried to attack those whom they labelled black leg labourers. Those were exciting times. I think everyone had considerable sympathy for the workers, but ruining the economy wouldn't have helped them or anyone else. I wished someone could explain to them that changing governments would make little difference to world trade, and they would only succeed in making things much worse for themselves and everyone else, much worse in fact than they already were.

'It's no good thinking,' Frank said, 'that ignoring what goes on in the world can protect one from the consequences. Business is very bad, this strike has made things much worse. I don't know how Teddy will get on with his new firm in the city in all this turmoil. As for Francis, he will go his own way.' 'A doctor is always needed,' I said, 'a doctor will always be able to earn a good living, he has plenty of rich patients.' Arthur is also a doctor, a qualified radiologist now, and I don't suppose it will affect him either, except perhaps he will have more broken bones to X-ray.' I had never heard Frank speak so before, he was usually gentle and optimistic, not a cynical kind of man at all. I began to wonder if perhaps he wasn't feeling quite well.

The strike was over, and the rich seemed hardly to have been touched by it. They had enjoyed playing at bus and train drivers for a short interlude, and now they continued their dancing, their wild parties, and their cruises in those luxury liners. It was no wonder the strikers felt bitter. When I was young it seemed to me that the well-to-do had a much stronger social conscience.

People kept flying about in aeroplanes and seaplanes. More and more people got telephones and wirelesses, and cars. Everything seemed to be moving around so fast, it began to make one feel quite giddy.

I was upstairs in the house in Nightingale Lane with Mollie, we were dressing Ruth the new baby ready to go out to the shops. 'Fire, help fire!' we heard the children shriek from downstairs. Mollie turned pale, stuffed Ruth into my arms, shouting get her out quickly, and ran. I've never seen Mollie run so fast, I feared she would trip on all those stairs. I just stood there, I am ashamed to say, transfixed, my heart thumping, I felt like fainting. It was remembering the fire when my shoulder was burned all those years ago. You never get over a real experience of fire. The pause was only momentary. I followed Mollie down as quickly as I dared, fearful lest I should injure the bundle in my arms.

'Don't be cross,' Mary was saying, 'I had to throw the towel on the fire when it caught alight. I couldn't think what else to do.' I could see the flames were still roaring up the chimney with the heat of the coals and the burning towel. 'You nearly let us get burnt,' young John said accusingly. 'When it's raining there is nowhere else to dry the towels except in front of the fire,' Mollie said, by way of explanation. 'The fire must have been hotter than I thought.'

Mollie refused to live in a house with so many storeys, so many stairs to climb up and down. I made no objection, how could I, thinking of her racing down those stairs, she was lucky not to have done herself an injury. They all moved into a modern house in Ellerton Road. True, there were the allotments at the back of the houses, and you never knew who might be lurking about in an allotment. But it was certainly more convenient, and much nearer to Frank and me. Not nearly so good a neighbourhood of course, and modern houses are more expensive, but as Mollie said what did that matter.

I liked to watch Frank with his grandchildren. I think he was fondest of the girls. He played bezique with Mary, took Ruth out for little walks, and did his best not to be put out by Nancy's tantrums. He always looked at her in a gentle puzzling way, but she wasn't to be wooed. But she and Mary both behaved beautifully when I took them to the House of Hope meeting where they presented charity purses to the Countess. They were both dressed in white, how pretty they looked. I was really proud of them.

Mollie was still unhappy to be living in London so Frank and I took them all for a country holiday to Ash, a pretty wooded place where the children picked wild raspberries and strawberries, and Frank cut himself a Holly walking stick from the woods. Teddy couldn't be there all the time, he was too busy, he worked far too hard. I don't think Mollie much liked the boarding house, but it was all right, if not luxurious. The food was not exactly exciting. Frank tried to improve things by putting hot pepper on his meat, and the top of the pepper pot fell off. 'You can't possibly eat that now,' I said, seeing the pile of pepper on his plate. 'Don't make a fuss,' he insisted. He even managed to eat some of his meal, but it must have made his mouth burn. Frank was never one for making a fuss.

Harold got his scholarship to Merchant Tailors School. Mary got on worse at school than ever. She was eight and still couldn't read much. 'The letters all get jumbled up when someone tells me to read out loud,' she explained. She didn't complain, but it was Nancy who told me when I fetched them from school one day that poor Mary had been made to read to the class below, the one in which Nancy was doing quite well, as a punishment for not trying hard enough. 'She's not stupid, you know,' Nancy said, 'she just doesn't like people looking at her.' I bought them both a frozen fruit ice from a passing Walls ice cream 'Stop Me and Buy One' tricycle. I didn't at all approve of children eating things in the street, but we were almost home.

I had great pride in taking my grandchildren to visit my friends. They were surprisingly well behaved as a rule. I took them one day to see my Jewish friend Jacob who lived down the road, I'd made his acquaintance while raising money for the House of Hope. He had been giving me very good advice on their money matters for some time now. The children enjoyed themselves, Jacob was a great entertainer. He made oranges and lemons appear out of nowhere, gave them the pennies he extracted from out of their ears, and made them believe in a mouse he was pretending to chase round the room.

'Do Jews come from far away like little black Sambo in my reading book,' Nancy asked as we walked home. I explained that Jews lived in England, just like us, but did some things differently. 'Can we be Jewish,' Mary asked, 'because then we could be different like them, and do magic tricks.'

I don't know why Mollie insisted the children would be better off living in the country. After all they had the allotments and the Common to play on, there were plenty of young children they could make friends with. Frank and I could always look after the children, should they wish to entertain , or to go out for the evening. Mollie wasn't always wise, I thought, to put the children before the needs of Teddy's business. He still had his way to make, and with all those children to feed, well they couldn't live on air.

A man came to the door offering to draw portraits of all the children from a photograph. Mollie was always inclined to accept suggestions from people calling at the door. I must admit I appreciated the drawings when they were done. Handsome Harold with his fair complexion; Mary with her solemn look and dark hair fringe; Nancy with her curls and obstinate mouth; John with his pert, interested expression, and Ruth sitting smiling among the daisies in the garden. Those pictures have given me much pleasure through the years.

Missing The Family

'We are moving back to Crookham,' Mollie announced one day. 'We have no reason to stay in London any longer, Teddy and I have agreed. Harold can be a boarder at Merchant Taylor's and there are schools near Crookham the other children can go to.' Crookham had always been where Mollie wished to be, she had never been really happy anywhere else. But how Frank and I shall miss the children. Who would have thought her wild adolescent behaviour would have resulted in this, a longing for the quiet life of the country.

'At least we are not likely to find thieves in the country,' Mollie said. She was still feeling upset by the loss of a cigarette box. One of the numerous down and outs trying to sell things at the door had gone off with it she thought. 'I know it wasn't real silver,' she said, 'but it looked like it. I hope he isn't too disappointed when he tries to sell it. It was a nice box, now I shall have to get another to pass cigarettes to our friends. I can't very well just offer them an open packet.' 'Teddy has his silver cigarette case I gave him, hasn't he,' I ask. 'Yes' she said, 'but then he is not always here, is he?'

They found a house at Crookham called The Haven, at the other end of the little lane where they used to live. It had lots of small rooms in it, with an old stables at the bottom of the garden where the children could play. 'Ideal', said Teddy, and Mollie has already found someone who will help in the house.'

I suppose it was quite a sensible house really, it had fire grates in all the rooms, although it seemed to have a lot of draughty corridors with, I remember, a green linoleum covering. I suppose it will be easy to wash them I thought, they will need to be kept clean when there are all those small feet about. There was ample gas lighting downstairs, although I still worried about the candles the children would have to carry about upstairs after dark.

A kind neighbour was soon commandeered to teach John and Ruth their letters. Nancy took a great liking to writing little poems, very imaginative some of them were I thought. Perhaps it was a way of her expressing her frustration. I told Mollie Mary should be given the chance to have a good education at a High school. Mary was enrolled at Farnham Grammar half an hour's bus journey to travel twice a day, and then she had to walk half a mile home. It meant she left home early and came back late, a long day for a nine year old. I remember one day she got scolded for accepting a ride with the milkman, coming home on the back of his motorbike. It remanded me of my childish ride with the coachman. She never seemed very happy at that school, I think she got teased a lot.

I persuaded Mollie to take in one of the unfortunate children the House of Hope home was responsible for, a boy who had been badly injured in a car accident. He came from the slums, and he had no family to care for him. He was a kind of curiosity to the children. I brought some pears to distribute on our arrival, much better than sweets, I thought. 'I ate my pear,' John announced. 'I loiked mine' said the boy. I could see communication might be difficult. He stayed an uneasy three weeks. The children, Mollie said, were polite but mystified.

I could see Mollie and Teddy felt at home now they were back in Crookham. They seemed pleased to be surrounded by those retired Indian army officers and their wives, with whom they often played bridge, even sometimes far into the night, I was surprised to hear from the children. They had a great friend, a Miss Cheetham, who lived at a house called The Kop. It amused her and Teddy greatly to suggest there must be something about Miss Cheetham, the retired Matron of an army hospital who lived at The Kop at Crookham. She should have been an army redcap, arresting people, they joked.

What energy young people have. Teddy travelled every day to London, sometimes he fell asleep in the train, and had an extra journey coming back from Basingstoke, the next station along the line. Quite often he had to spend the night in London. He went to a Turkish bath, he said, because he could sleep when he needed to, and which he said cost a great deal less than any lodging.

I began to realise Frank might not be too well. Not that he complained of anything. I did notice he kept getting hiccups. They usually were cured with a glass of water, we didn't think much of it at the time, he teased me about the cooking. But he seemed tired, listless somehow. It was while I was on a visit to Crookham, in the middle of distributing my small presents to the children, that a message came to say he was really ill. Of course I went straight back to London. It was serious, the doctor said, he had cancer of the pancreas, and probably only had a few weeks to live. How I wished I had stayed at home, to have been there when he was told the news. He was such an amenable patient, concerned about me rather than himself. He died a month later. Such a kind man, a saint almost, one could say. How alone I felt now. I began to realise more and more how much I had depended on him. He had never interfered, but he seemed always to be there when I needed him.

Why is it repeating lines of poetry to oneself seems to bring some kind of comfort in loneliness. I had taken sometimes to walking by myself across the common. One day I found myself repeating those forgotten words to myself.

Frosted diamonds greet the morning sun
As I walk lonely under listening trees.
The distant calls of waking birds relieves
The silence of a new day half begun
The yellow sun above the treetops stands
Brown frosted leaves are crushed against the ground
And twigs that snap the air with sudden sound
Breath misty breath. Chill morning understands
The touch of death. But desperation cries
Back from cold earth my stolen love. Quiet tears
Flow in desolation. A breath of hope
Stirs the dead past. Comfort the world denies
Nor gives a meaning. But in those happy years
We listened wondering at the blackbird's note.

How strange that I should bring back to mind those words after all these years. I suppose it was the blackbird singing.

I didn't feel like carrying on with the work of the House of Hope. For one thing there were all those titled ladies taking an interest. I suppose the publicity was good for funds, but now there seemed to be a different kind of atmosphere, of ladies feeling they needed a cause to be compassionate about. I didn't feel they were really interested in the mothers and their children. There is a subtle kind of difference between those who feel themselves to be philanthropic, and those who feel a genuine interest in individuals. I had been feeling a little uneasy for the last few years in such company. Now I regretfully admitted to myself that I no longer seemed to have any desire to continue. I resigned from the Committee saying I must leave the work to others.

I and my maid Florence lived a lonely isolated life together, so after a while I got a wireless and started to listen to the BBC. We liked listening to Jack Payne's and then Henry Hall's band music, and some of the Music Hall turns would make us laugh together. What I didn't like was that it seemed to bring the worries of the world closer, like the Wall Street crash in America and all those ruined people; Roosevelt; the Nazis in Germany; one got the impression that thugs and gangsters were getting the upper hand all over the world, there seemed to be a kind of collective madness invading people's minds. I didn't want to think about it. The King was ill. I was feeling old. The modern politicians in their usual inept way seemed to be making a muddle of the world again. God forbid there should be another war.

My family did come to see me sometimes, though they seemed increasingly like strangers. Francis came once, but seemed distant, it was like having a consultation with a family doctor. 'Let me know', he said, 'if you have further trouble with your bronchitis.' Teddy dropped in sometimes when he was staying overnight in London, and he always had something interesting to say. He had always liked talking about politics, and most of the time he was optimistic. 'I would like to stand for Parliament one day,' he suggested. He often seemed very tired and was liable to fall asleep in the armchair. Mollie was busy at home with all those children.

Arthur was working as a radiologist in a London hospital for a while, and came to talk about his plans. So many doctors and nurses in this family. I never knew if he would arrive bright and cheerful, or if I would find he was in one of his increasingly black moods of despondency. He was offered work in Edinburgh. Then he wrote to say he had met a girl called Martha and wished to marry her. He brought her to see me one day, she seemed nice enough, you could tell she had good manners and important family connections. I was a bit doubtful if such a marriage would last, there seemed something strangely missing in the way they regarded one another. I didn't feel like going to the wedding, Edinburgh is a long way to travel, but I gave them my blessing and hoped against hope that they would be happy together.

Connie came quite often, she was lonely like me. I was fond of Connie, she had had a difficult time. She could be very irritating, nevertheless I felt at home with Connie. She was always worrying about her son, his health, did he have the right clothes, did the school see that he was kept warm enough. At the same time, despite my expressing some anxiety, she insisted he should stay at his present boarding school although she knew he hated it. Her care for him was a strange mixture of over protection and an inability to understand his real needs.

Sometimes I would visit Fanny, especially if I knew her friend Annie would be out. Their patient Josey was a good-natured harmless woman, but those horrible little Pekingese dogs were always a trial.

*

Fanny is shaking me and asking me if I want my tea, as it will be cold by now, or shall she pour me another one. I hastily try to bring my thoughts back to the present. For a moment I am still in the past, I think I can hear one of those yapping dogs, and then realise it is the noise of our local Worthing postman putting letters through the door. I open a letter from Connie that Fanny hands to me.

Fanny and I have finished our breakfast.

"You haven't said a word" she says, "for the past half hour. You've been sitting there as if you were in another world."

"Well, I'm back in this one now" I say grumpily. I don't like having my thoughts interrupted.

I pick up the paper, and read the headlines about the Ground Nut scheme in Africa.

"The only difference between ordinary people and politicians is," I say "is that politicians have the power to make mistakes on an enormous scale. It isn't as if the government had that much money to spare. Indulging in such schemes is highly irresponsible."

It doesn't do for two people to shut themselves up together for too long, it only makes for bad temper and dismal thoughts, I ought to know. Fanny and I have words about that ground nut scheme.

"It's madness, I say, it will never work, just the government's way of wasting more of our money."

"At least they are trying to do something about the continuing food shortage," Fanny says, "you are always complaining they never have any new ideas."

"It's not much use having new ideas if they are the wrong ones" I retort.

"So you know better than the government, I suppose" says Fanny, and she mutters something uncomplimentary under her breath about my always knowing better than anyone else. I never take much notice of such little outbursts.

I have made a little plan to cheer us both up.

"We are going on a shopping expedition today" I tell her.

"What have you forgotten this time?" says Fanny critically, "We were at the corner shop only yesterday morning."

"We are going into town, into Worthing" I explain.

"Whatever for?" says Fanny.

"To do some shopping of course, and have lunch. I have ordered a taxi, it will be here any minute now."

"You go, I think I'd rather stay in."

I ignore her reluctance. I fetch Fanny's coat, and when the taxi arrives I give her no chance to refuse to get in. The taxi driver is very helpful.

"Let me help you two ladies," he says, and hands us in before Fanny can think of anything else to say. It is quite pleasant riding along in the taxi, we drive for a short way along the front.

"I'd forgotten," says Fanny "how well they have tidied things up. They have even planted out some of the flower beds. Everything looks so nice and clean these days."

I took Fanny into several clothes shops.

"You said yourself you needed something new for our visit to Mollie," I say encouragingly, "I don't suppose you have bought anything for yourself since clothes rationing began, or even before that."

Fanny never did take much pride in her appearance, yet I knew she was never quite satisfied with whatever she had on. Perhaps she could never afford to be adventurous enough.

"You can choose whatever you like you know, we don't need coupons any more," I said. I must admit everything she looked at seemed to be dull and uninspiring, or even ridiculous as so many designs are these days, all made for the young people with their "New Look" and flared skirts. Fanny was getting restless.

"Why do clothes always look better on someone else than on me?" she wanted to know.

"Just one more," I say, "We can't go and visit Mollie looking too frumpish, now can we? What about this?"

"I am too tired," she says, "to try on anything else. Each one I try is worse than the last."

We did find something. Fanny looked very nice in her new dress and coat and hat. She protested we were spending far too much money. I tell her not to talk nonsense.

I try to find something for myself. I have worn black ever since Frank died, and I insist on a reasonably long skirt. Being so short and not as slim as I once was, all the clothes seem either far too long, or too small round the waist. I give up.

"What a waste of money," Fanny says, as she looks at herself in the mirror. All the same, I detect a gleam of pleasure in her eyes but it would be foolish to remark on it.

"So what else would you spend it on?" I say. "Let's be extravagant for once. It's not so often these days that we go on holiday. Besides if the government can waste all that money on their mad ground nut scheme cutting down all those trees in Africa then I don't see why we shouldn't waste a little on ourselves."

"What day is it you said we were going to Crookham?" she asks. She is getting a bit forgetful these days.

"Next Monday," I say.

"Will any of the children be there, do you think?"

"The twins perhaps, I'm not sure."

Country Life

At bedtime I go rummaging in my drawer again. I find a scrap of paper with a little rhyme I wrote when the twins were born, I even gave it a title.

The Family

There was a young woman who lived in a shoe
She had only five children and that wouldn't do
We like a lot of children, we've plenty of bread,
She thought, as she counted and kissed them in bed
We must have another, I'd have two for two pins
And being in a hurry she ordered some twins
On the 19th of May 1930 they came
A daughter was first, and the second the same
And the father and mother a little aghast
Said seven's the perfect number at last
The children were as pleased as could be
And agreed that seven makes a perfect family

I remember the day I got the news very well. I was in bed with bronchitis. I often got bronchitis, I always put it down to the burn injury to my chest. The doctor ordered bed and rest, and plenty of fluids. Florence my maid always liked fussing over me. So many cups of tea. I was beginning to feel as if I were drowning.

Mollie with new twins, and all those children, how could she possibly manage. I was on the next train, my bronchitis apparently completely cured. I was soon with Mollie, helping to look after the new babies. Six weeks premature they were, so needed much more care than usual. Mollie not surprisingly was in no fit state to do everything for them that needed to be done. She was not so young any more, forty one is quite late on to give birth to twins. I must say Mollie had good neighbours. They saw the other children were fed and counted, and it was only a few weeks before things were more or less back to normal. I saw that little Mary did her best to help, but she was only eleven, and I thought perhaps her schooling might begin to suffer.

I persuaded Mollie to send John to a boarding prep school with his cousin Francis, I thought the two boys ought to get to know each other better, being of a similar age. The arrangement only lasted a few terms. The two boys seemed to hate each other, and John was miserable there in any case. So he left and for a while he went to school with his sisters at their new school in Fleet. Mollie said it was too complicated to continue to send Mary to Farnham. She had missed the bus home once or twice and worried everyone considerably.

I had warned Mollie that finding suitable schools at Crookham would be a problem, but the two well educated ladies who had moved into Fleet and started the Shrubbery School, seemed to have solved the problem. Mary will be much happier in a smaller school, Mollie said, and she and Nancy can cycle to school together. Harold, of course was away at Merchant Taylor's, he at least had got into a public school.

Those children had a lot of freedom, too much freedom I often thought. They roamed the countryside together, and I was sometimes worried they would come to harm. There were complaints from neighbours about Mary climbing high up into the trees in the garden and frightening the neighbours. Once I was there when they climbed up through the attic skylight and could be seen peering out at the world from the roof of the house. Sometimes they disappeared behind the eaves in the attic loft for hours on end. Mary said and I believed her, that she had practised climbing out of any window in the house should there ever be a fire. I think they had all been frightened by a local tragedy when an old lady they knew got burnt to death in her home.

Harold and the friends he brought home from school would take the whole family for rambles through the bogs and marshes, along the canal, or over the fields, and bless him, he taught them a considerable amount of botany. One day when I was visiting, they all, except for Harold, came back looking like drowned rats. Apparently they had failed in trying to jump across a stream and had fallen in instead. Mollie seemed quite unperturbed. One day Nancy fell into the canal. I saw the last bit of her leg disappearing under the water, Mary said, so I got hold of it and pulled. Mollie still seemed unperturbed.

They had a room they called the nursery, on which they practised their house decoration skills, no matter that some of the wallpaper was put on upside down. One of their playthings was a large fire guard, which they supposed a pulpit, and John would give sermons as we all sat listening solemnly to his words. Better sermons I think they were than many I heard at church when I was young.

I think Mollie had realised at last that they would be safer if they learned to swim. They all became expert swimmers. There were two young men who had teamed up together to build a swimming pool and tennis courts at the edge of the smaller of the two Fleet ponds. They became friends of the family, and all through the summer Mollie would push the twins in their pram the two miles to the club, so that the children could spend their school lunch break there, mostly as far as I could see actually in the pool. They could all soon swim like fish, the twins at four years old thinking nothing of diving in off the diving boards.

How lucky they are, I thought, as I stood looking at their happy faces one day. I had been sitting reading stories in the papers of the bread lines in America with all those starving workers and their families. It is bad enough here with the depression, but nothing like it is over there. Roosevelt had seemed to be improving things, I thought, but now they say he is being blocked in his plans for reform. There is no end to the folly of human nature. Politicians always make me feel depressed.

Don't put more into your mouth than you can swallow, I said sharply to one of the twins, I forget which. I was appalled sometimes by their table manners. It seemed as if they had no notion about saying please and thank you, waiting for their elders to sit down, asking to leave the table, or even how to use a knife and fork in an acceptable way. They would suddenly disappear under the table if they felt aggrieved. We are talking to our friends Peddy and Gentules they would explain. You can imagine how unsettling it was to have children crawling round one's legs.

I remember one day when I said they shouldn't answer their mother back, that one of them threw a lump of sugar at me, which hit me by chance on the end of my nose. After a few stunned moments of silence I began to laugh, I couldn't help it, seeing the look on that row of anxious faces. I worried though, when they often seemed so rude and antagonistic if I tried to correct them. However will they get on in company, I wondered.

I don't know where Mollie found the energy but she was soon involved in raising money for their local hospital. First it was a garden party. I gave her the script of a little play I once wrote for some children, called 'Prince Uglyface' which the family performed. The advantage of a large family is that they can so easily be coached to take the principal parts. The audience loved them. I watched once as John threw himself to the ground in pretended self disgust as he took the part of the prince whose bad temper made him seem so ugly. Ruth was a sweet Princess Charming. I remember the refrain that the Wise woman pronounced as a cure for the Prince.

> Three good deeds done every day
> Three kind words which you must say
> Three kind gifts either great or small
> Three bright smiles to sweeten all.

I went once with Mollie and the children to a sports day at Merchant Tailors school to watch Harold and his friends. The Duke of York was there with two little princesses. It was a difficult occasion for both the Headmaster and the Duke. They both stuttered terribly.

'Yourr Mmmajesty, wwwwwe are hhhonoured ttttto hhhhave yyyyou with uuus tttoday,' Mr Leeson the headmaster said.

'It ggives mmme ggreat ppppleasure tttto oopen this sssports day' The Duke replied. They had visitors' races, I remember and Mary won a silver teapot in the sisters' race.

Mollie started writing pantomimes, to be performed each Christmas. It seemed all the children in the village joined in as well as any visiting friends. I remember one little deaf boy who enjoyed himself tremendously. His part as Prime Minister consisted of a single line repeated at intervals. Whoever was standing next to him was instructed to give him a little nudge every time he had to repeat it.

Teddy opened an office at Fleet, and did not have to go to London every day, I was thankful to hear. Mollie let the children learn to ride a horse, as if they hadn't had enough hazards to contend with. 'They need the exercise,' she said, 'especially in the winter.' When Teddy joined them one day and fell off and quite badly hurt himself I said I told you so. But the children still went on riding.

I saw them all on horseback one day when the village was celebrating the King's jubilee. They represented all the Tudors in the village parade. Harold wasn't there, at school I suppose. John was Henry VII; Nancy Henry VIII; Mary, Mary Tudor; Ruth Queen Elizabeth, and the twins Edward VI and Lady Jane Grey. Nancy made a marvellous Henry VIII, but I wished she was not quite so plump. I decided to talk to Mollie about it, it is a handicap for a girl to be too plump.

It was soon after that I decided that there was no point in my staying in London any longer, living there on my own, feeling, as widows do, lonely and cut off from everything. I had one friend, true, a widow who lived next door, we would often be in each other's houses, and sometimes go out together. Her sons went to Dulwich College. But I was feeling restless, was this to be the pattern of things for the rest of my life? I decided something had to be done.

Teddy helped me to buy a house which was situated in the little lane which ran beside The Haven. The lady who had owned it (The one who had taught John and Ruth their letters) had just died. It was a curious house, built on a disused concrete roller skating rink, so that all round it was a kind of concrete terrace. But it had a garden full of apple trees, and seemed quite comfortable. I found my faithful Florence a new post in London, no way could I persuade her to move into the country with me. If she used the money I gave her wisely, she would be well provided for until her small pension became available. I rather regretfully said goodbye to my Wandsworth house, wondering at the last minute as one does, if I had decided to do the right thing.

It is quite an effort to move to new surroundings when you are seventy-four. Of course Teddy and Mollie were kindness itself, but I found the houseful of children rather overpowering. The children did come and visit me sometimes, they enjoyed picking up the numerous fallen apples in my garden. I pointed out that they should wash them before they ate them. They didn't come so often after that. Mary came and cooked for me sometimes. I didn't see so much of Teddy and Mollie as I would have liked. I felt somewhat de trop.

It was a few months later when I had a message from Penelope's housekeeper, a Mrs Draycott. It had been sent to my old London address some two weeks ago and had only just arrived at Crookham.

> *Dear Madam,*
>
> *I am giving in my notice as housekeeper to Mrs Winder. Her strange behaviour of late has made it impossible for me to stay longer. She has needed constant attention for some time now, and I do not feel I can provide for her as I would wish. I cannot get her to see a doctor. Her behaviour has become so strange I fear an injury to myself. It is urgent that some new arrangement is made for her.*
>
> *I am sorry for the trouble, but her lawyers said to get in touch with you and gave me your address.*
>
> *As ever your obedient servant,*
>
> *Mrs H Draycott. Housekeeper*

Those lawyers, I had been most particular in giving them my new address, though I might just as well not have bothered. I had impressed on them many times to inform me immediately should anything need attending to. You can never trust a lawyer.

I travelled up to St Anne's the next day and saw that drastic measures would immediately have to be taken. Penelope I found could be quite violent at times, and certainly should never ever be left on her own. The wonder was Mrs Draycott had stayed so long and managed so well up to now. I contacted the lawyers with some difficulty, and had a problem persuading them that extra money would be needed. A doctor's conference was arranged to certify as to her condition, and the necessary arrangements set in motion for the employment of two nurses.

Of course I felt guilty, had I not promised Arthur that I would look after Penelope. Not that I hadn't tried. Each time I had attempted to arrange a visit, I had been met with antagonism, and it was plain I would not be welcome. Indeed I did once travel all the way up North to have the door slammed in my face. 'All you want is my money,' she shouted at me. 'Get out.' So I went.

I could see immediately when I arrived that she was past ordinary medical help. Indeed she was so violent when the doctors came that they had to restrain her. I said that I would stay to see she was properly looked after. Fate seemed to have intervened once again. I was very grateful to Mrs Draycott for saying she would stay as housekeeper, a most capable woman was Mrs Draycott.

I left Teddy to sort out the house at Crookham. He and Mollie said they thought it best if they moved into Greengates for the time being. 'We can keep your furniture there for you,' they explained, 'and if ever you should need to come back, we can move out and let you live there once again.' 'Won't Greengates prove to be too small for all of you,' I wrote. 'The children are growing up', Mollie replied, 'we would soon be finding the Haven was too big. We'll manage, one way or another.' And so it was decided.

I do admit I was quite pleased to be feeling useful once again. It was a nice house my brother Arthur had bought when he retired there those many years ago, near the front at St Anne's. It was a good arrangement. I wouldn't feel I was tied too much, for I could soon have the nurses trained to my ways. I could go out whenever I felt like it. In a way I felt I had gained a new kind of freedom.

Freedom! Freedom for anyone for how long. There was a feeling of great dread about these days, even my two nurses talked about war fever, as we sat together in the evenings while they did embroidery. I had a plan to get them to make a bed cover for Mary, after all she would probably some day be married I supposed, and it would be such a lovely present for her. It didn't do for those women to sit idle every evening, and I had discovered they had quite a talent for embroidery.

Mary came to stay that summer. To entertain her I took her to the baths at Blackpool, knowing how fond she was of swimming. I wondered if I had done the right thing when I saw her dive off the high board, it looked so far up there above the water. Mollie would never forgive me if she came to any harm. She would stay in the water for hours, but would soon warm up again with a good cup of Horlicks. A daily visit to the baths soon became a kind of routine. Then they held a kind of gala with competitions and races, I remember, for which she seemed to gain a lot of prizes.

'They asked me', Mary said that day in a rather bewildered way, 'if I would like to join the English swimming team. I have to tell them if I can tomorrow. I could stay here couldn't I and train with them. It's an Olympic pool you know and there is something called the Olympic games.' 'I don't think your parents would approve', I say, 'and it might be difficult for you to live here all the time. In any case you may have to take more school exams if you haven't passed your school certificate this year.' I don't think she was all that disappointed. I would have been very worried about her in any case, mixing with all those strange young men.

Trying Not To Believe It

Our dear King George V died and Edward VIII was proclaimed king. Mary wrote to me describing how she had been to see the funeral procession as it wound its way through London to the Abbey, a very grand and solemn occasion she described it as, with people lining the streets in thousands. His death seemed to mark the end of any kind of stability.

The new King was decidedly controversial, an odd mixture, people said, of a playboy and a conventional monarch. He was photographed just wearing shorts, so unconventional, so somehow demeaning, yet at the same time insisted on protocol when a little less formality would have been appropriate. He made pronouncements about doing something for the unemployed miners, without consulting his ministers who were the only people who could try to make any such provision. He made Emily Pankhurst, that champion of Women's rights a Dame of the British Empire, yet treated women as his playthings. Prime Minister Baldwin didn't quite know what to make of him.

Besides world wide financial problems, there was increasing political unrest everywhere. India was asking for independence, with that strange man Gandhi wandering nearly naked round the streets of London. Japan had invaded that wild Chinese province of Manchuria. There had been grave news from Europe with Italy invading Abyssinia, and Germany reoccupying the Rhineland. Armies seemed to be on the march again everywhere.

In England rumours flew around about a certain married American lady called Wallis Simpson who it was said wanted to become Queen of England when she had managed to get a divorce from her present husband. Of course it was very easy to get a divorce in America. 'What is the world coming to,' I said to Teddy on the telephone. Teddy was a great respecter of the monarchy. For instance, he had listened every year since the broadcast of the first of the King's

Christmas messages as if it were a kind of annual ritual, and even stood to attention, I remember, when the National Anthem was played. I knew how upset he would be by all this speculation and gossip.

Even so the abdication came as a sudden shock, when Edward broadcast his message of abdication. 'His brother will make a much better King', Teddy said, 'he has the right notions of what the monarchy is all about. We can all settle down now, and the politicians can get on with trying to keep the world at peace.'

There was the coronation in the Abbey of George VI.

The new King and Queen went to America and were welcomed by huge crowds. The King had nearly overcome his stammer. The world seemed to hold it's breath. There was the Spanish civil war, as if the Germans were playing at making war, except of course such terrible events took place like the bombing of the town of Guernica I knew long ago when flying machines were invented, that they would be responsible for making such dreadful things as the bombing of towns a possibility. Everyone could now see what air power could do. Young men from England enlisted to fight in Spain partly because it offered them adventure, but also because they wished to prevent further atrocities.

The coronation was a spectacle which had somehow been overtaken by events, an almost empty gesture in defiance of the reality of the wickedness of man. More treaties were broken, as the Germans marched on. America became more isolationist, and everyone began to realise that once again war was probably inevitable, however unwilling we might be to admit it. 'The clouds of war are gathering,' someone said, it must have been Churchill. He was about the only politician who seemed to have any idea of what was going on. But of course everyone hoped against hope that something could be done to stop the axis powers from trying to take over the world.

Harold had almost got a scholarship to university. How I wished he had, the academic life was what would have suited him best I always thought. I offered to pay for him, but he would have none of it. Instead he had left school and went to stay with Francis and Connie while he worked in a firm in London. I know he hated it. All his energies went into playing the drums in a band in his spare time, with musicians such as Desmond Duprey. Perhaps he should have been a musician. His talents certainly seemed to be wasted in some kind of office routine.

Mary went to nurse in a hospital. If there is going to be a war, she said, I might as well get trained for something. She had passed her examinations, but had taken the wrong subjects to earn a university place. How philosophical the young people are. They have no idea what war entails. Perhaps it is just as well. John had a place at Blundells School in Tiverton. He was going to be a doctor he said. Nancy went to look after disabled children at Lord Treloa's Home at Alton. Why do most of the family, I wondered, still seem to have such an interest in medicine.

'Peace in our time,' pronounced Neville Chamberlain, waving a bit of paper as he returned from Germany. 'Peace in our time' declared the papers, and the news reels and the wireless bulletins. We knew it wouldn't be true, but preferred to believe it nonetheless.

I invited Mollie to stay at the holiday camp in Blackpool with Ruth and the twins. It might very well be the very last chance I would ever have to see them. War was coming, bombing of cities was coming, men women and children were about to be killed on a scale never before encountered in the history of the world. I didn't expect I would still be alive at the end of another war. Perhaps it was the last time those children would be able to have a happy carefree holiday.

Those three children won all the swimming races between them at that camp. Mollie had certainly fulfilled her promise to see that all the children would learn to swim. The day they gave out the prizes Poland was invaded, and war was declared.

It must have been a nightmare journey back home for them all. When Mollie wrote she described how the train had been filled with soldiers, how they had sat on their suitcases in the crowded corridor because no seats were available, how everything was blacked out and no one knew exactly where they were. It was a long and tedious journey, and they arrived at Fleet after midnight, faced by a three mile walk, with all their luggage to be carried home.

Mollie says to this day she doesn't know who the kind gentleman was who picked them up at the station and took them home. It was so dark she wouldn't have recognised him even had she known him well, as it was he might have been a total stranger, or on the other hand someone she might often meet, but someone to whom she could never acknowledge her debt. The disruption of war was becoming apparent, so too, which I suppose was a comforting thought, was the compensating kindness that somehow always seems to emerge in times of crisis.

*

Shopping is very tiring, especially when it is difficult to find what one wants. But Fanny seems pleased with her new clothes, and in the end I did manage to find myself a much needed new pair of shoes. We had a very satisfactory lunch at the Pavilion too, and we walked the short distance home from there.

After a cup of tea when we got back, we both fell asleep in our chairs. I shan't tell Fanny that I got lost in thinking of the past again, as she still thinks it bad for me to do all that reminiscing. I sometimes wonder what she thinks about all day long.

It is the doorbell that has wakened me. There on the doorstep stands my nephew Steve, and his daughter Claude, I always think of him and his sister Christine as they played with Mollie when they were children together at Forest Hill all those years ago. He lives at Brighton and that is not that very far along the coast from here.

"Now that we find we have got extra petrol I thought we would drop in and see how you two are getting along," he says cheerfully.

"Come in, come in," I say, "It is a pity you didn't phone to tell us you were coming, we could have had something ready for your tea." I suppose it is old age, but these days I don't much like being taken unawares. It's not that I am not pleased to see them, just that I like to have some idea of how to plan things out. Fanny wakes, and we all greet each other affectionately. I go and put the kettle on. There are a few stale biscuits in the tin. That is all there is, so that will have to do.

Steve looks tired. Like all civilian doctors he continued to work too hard throughout the war. Being an ear, nose and throat specialist his skills have always been much in demand. Fanny of course has always had a soft spot for him, as it was his father Tom she once hoped to marry. Tom died a few years ago some time after his wife.

It is sad but all the Allen family of boys are dead now – my Frank, Tom, William the artist, Charlie in Australia, and Walter and Edward who never married but stayed on at the family home of the Hermitage. I think of all those bright and adventurous boys as they played with the cranes on Dowgate wharf and it makes me feel I belong to a past generation, which I do of course. They are gone, all gone, and soon there will be no one left who can remember them any more. Of the next generation there are four cousins – my son Francis, Mollie, Christine with whom she used to have such fun, and of course Steve. Roland and Gordon are the sons of Charles, but they hardly count as they live in Australia and I have never met them.

I ask after the refugee girl Claude cared for during the war.

"Do you know, Aunt Minnie," she says rather plaintively, "I have not heard a word from her since she said she was going back to Austria to look for her family. You'd think she would have written at least, wouldn't you, after all the trouble I took with her." I feel sorry for Claude. Her Belgian mother had to be admitted to an asylum when she was only sixteen, and she has had to look after her father and brother ever since.

We talked a little about our families, I brought down one or two photographs and then we had tea, and then they left. I have always liked Steve, but I wish they had come another day when we were not quite so tired. I fell asleep again and went back to my reverie. Interruptions to my thoughts feel as if I am being woken from a dream I want to remember, but can't quite recall.

*

War

I had said goodbye to Mollie and the children as they left on that train September 1939 to get back home, and I didn't really expect to see any of them ever again. It seemed like the end of the world. Very little could survive the kind of onslaught that we all expected from the German bombs. Explosives, poison gas, even the spread of deadly germs was what everyone expected. The Germans were likely to attack all our cities and reduce them to rubble. The last war had been bad enough. This time it would be far worse. It wouldn't be only soldiers who got killed, but women and children as well.

I was sitting doing *The Times* crossword a few days later, just to keep myself occupied. I didn't want to dwell too much on fears about the war. The two nurses were sitting doing their embroidery, listening to music on the wireless. It was a silly jerky tune that kept going irritatingly round in one's head. The nurses said it soothed Penelope. Penelope was wandering rather restlessly up and down. Such restlessness was probably building up, as it often did, to a fit of violence. I was trying to concentrate on some clue in the puzzle about a Biblical musical instrument. 'Sound the loud cymbals,' Penelope suddenly ejaculated in her forceful way. I wrote cymbals in the crossword, it fitted. I know many people think the idea of telepathy quite unscientific, but Penelope, as she often did, seemed to have read my thoughts. Madness is a very strange condition. I sometimes wonder which if any of us are sane. Hitler for instance, he must be a madman.

'I said to the man that stood at the gate of the Year "Give me a light that I may tread safely into the unknown." And he replied "Go out into the darkness and put thy hand into the hand of God. That shall be to thee better than light and safer than a known way."' We had listened to those words which the King quoted in his broadcast as war was declared. They were not written by some well known poet, but by someone called Minnie Haskins who suddenly became famous. They are words I have never forgotten. They so exactly expressed how we all felt, Churchill had promised us 'nothing but blood sweat and tears.'

It was astonishing to me how well everything had been prepared for war. Soldiers had been called up and sent to France; the blackout enforced; air raid shelters available; people had been issued with gas masks and ration books and identity cards; children were evacuated; buildings commandeered for use as hospitals; factories turned to making aircraft and guns, all within what seemed like a matter of a few days. The government must have been preparing for war for months, years perhaps. Well, the last two years anyway.

We made an air raid shelter for ourselves under our stairs, equipped with torches and a first aid kit, though we thought we would be unlikely ever to use it in such an out of the way place as St Anne's. The Germans wouldn't waste their bombs on us. We practised with great difficulty the wearing of our gas masks, which frightened Penelope, and it was impossible to get her to put it on.

Teddy was called up and posted, not far from his home thank goodness. Harold looked most handsome in his army uniform, when he called in on his way to some posting or other. Mary was evacuated from her London hospital and arrived at a workhouse in Aylesbury. 'It felt strange,' she said when she wrote, 'for the workhouse inhabitants all seemed a little simple, and some of rather uncertain temper.' The day after she arrived there a bus load of expectant mothers arrived on the doorstep. 'Not that we had even a mug to give them a drink, or a pair of scissors with which to cut the cord if someone had actually had a baby,' she wrote, 'but things soon got sorted out.'

Connie had taken young Francis to Canada, much I think to the relief of his father. I was thankful when I heard they had arrived safely, with all those attacks on shipping that we read about. My son Francis said he was not to be called up, he was needed as a doctor in London. Arthur was working in London.

It is said that one tends to forget the immediate past as one gets older. I must admit that memories of the second World War are very muddled sometimes in my mind. Besides it is easy to think that some incidents from the first World War belong instead to the second. It is curious how so many parallels there are between the two. You must forgive an old woman for whatever historical inaccuracies occur. It is difficult to remember which event followed which. One's mind becomes blurred, things that seem important at the time fade from memory, while silly little incidents long forgotten spring to mind.

One doesn't forget things like those notices, they were everywhere. 'Careless talk costs lives', 'Colds and sneezes spread diseases'. People were asked to pull up railings and donate cooking pots and anything else metal to the war effort. People asked 'Is your journey really necessary.' Everyone walked about with little jars of their rationed butter and sugar whenever they were invited out to friends. Soldiers were everywhere, and so it seemed were concrete posts and barbed wire, especially along the coast.

Vera Lynne sang songs about the 'white cliffs of Dover,' and 'we'll meet again': there were other songs, like 'A Nightingale sang in Berkeley Square', or a more vulgar one called 'She'll be coming round the Mountain when she comes'. For some reason it was quite comforting to hear songs repeated over and over again. There was Tommy Handley and Itma, with 'that man again', and 'Funf speaking'. There was Lord Haw Haw, that arch traitor of ours, broadcasting from Germany. No one believed a word he said, which made us feel we had a better intelligence service than our enemies.

Ex-king Edward VIII and his American bride were sent out of the way to the Bahamas. Russia invaded places like Latvia and Estonia, and only Finland put up any resistance. Brave little Finland we all felt, struggling like us against the odds. Did Russia and Germany intend to take over the whole world?

There was a period during the first year of war when very little seemed to be happening at all. There was fighting in France of course on the Maginot defensive line, and people sang songs like 'Run, rabbit run,' or 'We'll hang out our washing on the Seigfried Line' in bravado against their fear of what might come next I suppose. Some casualties of course, but not nearly as many as there had been in 1914.

In that first year of war Penelope suddenly died. She had a cold, but then she got pneumonia, and within a few days she was dead. I couldn't feel any real grief, considering the state she had been in these last few years. But it was another step in the breaking of links with the past. And once more my life would have to change in a somewhat drastic way.

Mollie came to the funeral. When the will was read it transpired that everything, the house, money, goods, everything had been left to charity. We were instructed by the lawyer not to move anything from the house. Mollie and I didn't see why not. We packed a few of the things that we most valued, the money they would have fetched for charity was negligible. We needed to keep some souvenirs of the past.

Besides it transpired when matters were settled that there was very little money left, it had all been frittered away by those greedy lawyers. You would have thought my brother would have been a better judge of character then to have left those two crooks in charge of all that money. One of the partners had recently died, the other was obviously sick, and there was very little possibility of recovering stolen money. The charities got very little, because the money had had to be used to pay the debts the lawyers had incurred on behalf of the Trust. I don't understand these things. They knew what they were doing, Teddy said, in persuading Penelope to leave it all to charity, they had everything under their control. I am not surprised they took advantage of the situation.

We decided the best thing I could now do was to move to Worthing and live with Fanny, who had recently bought a house there. When Josey died the house she and Annie had lived in became their property by a long standing agreement. Annie had died soon after Josey, and Fanny was left with money enough to find somewhere to live of her own choice. 'I never liked Sanderstead,' she said. 'Why did you live there then,' I asked. 'It was what Annie wanted' she said simply.

Mollie helped me pack, and we travelled down by train. I think Fanny was quite pleased at the arrangement. 'We can bring any furniture you would like from Greengates, you have only got to tell us what you want,' Teddy explained. So Fanny and I, then Ada, settled down together in Worthing. You would have thought sometimes that there was no war on, except of course there was no chance of employing anyone to help us in the house. We could see the barbed wire defences put up along the seashore. Food rationing made providing for ourselves quite difficult because standing for hours in queues was not something we could manage very well. People began to call it the phony war.

Some lines come to mind, bull whether they are something I have once read, or something I have just invented I am not sure.

> Hope hovers trembling in the air
> Time holds its breath with fear.

The Dark Days

What did happen the following June of course was Dunkirk, the retreat before the German forces with all those French and British troops being chased into the sea. So many brave men saved by that sudden sea fog and that flotilla of little English boats that fetched so many of them home. I thought about those lines, putting your hand into the hand of God. That so many were rescued did seem like a little miracle, the hand of God. Somehow it made us feel as if God was on our side. Everyone expected an invasion, we were always looking out to see if we could see the Germans coming.

Bombs fell on London in August, and the air raids began in earnest in September. Hundreds of German bombers, escorted by hundreds and hundreds of fighters, droned across the sky. It was in London that the savagery of bombing civil populations was first demonstrated to everyone in England. London was on fire, the glow in the sky could be seen fifty miles away. St Paul's was bombed, there were news pictures of the cathedral in the middle of the smoke and fire of the raids. I had a great affection for St Paul's, it would be impossible to think of London without St Paul's. We heard the wailing sirens, even in Worthing at times, and then felt the relief when the all clear went. The Palace was bombed, and the King and Queen toured the devastated East End of London. Mary wrote sometimes from London. I have here a letter from her, undated, for some reason she seldom dated her letters.

> *Dear Banna,*
>
> *I am lying on a bare mattress in my clothes in the hospital basement which is our air raid shelter. Above me as I lie here are rows and rows of cables and pipes, small pipes, big pipes, straight pipes, angled pipes and I can't help wondering if we were hit what would come out*

of the broken pipes. Would I be scalded by hot water, deluged with cold, would I be gassed, would I be drowned in sewage, or would I be electrocuted by the cables criss-crossing the ceiling. The light is dim, but I am writing to you to try and get them out of my mind. We have had a lot of casualties, the burns are the worst, especially the children, but the hospital itself hasn't yet been hit.

I have three particular friends and we go out together when we can. I was home last week for one night. I had to ask the train driver where the train was supposed to be going, since no one else seemed to know. It was midnight when I got to Aldershot. I walked back the seven miles to Crookham across the camp fields of Tweezledown.

Give my love to the Aunts.

I suppose if you have the fear of bombs to contend with, you don't think about the dangers of troops molesting you, especially with so many foreigners about. But I remember worrying about her. Harold got married to an Australian girl called Sheila who could sing rather well, and then he got posted to Burma.

During those years the sky always seemed to be full of planes. One soon learnt to differentiate between the sounds of ours and theirs, between bombers and fighters. Our hearts sank each time we saw one of ours with a great trail of smoke behind it as it was hit. Those brave airmen, the same young men I suspect who only a few years ago were signing a pact between themselves never to take part in any war. I recall a line quoted by J B Priestley on the wireless. 'London the centre of the hopes of all free men everywhere.' Our brave airmen, 'the centre of the hopes of all free men' I misquoted to Fanny.

We got used to remembering what various letters stood for, the army ATS, the navy WRENS, the air force WAFFS, the army nursing QAs. As for the number of allied troops, it was quite bewildering. It was not just the Australians and the Canadians, the South Africans, the Indians, West Africans, and other commonwealth troops, but the free Poles, French, Dutch, Norwegians, and Czechs who seemed to be scattered everywhere. Food seemed to get scarcer: clothes were rationed: petrol was strictly rationed. Everyone was singing Lilly Marlene, a song our troops took over from the Germans. Germans chased our troops through the Egyptian deserts, and we chased them back again.

I had another letter from Mary, quite a long letter but the parts of it of which I took particular note were those concerning the air raids.

It is more difficult in London just now, the sirens seem to be going most of the time. People were killed and injured when someone tripped and fell on an escalator, as they were going to the Underground shelter and everyone fell on top of one another. There were not nearly as many casualties as rumour seems to suggest.

The hospital has been bombed, but not badly. I was working in casualty and the water pipes broke, and in a matter of minutes we were knee deep in water trying to rescue the equipment. Only a few people were hurt but it became quite difficult to treat them efficiently.

The Germans invaded Russia. I felt more optimistic. I would have thought history would have taught anyone that to invade Russia with winter coming on would turn out to be a disastrous adventure. Just remember how Napoleon had had to retreat from Russia. Pearl Harbour happened with all those American war ships blown up by the Japanese. America was really on our side at last.

Personal things do not seem to be of so much consequence during wartime. My son Arthur got divorced from his nice Scottish girl: I knew it was hopeless from the start. I think any girl would have found it difficult to cope with his dark moods. Francis got divorced from Connie and married his actress friend. I told both those girls that consenting to divorce would mean they would find themselves badly off financially when the war was over. Connie would at least have a son to support her.

I suppose we were not very different from most other families, but I was finding it difficult to remember where everyone was and what they might be doing. Harold seemed to be lost somewhere in Burma; Mary had joined the QAs and was wandering round the Middle East; John was restless and wanted to join the Forces before he was fully qualified as a doctor, but was dissuaded. He was still in London with the bombs. Nancy was working for the Red cross: Mollie commanded a red cross platoon at Crookham; Ruth was now a WREN. Teddy was invalided out, following an operation for the removal of shrapnel left over from the first world war. We three old ladies felt we would like to be doing something more but at our age we would probably be more a liability than a help. Fanny had been knitting for the forces of course, and I had done some sewing for a local Children's Home. It is rather humiliating feeling so helpless. All we can do is give donations to whatever charity we feel most needs our support.

It Is Not All Gloom

I feel rather helpless now, waiting to hear from Teddy about our proposed visit to Stranger's Corner. A strange name, Stranger's Corner, one of artist William's ideas. He built himself a house at Farnham called Stranger's Corner. When he died I suppose Mollie liked the sound of it, and transferred it to their new house. I puzzle sometimes as to whether the name should make one feel more welcome or less.

Teddy phones this morning to say he will fetch us about eleven o'clock. I have been so busy thinking of the past lately, that I had almost forgotten this was the day for our arranged visit to Crookham. I get agitated trying to think of what to take with me.

"What about food?" I say. "We shouldn't waste anything. If there is anything left in the larder we should take it with us."

"Don't get yourself in a muddle," Fanny says. "We have used up everything here, and Teddy will see we get something to eat on the way. He knows someone who owns a little place about half way there."

I take with me some of the photographs, I want to ask Mollie about some things I can't quite remember. Packing doesn't take much time, I've only two dresses I can still wear, and I must take my all important two cardigans so that I will be warm enough, Stranger's Corner may be very picturesque, indeed it is, but it is very draughty. I remember feeling quite cold when we were there for Mary's wedding.

The drive is a very pleasant one, as Teddy promised. We have some coffee and sandwiches with his friend at Petworth. Teddy talks about the painter Turner, and then about the Manor House.

"We can call in and have a look at the old house perhaps on your way back" he suggests. Fine old building. Teddy always was interested in history and old buildings.

Mollie is standing at the gate waiting for us. The sun catches her hair where the wind has been blowing it untidily, she looks about eighteen from a distance, the way she stands. The house is just as I remembered it, long and low and white, with that little stream running in front of it. Koobah the dog comes to greet us, I don't much care for animals, but as dogs go he is friendly and not too obtrusive. Mollie has always been fond of dogs. This one was left behind when Nancy and her family recently emigrated to Canada.

We enjoy our week's visit. Harold brings Sheila and his two little girls Joanna and Sarah to see us, they are now living in my old house of Greengates. Harold doesn't look all that well I know he had a lot of fever while he was in the Burmese jungle.

I did offer to pay for him to go to university when he came out of the army, but he refused, I think he didn't want to be beholden to anyone. He got a grant to do accountancy instead, I suspect organised by his father. He is taking over Teddy's business in Fleet. He doesn't look too happy poor boy, but never says what can be the matter. He looks bemused. I almost think sometimes he would like to be back in the jungle with his men, his Indian troops. But you can see he is very proud of his children. It must have taken him some time to get to know Joanna, he never even saw her until she was four years old. So many returning soldiers haven't seen their families for years. Such a sweet pretty child is Joanna, I so enjoyed her company when she was in Worthing earlier this year while Anthea helped her convalesce from whooping cough.

Mollie has quite an estate. They have chickens, so we can all have fresh eggs for breakfast. there are cows in the field.

"We even kept a pig during the war," she tells us , "he was called Henry. We managed to feed him and the chickens on our scraps. But we couldn't eat Henry in the end, because the twins flatly refused. So we sold him to the butcher."

"You have such a pretty garden" I compliment her, 'but it must be such a lot of work." We walk round the estate. There is a big vegetable garden , we meet the man working there.

"It certainly pays to grow your own vegetables," I say. Fanny and I have been enjoying those tasty fresh vegetables ever since we arrived.

Teddy takes us to Winchfield church on Sunday. Fanny and I haven't been in a church for years. I used to go sometimes on

Armistice Day, but that is a long time ago. Fanny seemed reluctant, but I could see Mollie might be quite glad to have us out of the way for a bit. Mollie never goes to church, not for so long as I can remember. Except of course for things like funerals and christenings and weddings, there have been quite a lot of those. The church is very pretty, Norman, Teddy explains. Teddy is what I call a real Christian. He introduces us to the vicar. They have been planning together to try to encourage more children to come to church.

I manage to see most of Mollie's children. Anthea comes home for her day off from Great Ormond Street Hospital, she will soon be qualified as an expert children's nurse she tells me. She is such a kind thoughtful girl, bless her, she must make an excellent nurse. Ruth is home for the day from the Middlesex Hospital where she is training. Sylvia drives over from the stables where she looks after horses. Not a very suitable occupation for a girl I can't help thinking but these days girls seem to do almost anything. John is home too, he is now qualified and he too works at Great Ormond Street. All these doctors and nurses in the family, they say medicine runs in families. Even Sylvia is caring for patients of a kind, horse patients in her case. What delightful young people they all are to be sure, so caring of others.

Teddy takes us for drives. He took us to Crondall, 'the ancient capital of this whole area' he explains and then on to Farnham where William was once head of the art College, and where Mary went for a while to the grammar school she so hated. He points out old houses; we get out of the car to look at the canal; "the canal has never been used for transport" he explains, "only for recreation. By the time it was finished it was no longer really needed." Harold once explained to me that on its banks was the best place to find rare plants and animals. It is very pretty countryside, Fanny and I agree when we return, with all the hills and woods and streams, very different to the sameness of the seashore we are so used to at Worthing.

I am rather frightened of the stairs, there are no rails, only a rope to hold on to. There is one room downstairs where Fanny sleeps, while I have the room above her under the beams of an old slanting ceiling. Very comfortable, but it takes me a long time to negotiate those stairs each day. I have to be very careful.

The week has gone all too quickly. Teddy drives us back, we stop again at Petworth and we stay to admire the façade of the old Manor House. But I think we are both glad to be back home.

Farewell

We were at home in Worthing, all three of us listening to the six o'clock news as everyone did during those war years, when we felt the 'tide of war was turning' as they say. It seemed the first piece of really good news since the war began. Up to now we had been told of aircraft missing, ships being sunk, prisoners captured in the far East, everything had seemed all doom and gloom. But we had routed the Germans at El Alamein, and now at least in Africa we were driving the enemy into the sea and capturing so many prisoners no one knew what to do with them all.

We started gaining ground in Italy; there was the battle of Monte Casino; the Russians defeated Hitler at Stalingrad. Whatever else you could say about the Russians, they were tenacious fighters when their own country was invaded. Japan was being defeated in the far East at a place I had never heard of.

A quotation, 'The dark sense of duty, greater than that of love' comes to mind as D-Day approached with the invasion of France. Too many casualties, especially as airborne troops tried to capture a bridge at Arnhem. What a waste of life, when the Germans must already have known they were defeated. Liberated people lined the streets and cheered. Paris was free. Resistance fighters all over Europe rejoiced. The Russians were beginning to have it too much their own way, and now it was Russia we were beginning to be frightened of. There was talk of the United Nations, and the trial of war criminals. Roosevelt had died.

Arthur, my son Arthur is dead. What is it the letter says, 'died on board of a fever and an overdose of pills.' I asked Teddy what exactly he thought that might mean. Poor Arthur, he was just as much a victim of the wars as anyone else. I remember his distress the day he got his papers to say he must report for a journey to the Middle East. He was to relieve medical officers coming home at last from those far off desert places. He so hated war, he used to say that desert places produced in him a strange kind of melancholia. I knew how distressed he was.

The letter from the officer praised his medical skills, and said how much he would be missed by his fellow officers. It was a kind letter. Mollie was most upset, she was always fond of Arthur.

If any one ever had any doubts about the need for us to have fought this terrible war, they were dispelled by the stories coming out of Belsen and all the other concentration camps. Nancy as a red cross nurse was sent to Belsen to help the survivors. She has never spoken much about it. Wickedness on that scale is hard to comprehend.

VE Day, with parties and dancing in the streets, victory in Europe. Bells were peeling in Worthing, all the street lights came on. How bright everything suddenly seemed. Lights went on, bells rang. Then that strange phenomenon called an atom bomb, so destructive it brought fears of the end of the world to mind. One should never give children matches to play with: one should never give wicked men the chance to play with atom bombs. It was said it had shortened the world war and saved many lives. We had VJ victory in Japan day.

'You would think,' I said to Fanny and Ada, 'that the world could have some peace after such a terrible war.' News this time was about Jews blowing up people in Palestine. 'I am tired of the foolishness of us human beings, I said, 'I have just been reading that book by Orwell called *Animal Farm*. It's much too perceptive, I despair of human nature. There's never going to be a war to end wars, men will never be cured of their wickedness. I feel sorry for my great grandchildren, one can only foresee just a succession of struggles with weapons becoming ever more deadly. I'm glad I won't be here to see the world utterly destroyed.' 'Don't be so gloomy', Fanny says. 'The best thing is never to think about it any more.' So we never speak about the news to one another now. We still listen to it every evening, one needs to know what goes on in the world, but we never talk about it.

What More Is There To Say?

I am writing to Mollie to thank her for our holiday. I wonder shall I ever be able to visit Stranger's Corner again. I will be ninety soon. It is wonderful to me that I can still see and hear as well as I can, I need no glasses or hearing aid. True my handwriting is getting somewhat wobbly, but it is not too bad considering. I am sure Mollie will be able to read it.

How do I start this letter, I wonder, perhaps it will be the last I ever write, you never know at my age. I need to say so much, yet Mollie would hate it were I to become sentimental. It is strange how things work out. My sons Harold and Arthur both dead, and Francis seeming like a stranger almost. Yet when they were young it was Mollie whom I found most difficult. She was always up to some escapade or other. Besides in my ignorance I had always felt uneasy about the way she brought up her children. But how could I criticise now with the success they all seem to be making of their lives despite the war. Such delightful young people, all of them, a pleasure to be with, so able to take care of themselves.

> *Dearest and Best of Daughters,* [I write.]
> *I feel hundreds of miles away from you and miss you dreadfully. Not of course that there is anything wrong here, we found everything in good order and nothing lacking to make us comfortable. But I find it difficult to be quite happy without you and the charming family.*
>
> *I was so very happy at SC and feel I cannot thank you enough for the perfect holiday I spent with you and yours. Please thank Teddy for all he did for us.*
>
> *I still feel guilty that you would not let us help with anything, even the washing up. I suspect we would have*

only been in the way. Nor would you let us pay back
various expenses you incurred on our behalf.
Did you see an article on Juvenile Delinquency by a
London Magistrate, a relative of one of our erstwhile
gentlemen friends. I think Teddy might be interested.
Our best love to you one and all,
Your loving mother. Banna
Mary Allen

I read it through many times, that letter, altering this or that, but in the end decide to say less rather than more. Anything I try to add seems to make my thanks and pleasure sound somewhat false.

Fanny and I walk down to the corner to post it. There seems to be a cold wind blowing.

I have noticed recently strange little shivers that run up and down my arms. Nothing to worry about I don't suppose.

It seems warmer today. I have been turning out my things again, and I have been looking at the bracelet George gave me all those years ago. Fanny says I am getting morbid.

Mary and David arrive in their little car, paying us a flying visit.

"We can't stop, I am afraid," Mary says. They have come quite some way I realise, all the way from Leeds.

"We are down this way to go to a University conference," explains David.

"We could not come this far without saying hallo to you both, now could we?" says Mary.

I feel a very stupid little pang of jealousy in that both Fanny and I are included as the reason for the visit. One should never assume proprietary feelings over one's family, I know, and I am ashamed of the momentary lapse, quite irrational of course. We provide them with a cup of tea. All these young things, they all look so enthusiastic and hopeful these days, I am glad to say. They do seem to be shrugging off the horrors of war without too much effort.

They say they must go.

"Just a moment", I say to Mary. Of course I have to rummage about a bit to find that bracelet, one can never find what one wants when one is in a hurry. I don't like to keep them waiting.

I hold out the bracelet to her as David goes down the path to the car.

"I just thought I would show you this, it was given me when I was a young girl by a man I was deeply in love with, a man I was once going to marry. He died of TB. It's pretty, isn't it?"

We kiss each other goodbye. I was left standing there with the bracelet feeling rather foolish. I wondered what that sudden impulse of mine had been all about.

Nine Lives Is Quite Enough

I am not sure how I came to be here, lying in my bed with the sunlight gleaming in the window. Fanny is standing on one side of me, Mollie on the other. There is a man at the foot of the bed, I assume he is the doctor. Because you see, I can't move one of my arms. My legs don't feel as if I could stand on them either.

I try to say something but that too is difficult. It is more than disconcerting when one tries to say something, and strange noises come out of one's mouth, rather than the words expected.

"How are you feeling?" Mollie asks. Since I can't say anything I try and smile. Judging by her reaction this is not a very successful attempt at communication.

"You'll be feeling better tomorrow" Fanny says. I nod, yes, I find I can nod, only a little nod, but I can see it is understood.

The doctor examines me. I don't really like Mollie and Fanny to see me in such a helpless state.

"A stroke," the doctor says, "only a mild one as far as I can judge. We'll know more tomorrow. She should be kept warm, give her a warm drink too if she can manage it." I do so hate doctors who talk as if one were not there. I feel quite glad that Fanny is a nurse, she will know if I can manage a drink or not. She always has had a way with sick people.

My thoughts drift about. I am glad I am not ill with a fever. I remember when I had smallpox and I was quite convinced I had murdered Aunt, and buried her on the moors in Rochdale. It took me some days to realise it wasn't so. At least this time I can think clearly, even if I am the only one who knows it.

Mollie smiles at me, I am glad. I have never known with Mollie whether she even likes me. Now I think I know she does care about me a little. We have enjoyed doing things together at times after all.

Some lines come into my mind, Tennyson I suspect.

> I have lived my life and that which I have done,
> May He within himself make pure

I suppose everyone makes mistakes bringing up one's children, me more than most I am afraid. But one can't undo what has been done, I hope they will find it in their hearts to forgive me.

Francis comes to see me, the doctor as ever.

"Not too bad," he says, "just rest and take things easily. You will probably find in a day or two you can start to move around a little." He gives me a little kiss on the cheek as he goes. It's years since he did that.

Fanny brings me a drink of tea, which I manage in a fashion with her help. I was getting very thirsty, I realise.

"We will leave you to rest now," she says.

I feel rather strange all of a sudden.

Some words come into my mind.

> As unto dying eyes,
> The casement slowly grows a glimmering square
> And leaves the world to darkness and to me.

They seem to wander through my dying brain.